Has History Ended?

Has History Ended?

Fukuyama, Marx, Modernity

EDITED BY
Christopher Bertram
AND
Andrew Chitty

Avebury

Aldershot • Brookfield USA • Hong Kong • Singapore • Sydney

© C. Bertram, A. Chitty and Contributors 1994

All rights reserved. No part of this publication may be reproduced, stored in a retrieval system, or transmitted in any form or by any means, electronic, mechanical, photocopying, recording or otherwise without the prior permission of the publisher.

Published by
Avebury
Ashgate Publishing Ltd
Gower House
Croft Road
Aldershot
Hants. GU11 3HR
England

Ashgate Publishing Company
Old Post Road
Brookfield
Vermont 05036
USA

British Library Cataloguing in Publication Data
Has History Ended?: Fukuyama, Marx and
  Modernity. (Avebury Series in
  Philosophy)
  I. Bertram, Christopher, II. Chitty,
  Andrew III. Series
  901
ISBN 1 85628 959 1
Reprinted 1996

Library of Congress Cataloging-in-Publication Data
Has history ended? Fukuyama, Marx, modernity / edited by Christopher
  Bertram and Andrew Chitty.
      p. cm. -- (Avebury series in philosophy)
  Includes bibliographical references.   ISBN 1-85628-959-1
  1. Fukuyama, Francis. End of history. 2. History--Philosophy.
I. Bertram Christopher, 1958–   . II. Chitty, Andrew, 1953-
III. Series.
D16.9H3675   1994   94-34534
901--dc20   CIP

Typeset in Monotype Bembo by Lucy Morton, London SE12.

Printed and bound by Athenæum Press Ltd.,
Gateshead, Tyne & Wear.

Contents

Acknowledgements   vii

Introduction
Christopher Bertram and Andrew Chitty   1

Part I   Fukuyama

1   Shaping Ends: Reflections on Fukuyama
Joseph McCarney   13

2   The Enthronement of Low Expectations:
Fukuyama's Ideological Compromise for Our Time
Frank Füredi   31

3   The Cards of Confusion: Reflections on Historical
Communism and the 'End of History'
Gregory Elliott   46

Part II   Marx

4   The End of History or the Beginning of Marx?
Keith Graham   67

5   On Societal and Global Historical Materialism
Paula Casal   87

6   Marx, Moral Consciousness and History
Andrew Chitty   112

Part III Modernity

7   The End of History and the Metastructure of Modernity
    Jacques Bidet   135

8   Socialism and Modern Times
    Alex Callinicos   154

9   The End of History: One More Push!
    Christopher Bertram   167

Notes on the Contributors   181

Acknowledgements

We should like to thank Robin Gable and Lucy Morton for producing camera-ready copy and for their support and assistance during some difficult episodes in this project's history. We should also like to thank all the contributors to this volume for their patience and support.

The contributions to the book appear here for the first time in English, with the exception of the following: Chapter 1 was written for this book but first appeared in *New Left Review* 202, November–December 1993, pp. 37–53; Chapter 3 first appeared in *Radical Philosophy* 64, Summer 1993, pp. 3–12, under the title 'The Cards of Confusion'.

Introduction
Christopher Bertram and Andrew Chitty

In the summer of 1989, a political analyst with the US State Department named Francis Fukuyama published an article entitled 'The End of History?' in the conservative journal *The National Interest*.[1] The article makes the sweeping and somewhat startling claim that events in Eastern Europe and the Soviet Union mark not simply the collapse of a particular attempt to implement socialism, nor even just the collapse of the idea of socialism itself. More than either of those two things, they mark the end of humanity's social and political evolution: the end of history.

For what was disintegrating in the East was the last feasible alternative social system to 'liberalism'. By 'liberalism' Fukuyama means liberal-democratic capitalism: roughly speaking, a free-market economy plus individual rights and parliamentary democracy. Since the American and French revolutions first began to establish it, 'liberalism' has successfully seen off the challenges of predecessors or alternatives such as medieval theocracy and fascism. Now the last such contender, communism, is disappearing from the stage. With that disappearance, 'history' – in the sense of the struggle between competing social forms and their underlying ideologies – comes to an end. Liberal-democratic capitalism represents humanity's solution, at last, to the problem of social coexistence. This problem solved, there is no longer a need for ways to formulate dissatisfaction with social systems. Art and philosophy will therefore lose the essential function they have hitherto possessed. Human beings will turn their attention elsewhere: in particular to the development and satisfaction of ever more elaborate consumer desires.

In his article Fukuyama offers only brief arguments to support his thesis that liberalism represents the terminus of history. First, he argues that no alternative to liberalism has the backing of any constituency of intellectuals, nor is any such alternative embodied in any significant social movement. Of those counter-examples that might spring to mind, he dismisses Islamic fundamentalism as posing no serious threat to liberalism, and nationalism as not really qualifying as an alternative at all. The defeat of those societies that had once been claimed to be preferable to liberalism and the absence of any new challengers signify that human beings have discovered that liberalism cannot be bettered.

Second, Fukuyama argues that different forms of society have been more or less successful in providing material well-being and security for the people living under them, partly as a result of the ways in which the ideologies corresponding to the social forms affect economic motivation. In this, liberalism has outshone all its rivals. The main reason for the abandonment of the Soviet system lies in its failure to satisfy consumer desire. Liberalism, by contrast, has proved in practice that it can generate unprecedented material abundance.

The third and final reason Fukuyama offers is that human beings desire not only the satisfaction of their material needs but also 'recognition' by other humans. Referring to the prewar French interpreter of Hegel, Alexandre Kojève,[2] he suggests that the rise and fall of social systems has not just been conditioned by the struggle for physical well-being but also by this struggle for recognition. With liberal society a stage has been reached where all human beings can accord and receive recognition. The satisfaction of this second dimension of human desire means that another of the impulses that have driven people to reshape their social arrangements has been discharged.

Recognition and Liberal Democracy

'The End of History?' was perfectly timed. Published a few months before the opening of the Berlin Wall, it provided an interpretation of the events of 1989 that was accessible and was painted on the largest canvas. For a few months Fukuyama's thesis enjoyed wide publicity and in some countries his name came close to being a household word. Fukuyama amplified and defended his thesis in further articles and before long had contracted to produce a book-length elucidation.[3] When it appeared in the spring of 1992, *The End of History and the Last Man* provoked a fresh round of debate, although the events of the intervening two years (most notably the Second Gulf War and the collapse of Yugoslavia) meant that the discussion was less exhilarated than before.

The book develops the arguments of the article into a complete, though schematic, theory of historical development. Once again, Fukuyama relies on the mechanisms of economic competition and the struggle for recognition to underpin his thesis. But the emphasis has shifted. Whereas the central mechanism invoked by the original article was the differential capacity of forms of society to promote technological progress and material abundance, the book foregrounds the psychic need that each human individual has to be recognized as a person by others. Adapting a term from Plato, Fukuyama derives this need from the individual's *thymos* ('spiritedness'), a sense of one's own worth as a free originator of actions. Thus a crypto-Marxist explanation has yielded pride of place to a neo-Hegelian one.

According to this new account, *thymos* was responsible for the earliest class systems, as the courageous forced the weak to serve, and thus to recognize, them: a process dramatized in Hegel's master–slave dialectic. But the resulting unequal recognition could not even satisfy the masters, who were recognized only by creatures for whom they had no respect. In the end it was the struggle for recognition by the subordinated 'slaves' that had to succeed. With the advent of liberal democracy they finally managed to impose on their masters a system that accords universal recognition to each individual, for here each is an equal citizen in a democratic state. Liberal democracy triumphs principally because it dispels for ever the anxiety created for each by the need to live in the opinion of others. It assures each person of their worth and enables each to think they are 'as good as the next'. The struggle for recognition that has driven 'history' forward has come to an end.

This change of emphasis is not the only way in which the book differs from the original article. Despite some explicit reservations, the article conveyed a sense of exultation in the victory of the West. Two years on, the mood has become much more sombre. In the final section of the book Fukuyama registers an array of doubts about the ability of the liberal-democratic form of capitalism to satisfy the twin desires of material satisfaction and interpersonal recognition. Perhaps authoritarian forms of capitalism are more productive – Fukuyama cites the Singaporean model. Perhaps the formal recognition accorded by liberal-democratic societies is empty and unsatisfactory by comparison with the differential respect given to individuals with real merits and demerits in societies with strong codes of social behaviour, such as Japan. More generally, it may be that liberal-democratic societies cannot satisfy the demand for absolutely equal recognition without becoming unworkable. Or they may be unable to respond to the desire of some to be recognized as superior, a desire that finds expression in boredom with consumer society and in a Nietzschean contempt for its inhabitants, the 'last men'. These doubts, which are summarized in Fukuyama's paradoxical suggestion that history, having ended, might start again, do much to undermine the clear-cut thesis of the original article and the first part of his book.

Fukuyama and the Left

The present volume results from the editors' view that the left has failed to formulate a response to Fukuyama which takes seriously what he has to say. It may be tempting to forget Fukuyama now that the initial wave of interest has died down, but the challenges which his writings pose to Marxism and to a left still deeply indebted to Marxism need to be confronted.

What do these challenges consist in? First, Marxists have always adhered to an account of history involving the growth of scientific and technical knowledge and a progress through different social forms. The central Marxian idea about history is that, following the demise of primitive communism, a succession of class-divided social forms rise and fall according to their tendency to promote or impede technological progress. Finally, when the 'springs of co-operative wealth flow more abundantly', class society will be superseded by communism. By contrast, conservatives have traditionally opposed any progressive philosophy of history, and liberals have increasingly abandoned such a view during the twentieth century, suspecting that it carries with it the germ of totalitarianism. Whilst it is true that over the past twenty years some thinkers on the left, suspicious of 'grand metanarratives', have taken the same route, a tacit view of history as the progressive emancipation of humanity continues to underlie the thinking even of many who think of themselves as post- or non-Marxist. One of the striking differences between Fukuyama and the average liberal or conservative critic of Marxism is that, instead of condemning 'totalizing historical thought', Fukuyama boldly engages in such thought himself. Indeed there is a deep affinity between Fukuyama's view of history and the conception held by Marx. Both envisage history as the adaptation of social forms to the development of the economic productive forces, and as the progressive liberation of the subordinated classes of mankind from their enslavement. Yet Fukuyama's account culminates not in the victory of communism, but of liberal-democratic capitalism. Historical communism is allotted the role of helping to bring about the liberal-democratic end by giving a convincing demonstration of its own bankruptcy. Supporters of a Marxian theory of history have to say something about why history on that account should end with their preferred conclusion rather than Fukuyama's.

Second, the collapse of the Soviet-style regimes is an event that cries out to be fitted into any 'philosophical history' worth the name. Fukuyama has at least risen to this challenge, whilst the left has hardly reacted in a way consonant with the magnitude of the events. Someone who still adheres to a Marxian conception of history should surely try to make sense of recent events within that framework. For Marxists, the twentieth century has been a time of heightened expectations and bitter disappointment. In the early years of the century many believed the development of the productive forces under capitalism was already sufficient to underpin a successful transition to a communist society. But the isolation and failure of the Bolshevik experiment led to fragmentation on the left. Some rejected the Soviet Union completely; others clung to it to different degrees. Some were sustained by self-deception and wishful thinking; others had few illusions in the actuality of Soviet regimes but held onto the possibility of future reform, or simply insisted on a residual difference between a progressive Soviet social form and the imperialist states. The final demise of the Soviet Union transforms the landscape and poses the obvious question: 'What is the historical significance of this demise for the socialist project?' Fukuyama has given his answer: that it signifies the end of that project. Socialists need to provide their own.

Third, Fukuyama provides a defence of the Western status quo that goes beyond the familiar homilies of free marketeers on market efficiency or the warnings of Burkean conservatives of the dangers of disrupting long-established institutions. The real weight of Fukuyama's case lies in his claim that liberal-democratic capitalism alone can satisfy the 'deepest and most fundamental longings' of human beings, namely their desire for recognition as agents. This is a claim that rests on a philosophical anthropology not so distant from Marx's own and represents another example of Fukuyama reasoning from quasi-Marxian premisses to anti-Marxian conclusions. Anyone who shares a broadly Marxian conception of human beings as active self-defining creatures needs to explain why such creatures would achieve a greater degree of self-realization in a communist society than in the liberal-democratic capitalism that Fukuyama favours.

Finally, the Nietzschean theme in Fukuyama's book needs some comment from the left. For Fukuyama, the attainment of a social form that provides for universal mutual recognition is far from an unambiguous reason for celebration. The problem of recognition having been solved, there is no longer a place for the heroism of those who seek to attain or resist individual pre-eminence, nor for the courage and inspiration of those who would fight for liberty, equality and fraternity. All that is left to do is to resolve the technical problems that lie in the way of a universal life of bovine contentment, and to simulate the struggle for supremacy through sporting and similar activities. In short, the end of history opens the prospect of 'centuries of boredom'. For Marxists, of course, the end of history does not come with capitalism but with communism. But if communism is the final form of social organization then, *mutatis mutandis,* does communism itself not threaten humankind with the kind of meaninglessness to which, according to Fukuyama, liberal-democratic capitalism already condemns it?

In the face of Fukuyama's challenges, the reaction of the left to Fukuyama has been largely dismissive.[4] On the one hand there are those who have challenged the very coherence and possibility of grand theorizing about history that is presupposed by something like the 'end of history' thesis. As we have suggested, this is hardly a stance that is available to Marxists. On the other hand there are those who have insisted that liberal-democratic capitalism as we know it in the West today is riddled with inequality, sexism, racism or environmental destructiveness and so cannot be the 'end of history'. These are points that Fukuyama could easily accommodate by noting that they tacitly acknowledge his criteria for a social form that can qualify as the last in history (economic efficiency and equal recognition), and then by arguing that in so far as liberal democracy falls short in these areas it is not as a consequence of its essential nature, and that where it has been established for longest these failings are gradually being overcome.

The contributors to this volume attempt to address more squarely the issues that Fukuyama has raised – directly or indirectly – for the left. What is the meaning of the 'post-historical' mood in the West that Fukuyama exemplifies? What is the significance of the collapse of the Soviet Union for the socialist project? How important to that project is a Marxist theory of history based on the development of the productive forces? Are there other forces pushing us beyond capitalism towards socialism? Or must we abandon the tacit support of a philosophy of history and become 'utopian' again?

A Rational Kernel

The first three articles – by McCarney, Füredi and Elliott – all attempt, in different ways, to discover a rational kernel to Fukuyama's ideas or a truth which he expresses about the age in which we live. Joseph McCarney contrasts Fukuyama's official theme, which dominates the early part of his book, with the very different one that emerges towards its end. McCarney argues persuasively that whereas the source of the first theme is Alexandre Kojève, the indirect source of the second is the American conservative mentor Leo Strauss, with whom Kojève carried on a 32-year-long correspondence. Against both of Fukuyama's prognoses, McCarney argues that the desire for recognition is profoundly egalitarian. So if Fukuyama is right that human beings will not be content until they satisfy that desire, the deep implication of his theory is that capitalism of any kind must ultimately give way to a genuinely classless society.

Frank Füredi sees Fukuyama as expressing both the ideological exhaustion of the capitalist West and its continued determination to dominate the rest of the world in its own interests. He discerns beneath Fukuyama's triumphalism an underlying sense of historical pessimism that places him in a tradition of 'endist' writing running from Spengler's *Decline of the West* via Bell's *The End of Ideology* to today's fashion for postmodernism. He diagnoses this pessimism as expressing the anguish of adherents of a capitalism which they recognize can contribute nothing further to human development, but to which they can contemplate no alternative. At the same time, Füredi perceives in Fukuyama's distinction between a West where equal recognition has been achieved and a Third World 'mired in history' a new variant on the West's traditional claim to moral superiority. Such a claim, both now and in the past, has been used to justify the West's prosecution of violence in the rest of the world. Füredi sees Fukuyama's stance as symptomatic of a West in the process of moral and physical rearmament for war on the Third World.

Gregory Elliott also sees a truth in Fukuyama's writings, which he argues much of the left has been unwilling to admit: that the collapse of the Soviet-style regimes has been a massive historical defeat for the socialist project. Elliott is very far from denying the shortcomings, indeed the crimes, of Stalinism. But, taking his cue from Isaac Deutscher, he urges us not to forget the counter-hegemonic role of the Soviet Union. Its collapse – and that of the international communist movement – leaves the world denuded of any functioning alternative to capitalism and, given the concurrent crisis of social democracy, of any serious force capable of resisting attacks on workers' rights and living standards in the West. A powerful disincentive to the deployment of Western military force throughout the rest of the world has also disappeared. If only in such negative ways, and despite their extensive brutality, the historical communist regimes represented an advance on capitalism. There was always the possibility that some of them might eventually be converted into democratic socialist societies. Now that they have gone, socialists are deprived of any sense that the tide of history is on their side and have nothing to resort to but their will and imagination.

The Theory of History

Elliott implicitly raises a question that the next three contributors examine from a variety of standpoints: what is the status of Marx's theory of history today? In particular, what is its relevance to the Marxist critique of capitalism? Until five or ten years ago world history could still have been seen as moving naturally towards socialism, with the Soviet-style regimes in the East and the social-democratic forms of capitalism in the West construed as transitional forms. The reversion of Soviet-bloc regimes to a form that everyone can agree to be capitalist and the accompanying retreat of social democracy in the West now make such a perspective look naive, and force a re-examination of the theory of history on which it is implicitly based.

Keith Graham argues that for Marx the critique of capitalism was the critique of market society as such, and that Marx was committed to radically democratic methods both in the overthrow of capitalism and in the administration of its successor. A regime such as the Soviet one had, by these criteria, no connection with Marx's intentions. Indeed, Graham argues that the Soviet experience constituted an obstacle to socialist progress in the twentieth century. With the Soviet monolith gone, it may be possible at last to build a movement that takes seriously – as Graham believes Lenin and Leninism did not – Marx's commitment to the emancipation of the working class as the task of the working class themselves. But the removal of this obstacle is very far from being a sufficient condition for the transition to a new social order and Graham believes that Marx underestimated the difficulties in the way of the proletariat achieving the necessary degree of self-consciousness to effect such a transition.

Graham, then, draws the opposite conclusion to Elliott on the implications of the collapse of the Soviet regimes for socialist politics. However, he agrees with Elliott on one point: the Marxist critique of capitalism has to come apart from the Marxist theory of history. For the theory of history is based on the development of the productive forces, and the real force of the critique of capitalism is not that it fails to develop the productive forces but rather that it is inimical to human well-being and self-realization.

Paula Casal reaches a similar conclusion at the end of a careful examination of Marx's theory of history as interpreted by G. A. Cohen. According to Marx on Cohen's interpretation, a social form remains in existence for as long as it is propitious for the development of the productive forces. But a point inevitably comes when that social form ceases to favour their future development and instead turns into a 'fetter' on such development. At this point the fettering social form is replaced by another, which once again permits the onward and upward development of the productive forces. Casal argues that the theory fails to provide persuasive reasons to expect the predicted replacement to come about. She goes on to examine two 'global' versions of the theory: one proposed by Cohen and another by Christopher Bertram. In these versions, social forms propitious for the development of the productive forces emerge and sustain themselves through intersocietal processes of competition and transmission. The theory operates here on the scale of the whole world rather than relying on each society undergoing endogenous change. In Casal's view these globalized versions are no more successful than the original, and accordingly the theory as a whole must be abandoned. But she suggests that an ecologically aware socialism is anyway better off without a theory of history that makes the capacity to promote economic growth the criterion of historical success.

Graham and Casal, then, dissociate the justification of socialism from Marx's theory of history. Andrew Chitty, by contrast, proposes a reinterpretation of Marx's theory of history under which the two may not fall apart. This view draws indirectly on the idea of recognition to explain how the development of the productive forces can lead to the replacement of one social form by another. According to it, the development of the productive forces leads to the overthrow of capitalism not because a point is reached at which the capitalist shell prevents further growth, but rather by producing a new sense of self amongst workers. This sense of self is incompatible with their status under capitalism as individuals who have no control over the use of their own productive powers. As workers develop such a sense of self, they come to find the social relations of capitalism intolerable, and must attempt to replace them with social relations of their own design. Drawing on Hegel, Chitty suggests that this new sense of self is at the root of a new standard of 'right' which develops among workers under capitalism, and that Marx draws on this standard in his 'moral' condemnations of the capitalist system.

Recognition and Modernity

The final three contributors to the collection focus directly on the idea of recognition. Whereas Fukuyama's initial position is that the desire for recognition can only be satisfied by liberal-democratic capitalism, these articles focus on the suggestion that such a desire may be inherently incompatible with capitalist social relations. Specifically, they examine the possibility that capitalism may contain the seeds of its own supersession in the form of the conception of the person and of the rights of the person which develops among its individual members.

In his contribution, Jacques Bidet develops the searching analysis of the modern condition found in his book *Théorie de la Modernité*.[5] Via a close reading of Marx, and drawing on the corpus of political philosophy from Rousseau to the present, Bidet provides us with an image of 'modern' societies as the imperfect realization of a normative 'metastructure' that has three aspects. Modern societies recognize the freedom of individuals to structure their relations with others through voluntary agreement, but this pattern of 'interindividuality' calls into being (for familiar Hobbesian reasons) the authority of a central state power that must itself be legitimated by the idea of a social contract. Furthermore, individuals are not limited to contracting with one another in the market; they may also associate together, especially in order to improve their bargaining position.

These three elements, 'interindividuality', 'centricity' and 'associativity', constitute different aspects of a 'contractuality' which underlies all modern societies. However, they do not form a stable ensemble; rather, a dialectic results. The untrammelled expression of interindividuality in a free market leads to the domination of the capitalist over the wage labourer. In reaction, workers' associations attempt to use the central (state) power to counteract the effects of interindividuality, and in the limit case ('historical communism') interindividuality is almost completely extinguished in a state-planned economy. Almost, but not quite, since all modern regimes must pay lip-service to it. The result is again a regime of domination, this time of state functionaries over the rest of the population. Faced with the failures of large-scale central planning and with the state's interference in individual transactions, the population eventually reasserts the principle of interindividuality. The circle begins again. Whether in the form of capitalism or of 'historical communism', modernity's promise of a society as a system of voluntary co-operation between free individuals is broken, and contractuality turns into domination. According to Bidet, socialists have to learn to step outside this circle. Instead of affirming one part of the metastructure against another, socialists have to see both market and plan as technologies subject to democratic choice. Only such a democracy can finally redeem the 'promise of modernity'.

Alex Callinicos, in an appreciation and critique of Bidet's work, focuses on its central concept of contractuality. Callinicos allows that there may be a place for a concept of modernity that includes both Western capitalist and Soviet-style societies. But he argues that Bidet's identification of contractuality as the essential element of all modern societies is driven by considerations of political philosophy rather than sociology: specifically by his reliance on an adaptation of John Rawls's theory of justice. The idea of contractuality is not the only way in which to capture the egalitarianism which is inherent in modern societies. By giving it such a central role, Bidet effectively commits himself to a form of market socialism. Yet such a political stance fails to appreciate the degree, emphasized by Marx, to which the market and capitalism are indissociable.

Finally, Christopher Bertram explores the idea that the concept of the person as free and equal which is developed by liberal-democratic capitalism may be incompatible with the institutions of capitalism itself. Liberal-democratic societies give rise to the demand that each be accorded recognition as a moral person by others and by the political order. However, it is one thing to generate a normative order and another to satisfy its claims. The free and equal individuals of liberalism are anything but free and equal in the real world of liberal-democratic capitalism. Bertram illustrates this line of thought by describing how John Rawls's theory of justice, based on such individuals, can imply an economic egalitarianism that is scarcely compatible with capitalist economic organization. This mirrors McCarney's conclusion that the logic of the desire for recognition is radically egalitarian. If this is correct, we have not reached the end of history, where 'end' is understood to be the completion of a process. That completion would require a much more materially egalitarian society than our own. At the same time, Bertram suggests that the conception of the self as free and equal is not the only one characteristic of capitalism and that another such conception, that of the self as rational utility-maximizer, has very different political implications.

Conclusion

Near the end of the twentieth century, socialists have to contend with a capitalism that has been more successful at developing the productive forces than any social form in history, and that may even be better at doing this than a socialist alternative. It has become hard to envisage this development reaching a point at which the replacement of capitalism by socialism is positively necessary in order for the development to continue. But one alternative line of thought, that of moralistic socialism, also looks unpalatable. We can rely neither on the productive forces alone nor on denunciations of the inequities of capitalism to underpin the transition to a socialist society. However, perhaps all is not lost. Human beings desire material well-being, and no doubt in conditions of acute scarcity this desire takes precedence for most people much of the time. Nevertheless, as Fukuyama has pointed out to us, there is another dimension to human desire: the desire to count, to have significance for another. This social desire, to which both Rousseau and Hegel were keenly alive, can, in the right conditions, move people to collective action. This is, of course, the very same idea that Fukuyama relies upon to demonstrate that capitalism is untranscendable. But ideas can outflank their formulators just as desires can overthrow the societies that give rise for them. If only for foregrounding this particular desire, Fukuyama demands more attention than he has received until now from the left.

Notes

1. Francis Fukuyama, 'The End of History?', *The National Interest*, no. 16, 1989.
2. In particular, Kojève's *Introduction à la Lecture de Hegel*, Paris: Gallimard, 1947.
3. Francis Fukyama, *The End of History and the Last Man*, London: Hamish Hamilton/New York: Basic Books, 1992.
4. Although there have been some notable exceptions such as Perry Anderson, 'The Ends of History' in his *A Zone of Engagement*, London: Verso, 1992.
5. Bidet's impressive study is really two books in one, *Théorie de la Modernité suivi de Marx et le Marché*, Paris: Presses Universitaires de France, 1990.

PART I

Fukuyama

1

Shaping Ends: Reflections on Fukuyama
Joseph McCarney

Francis Fukuyama's *The End of History and the Last Man* has been widely regarded as a celebration of the triumph of the West.[1] Its message, on the accepted view, is that, with victory in the Cold War and the death of Communism, the Western way of life has emerged as the culmination of humanity's historical evolution. As the end state towards which that evolution has been tending, it represents a pattern of universal validity, a light to itself and to all non-Western societies still struggling in history. It will be argued here that this interpretation is wholly misconceived and, indeed, that it must be stood on its head to obtain the true meaning of the book. The distinctive core of what the West stands for, in Fukuyama's view, is liberal democracy. What his book really tells us is that this is itself a transitory historical form, the process of whose dissolution is already well advanced. It is a verdict that follows inescapably from the logic of Fukuyama's argument, from the fundamental tenets of the philosophy of history he espouses. Thus, in the classic style of that subject, he arrives on the scene too late, when a way of life has grown old beyond hope of rejuvenation. There is a sharp irony in the fact that philosophy's grey on grey should be taken in this case as an expression of maturity and vigour. Something is owed here to the complex perversity of the times, but something also, it must be admitted, to the strangely half-hearted, double-minded and inadequately self-conscious way in which Fukuyama has approached his task. All this constitutes, however, a reason not for abandoning the agenda he has set but for taking it forward towards completion.

Liberal Democracy in Question

The thesis of Fukuyama's book on the usual reading is that history has now come to an end with the definitive victory of what might be called capitalist democracy or democratic capitalism; that is, of the combination of capitalism and liberal democracy. Although this reading cannot be sustained, it must be acknowledged to have some rather obvious textual support. For a preliminary view of the scene, the evidence for it, and then the evidence that tells just as plainly against, will be sketched. These conflicting indications fix the terms of the discussion that follows.

Fukuyama tells us, in the course of restating and defending an earlier version of his position, that what he had suggested had come to an end was 'not the occurrence of events, even large and grave events, but History: that is, history understood as a single, coherent, evolutionary process, when taking into account the experience of all peoples in all times'.[2] The process is one that 'dictates a common evolutionary pattern for *all* human societies – in short, something like a Universal History of mankind in the direction of liberal democracy'.[3] Fukuyama is, quite generally, still more confident that it is an evolution in the direction of capitalism, an outcome 'in some sense inevitable for advanced countries'.[4] Hence it is that 'We who live in stable, long-standing liberal democracies ... have trouble imagining a world that is radically better than our own, or a future that is not essentially democratic and capitalist.'[5] This inability to imagine alternatives is itself a large part of the substance of the belief that we in the contemporary West are living at the end of history. It seems clear that Fukuyama's commitment to this belief is sufficiently well advertised as to explain and excuse what was referred to earlier as the usual reading of his book. Indeed, it is reasonable to speak in this connection of its official doctrine or, more strictly, of the first version of that doctrine.[6]

The book also contains formulations which cannot be reconciled with this version or, indeed, with any end-of-history thesis. They seem to gain in urgency as it proceeds so that its final chapter is ready to suggest the following conclusion:

> No regime – no 'socio-economic system' – is able to satisfy all men in all places. This includes liberal democracy ... Thus those who remain dissatisfied will always have the potential to restart history.[7]

The last paragraph of the book points the moral by affirming that 'the evidence available to us now' concerning the direction in which the wagon train of history is wandering 'must remain provisionally inconclusive'. Fukuyama takes leave of us on the following still more judicious and sombre note:

> Nor can we in the final analysis know, provided a majority of the wagons eventually reach the same town, whether their occupants, having looked around a bit at their new surroundings, will not find them inadequate and set their eyes on a new and more distant journey.[8]

This scepticism embodies what might be called the second version of Fukuyama's official doctrine. It seems plain that his book contains some large, even structural, tensions. What we need is a principle that will render these conflicting appearances intelligible, some key to the underlying predicament to which they are a confused and confusing response. To obtain it might even enable us to see which appearances can claim the greater authenticity, in the sense of being closer to Fukuyama's primary intellectual impulse and orientation. If any progress is to be made we shall have to consider the 'mechanisms' he relies on, in his role as a philosopher of 'Universal History', to provide a motive force and a direction for the historical process.

There are two such devices. The first is the logic of modern natural science, establishing a 'constantly changing horizon of production possibilities', possibilities which capitalism has proved to be the most efficient means of realizing.[9] Then, to take the story on from capitalism to liberal democracy, there is the age-old struggle of human beings for 'recognition'. The claims Fukuyama makes for the first of these mechanisms, though no doubt contentious enough in themselves, do not give rise to the kinds of internal difficulties we now seek to explore. They constitute what he is content to allow is essentially an economic, indeed 'a kind of Marxist', interpretation of history. It leads, however, he insists, to 'a completely non-Marxist conclusion', to capitalism and not communism as the end state.[10] This position is confidently and consistently maintained. Things are different with what Fukuyama acknowledges to be the 'most difficult' part of the argument, the transition to liberal democracy.[11]

The theme of the desire for recognition is, according to Fukuyama, as old as Western political philosophy. Its first major statement is Plato's account of *thymos*, the 'spirited' aspect or part of the soul. Thereafter it emerges in various guises in the thought of, among others, Machiavelli, Hobbes, Rousseau, Alexander Hamilton, James Madison, Hegel and Nietzsche.[12] The immediate source of Fukuyama's use of it is, however, Alexandre Kojève's reading of Hegel where it has a central role. The classic formulation of the theme, in Kojève's view, is the master–slave dialectic of *The Phenomenology of Spirit*, an episode that is for him the key to Hegel's entire philosophy of history. In Kojève's version of that philosophy the substance of human history is constituted by the struggle for recognition of fighting masters and toiling slaves. These struggles are necessarily unavailing, essentially because the slave, being a slave, can neither receive nor confer a humanly satisfying recognition. In the course of historical time, however, and specifically through the French Revolution and its aftermath, the contradictions of mastery and slavery are dialectically overcome. Both are transcended in equal citizenship in what Kojève calls the 'universal and homogeneous state' whose prototype is the Napoleonic Empire. Here every individual receives 'universal' recognition as 'a Citizen enjoying all political rights and as a "juridical person" of the civil law'.[13] The achievement of this fully satisfying form of recognition brings history to an end by, as it were, switching off the motor of its movement.

For Fukuyama to appropriate this body of thought he has to make a simple, strategic assumption. It is that 'we can understand' Kojève's universal and homogeneous state as liberal democracy.[14] The crux of the matter is then easy to state: 'Kojève's claim that we are at the end of history ... stands or falls on the strength of the assertion that the recognition provided by the contemporary liberal-democratic state adequately satisfies the human desire for recognition.'[15] The incisiveness of this formulation is, unfortunately, not matched by Fukuyama's response. Indeed, he never manages thereafter to hold the question steadily in his sights, still less to provide an unequivocal and authoritative answer. This failure is the chief source of the impression of systematic ambiguity left by his book. For the issue at stake, the satisfactoriness of liberal-democratic recognition, is the best clue to the array of conflicting appearances it presents. Moreover, to survey the variety of views Fukuyama seems to endorse on this issue is not simply to encounter a medley of contending strains, all with much the same claim to be the true voice of their author. Instead we find on one side a line of thought that seems lifeless, blinkered, without much sense of personal involvement. On the other there is a strong thread of argument, drawn out with energy, individuality and full awareness. It confronts and seems able to rebut in its own terms the claims of the first side without meeting any answering denial or even engagement. Hence, the theme of recognition can shed light on the question raised earlier of authenticity, of which are the deep and which the shallow features of Fukuyama's position.

The Influence of Leo Strauss

There is, to begin with, a line of thought comprising the indications that Fukuyama accepts the essentials of Kojève's case. That he is in some measure disposed to do so is hardly surprising since they provide the theoretical basis of his official doctrine in its first version. Thus, for much of the time he seems content to take over the substance of Kojève, giving it a liberal-democratic gloss. In this frame of mind the liberal-democratic state is conceived of as providing a fully satisfying recognition on Kojèvian lines. That is to say, it recognizes all human beings universally 'by granting and protecting their *rights*'.[16] Recognition becomes reciprocal 'when the state and the people recognize each other, that is, when the state grants its citizens rights and when citizens agree to abide by the state's laws'.[17] At times Fukuyama even outdoes Kojève in propounding the merits of this arrangement, as in the claim, surely absurd on any literal reading, that 'The liberal democratic state values us at our own sense of self-worth.'[18] We seem here to be firmly grounded in the brave new, and historically final, world of liberal democracy.

Yet a different and deeper note soon intrudes, growing more insistent as the discussion proceeds. To appreciate it fully one has to take account of another element in the intellectual background of Fukuyama's work. This is the presence there of Kojève's major critic and interlocutor, Leo Strauss. Their debate was sustained for over thirty years, chiefly by means of a correspondence which has now reached the public realm in the second edition of Strauss's *On Tyranny*.[19] The influence of Strauss on Fukuyama is much less prominently advertised than is that of Kojève, surfacing only in copious footnotes. Yet it is no less significant.[20] Indeed, Fukuyama's book may be read as the record of a struggle for his soul between Kojève and Strauss, a struggle in which the latter has the better of things in the end. To read it in terms of this unacknowledged drama is to gain an otherwise unobtainable perspective on its many evasions and equivocations.

A striking feature of the Strauss–Kojève debate is the urbane yet implacable resistance Strauss offers to the idea that recognition by the universal, homogeneous state brings history to a credible or satisfactory end. Against it he mounts a whole battery of objections which are for the most part not fully worked out or integrated but still ingenious and fertile in a high degree. They anticipate Fukuyama's discussion with considerable exactness and prove to be the basic instrument by means of which his attachment to Kojève is undermined. When doubts about Kojèvian recognition begin to arise for Fukuyama it is plain that Strauss's contribution is in the forefront of his thoughts. He refers to it in a note, and the text provides what is essentially a restatement.[21] His doubts centre, just as Strauss's did, on the issue of universality. The question, as formulated by Fukuyama, is whether recognition that can be universalized is 'worth having in the first place' and whether the quality of recognition may not be 'far more important' than its universality.[22] Echoing Strauss's concern with 'great men', he asks whether the 'humble sort of recognition' embodied in the granting of liberal rights would be satisfying for the few who had 'infinitely more ambitious natures'.[23] These are people driven by what Fukuyama calls *megalothymia*; that is, 'the desire to be recognized as better than others'.[24]

The Straussian movement of thought is re-enacted at the next stage when Fukuyama wonders whether even if everyone was fully content merely by virtue of having rights in a democratic society, with no further aspirations beyond citizenship, we would not in fact find such people 'worthy of contempt'.[25] Following Strauss, he invokes Nietzsche's image of the 'last man' to convey the spiritual emptiness and torpor of this situation. It is a world in which, for Strauss, 'man loses his humanity', that which 'raises man above the brutes', and in which, for Fukuyama, there are 'no longer human beings but animals of the genus *homo sapiens*'.[26] The moral is succinctly drawn by Strauss: 'If the universal and homogeneous state is the goal of History, History is absolutely "tragic".'[27]

Taken together, Strauss's objections constitute a formidable case. Yet it is one which Kojève never seriously attempts to address.[28] Indeed, the strangely inflexible, all-or-nothing cast of his thought makes it difficult to see how he might have done so. The entire structure rests on an analysis of Hegelian desire which sees what is distinctively human as 'Desire that is directed towards Desire as Desire'; that is, according to Kojève, desire for recognition.[29] This can, he argues, be 'definitively' satisfied only by realizing a universal recognition whose uniquely appropriate source is 'Universality incarnated in the State as such'.[30] Thus we arrive at a vision of the end of history whose formalism, abstraction and simplicity have aroused much comment.[31] In it only two kinds of entity figure, individual citizens and the state, each accepting and confirming the juridical status of the other. The push towards extremes in Kojève's thought is, as Strauss perceived, most fully realized in the conception of the individual in the end state. Human action is properly speaking, for Kojève, the negation of the given in the service of desire. Where desire is definitively satisfied this motivation loses its force, and action in the full, historical sense fades from the scene. Since, however, negating action is the hallmark of our humanity, what this implies is nothing less than 'the disappearance of Man at the end of History' and the emergence of an 'animal in *harmony* with Nature or given Being'.[32] Thus, Kojève is, at least sometimes, prepared to accept, even to celebrate, the condition of the 'last man' so deplored by Strauss. The pure, intense character of this eschatology is achieved, it must be said, only at the cost of an aridity and brittleness that seem unlikely to commend it widely. At least the strain of maintaining it proves too much for Fukuyama as he comes under the pressure of Straussian scepticism. His retreat may be seen from one point of view as a tribute to his realism and sensitivity to a range of conflicting considerations. Yet it shows also his curious tendency to register them by simply incorporating the alternatives into his text, so that they lie down side by side without any movement of integration or mediation. Thus the thin consistency of Kojève is replaced by a richer incoherence. More significantly for immediate purposes is the consequent erosion of the basis of Fukuyama's first official doctrine, a process one may now trace to its conclusion.

Cold Monsters

A second Nietzschean tag invoked by Fukuyama will convey the spirit of the discussion. It is the reference to the state as 'the coldest of all cold monsters', an estimate whose implications for hopes of satisfying recognition are easy to gauge. Recognition by the state, Fukuyama tells us in drawing them out, is 'necessarily impersonal'. The contrast is with 'community life', which involves a 'much more immediately satisfying', 'much more individual', sort of recognition, based not just on universal 'personness' but on 'a host of particular qualities that together make up one's being'.[33] What we really want, it seems, is an individual and inescapably heterogeneous recognition, geared to the specificity of our particular existences, which the state by its very nature, its universal, homogeneous mode of operation, cannot provide. Significantly, Kojève comes in for direct criticism at this point in the argument. In modern times, Fukuyama suggests, citizenship is best exercised through 'so-called "mediating institutions"', the vast range of civic associations from political parties to literary societies.[34] This is a truth which was well understood by Hegel, though not by Kojève:

> In this respect Hegel is quite different from Kojève's interpretation of him. Kojève's universal and homogeneous state makes no room for 'mediating' bodies like corporations or *Stände*; the very adjectives Kojève uses to describe his end state suggest a more Marxist vision of a society where there is nothing between free, equal, and atomized individuals and the state.[35]

The question of what is 'more Marxist' about such a vision may be set aside here, except to note the obvious distancing function of that description. What is important is that we appear to be at a strategic turning point in the argument. For Kojève's abstract statism is surely being decisively rejected. The comments on it have every appearance of constituting a considered verdict, reached through a prolonged engagement, not to say infatuation, with its object. It crowns a spirited and committed movement of thought and the position being criticized is never rehabilitated thereafter. This is as close as we shall get to noting an authentic, principled shift in Fukuyama's thinking. It provides both an obituary for his Kojèvianism and a clear indication of an alternative way forward. If the thesis that history ends in liberal democracy is to be sustained, it is plainly not to the liberal-democratic state that we should look for a consummating satisfaction. Instead we have to turn to the sphere of community life with its host of mediating institutions, to what is today generally referred to as 'civil society'.

This move runs immediately, however, into difficulties of its own. Although a strong community life may be 'democracy's best guarantee that its citizens do not turn into last men', it is, Fukuyama observes, 'constantly threatened in contemporary societies'.[36] What he has in mind are the societies of 'Anglo-Saxon' liberalism in particular and of Western liberal democracy more generally. The root cause of their plight, as seen by Fukuyama, is the tendency to conceive of community in purely contractual terms, as a device to safeguard the rights and minister to the interests of individuals. These rights are themselves interpreted in ways that are destructive of the possibility of a rich common life. The democratic principle of equality is, in its boundless tolerance of alternatives, opposed to 'the kind of exclusivity engendered by strong and cohesive communities'.[37] The principle of liberty ensures, among other things, that any contract of association may be freely abrogated when it fails to bring the expected benefits to the individual contractors.[38] Matters are made worse by the workings of liberal economic principles which 'provide no support for traditional communities' but, quite the contrary, 'tend to atomize and separate people'.[39] Hence it is that all forms of associational life from the family to 'the largest association, the country itself', come to lead a precarious existence, at constant risk of being emptied of their substantial, inner meaning. This is a disappointing outcome of the shift in Fukuyama's argument. The search for satisfying recognition had led away from that cold monster, the state, towards the promised warmth of community life. In Western societies, however, this promise has turned out to be illusory. All we encounter is the chilliness of contract, of arrangements instrumentally calculated to meet the needs of self-interested, atomic individuals. The true spirit of community, and hence the possibility of recognition in and through community, cannot reside in, or be sustained by, such arrangements.

Fukuyama's thinking about these matters has another important dimension to consider. It consists in his awareness of a viable, indeed flourishing, alternative, even at the supposed end of history, to liberal democracy. Earlier he had noted that Asian societies offer a sense of community conspicuously absent from the contemporary United States.[40] Their 'community-orientedness', it now appears, is grounded not in contracts between self-interested parties but in religion or some near-substitute such as Confucianism.[41] The recognition they provide is a kind of 'group recognition' that is vanishing from the West. What the individual works for is the recognition that the group accords him and the recognition of the group by other groups.[42] He derives his status 'primarily not on the basis of his individual ability or worth, but insofar as he is a member of one of a series of interlocking groups'.[43] The resulting emphasis on group harmony has, Fukuyama acknowledges, implications for political life. Even Japanese democracy looks, he observes, somewhat authoritarian by American or European standards, while elsewhere in Asia authoritarianism of a more overt variety is widespread.[44] Here we witness the raising of a spectre that comes increasingly to haunt the pages of Fukuyama's book. The manner in which his focus gradually shifts from West to East in pursuit of it is itself a major aspect, as well as a symbol, of the complex dislocations that characterize the work.

The haunting power of this vision can be fully appreciated only if one notes another factor in the situation. It takes one back to the first of Fukuyama's historical mechanisms, 'the logic of advanced industrialization determined by modern natural science'. It is a logic which, according to a constant theme in his work, 'creates a strong predisposition in favour of capitalism and market economics'.[45] He is equally constant in holding that it has no such tendency to favour liberal democracy. Indeed, democracy is, he assures us, 'almost never chosen for economic reasons'.[46] More emphatically still, it has 'no *economic* rationale' and 'if anything, democratic politics is a drag on economic efficiency'.[47] The reasons for this are in part rather familiar ones which have been articulated by Lee Kuan Yew and, in a more sophisticated form, by Joseph Schumpeter. The basic idea is that democracy interferes with economic rationality in decision-making. It does so through its tendency to indulge in policies that sacrifice growth and low inflation to requirements of redistribution and current consumption.[48] In addition Fukuyama employs a more interesting and distinctive line of reasoning. It holds that 'the individual self-interest at the heart of Western liberal economic theory may be an inferior source of motivation to certain forms of group interest.' Hence it is that 'the highly atomistic economic liberalism of the United States or Britain' becomes 'economically counter-productive' at a certain point. It does so when it begins to erode the work ethic on which capitalist prosperity ultimately depends.[49] Thus, the logic of the industrialization process would seem to point neither to liberal democracy nor to socialism but to what Fukuyama calls 'the truly winning combination' of liberal economics and authoritarian politics; that is to a 'market-oriented authoritarianism'.[50] This projection of theory is, in his view, fully in line with the empirical evidence, for instance, the historical record of authoritarian modernizers as against their democratic counterparts.[51] It is borne out most strikingly by the contrast between the lack of 'economic functionality' shown by democracy in America in recent years and the economic success, indeed economic miracle, achieved by neo-Confucian, authoritarian capitalism in Southeast Asia.[52]

It is time to draw some threads of this discussion together. The nub of the matter, it is now clear, is that both of Fukuyama's historical regulators lead decisively away from liberal democracy. That system is economically dysfunctional and cannot provide satisfying recognition either. In each case the root cause of failure is the same, the radical individualism that corrodes the ties of community on which, ultimately, meaningful recognition and economic success alike depend. A less triumphal message would be hard to conceive. It tells us that the contemporary Western way of life is doomed, just as communism was and for essentially the same reason, an inability to resolve the fundamental contradictions of desire which have driven human history up to now. To point this out is in a sense to reach the outer limits of a programme of showing what may with confidence be inferred on the basis of Fukuyama's argument. It is, however, a verdict of a somewhat negative kind. Given that we in the contemporary West are not experiencing the end of history, it is natural to wonder whether anything more positive might be said about the significance of the stretch of historical time through which we are passing. The complex theoretical apparatus Fukuyama has assembled might after all be expected to have some kind of intelligible perspective to offer on the current wanderings of history's wagon train. To raise this issue is to be brought up at once against the looming presence of the alternative form of capitalism he calls 'market-oriented authoritarianism'. The status of, and prospects for, this system need a closer look.

Western Weakness/Eastern Strength

A background is provided here by the speculation Fukuyama engages in concerning the present outlook for world history. It centres on what he plausibly takes to be the key issue, the future of Asia, and in particular of Japan. The position of Japan is consistently ambiguous in his scheme, being sometimes treated as a representative liberal democracy and sometimes held apart from that category. The ambiguity has a dynamic aspect. For Fukuyama believes that Japan, and Asia more generally, are 'at a particularly critical turning point with respect to world history'. On the one side lies the Western road of universal and reciprocal recognition, the universal rights of man and of woman, formal liberal democracy, personal dignity, private consumption, and a decline in the importance of groups. On the other side, 'a systematic illiberal and nondemocratic alternative combining economic rationalism with paternalistic authoritarianism' may gain ground.[53] Formally at least, Fukuyama wishes to treat these options as genuinely open. The tone and tendency of his account are, however, decidedly pessimistic. Thus he lists certain conditions under which the authoritarian option would become the more likely. Yet on his own showing the important ones are already firmly in place. These are faltering economic growth in America and Europe relative to the Far East and the continuing progressive breakdown in Western societies of basic social institutions like the family. It is entirely in line with this strand of thinking that he should suggest that 'the beginnings of a systematic Asian rejection of liberal democracy' can now be heard.[54] Plainly he is deeply alarmed by this prospect. A satisfactory response cannot, however, be yielded just by empirical speculation concerning likely and unlikely scenarios. It is necessary to ask what theoretical resources there might be for meeting the challenge. The question is whether Fukuyama has a principled means of rebutting the claim of market-oriented authoritarianism to represent the direction in which world history is currently moving, or even to constitute its final destination. For the spectre that haunts the later part of his book is in its most chilling form the possibility that he has simply misidentified the end state, that the end-of-history thesis will stand provided that authoritarian is substituted for democratic capitalism as the final form of human society.

At first sight it may seem that Fukuyama does have theoretical means of resisting the claims of authoritarian capitalism. This is suggested by the charge, apparently directed at the very roots of that system, that 'Recognition based on groups is ultimately irrational.'[55] On some accounts of the role of reason in history it must be allowed that this charge would have considerable weight. Indeed, if it could be upheld it would be decisive for the crucial issue of whether a system founded on irrational recognition might be indefinitely self-sustaining. Fukuyama's conception of reason lays claim, however, to no such ontological significance. Although never laid out systematically, it has in practice both a Humean and a Kantian aspect. In the first of them, the 'slave of the passions' view, reason figures as the minister of desire, a device for adapting means to ends set independently of it.[56] Where recognition is concerned it is, however, the second aspect that is important. Rational recognition, Fukuyama tells us, is 'recognition on a universal basis in which the dignity of each person as a free and autonomous human being is recognized by all'.[57] It is, one might say, the equal recognition of all persons as Kantian moral subjects. Fukuyama is fully aware that group recognition does not meet this specification. It is by its very nature restricted, not universal, and granted in virtue of group membership, not of free, autonomous individuality as such.[58] Given the theoretical assumptions at work here, the assertion that group recognition is irrational emerges as a conceptual truth, indeed virtually a tautology. It can yield no substantive grounds for doubting the viability of a social system based on such recognition. Neither does one obtain such grounds if, like Fukuyama, one supplements it with a normative preference for universal over group recognition. Adding a Kantian thought to a Kantian definition in this way may well seem natural, even self-evidently justified, to people of a liberal outlook.

Moreover, it might well provide a starting point for a critique of group recognition, a set of reasons for thinking it undesirable or unworthy. Such an argument would not of itself, however, comprise or form part of an explanation of why a system founded on it could not sustain itself, or even why it might not prove to be the final goal of human history.

The search for that explanation is in any case radically subverted by another feature of Fukuyama's account. This is the recurring suggestion that rational recognition cannot exist on its own since 'the emergence and durability of a society embodying rational recognition appears to *require* the survival of certain forms of irrational recognition.'[59] In slightly more concrete terms we are told that 'it appears to be the case that rational recognition is not self-sustaining, but must rely on pre-modern, non-universal forms of recognition to function properly.'[60] For real vitality and staying power we have, it seems, to look to irrational, that is group, recognition. The rational, universal kind appears by contrast as a parasitic form, dependent on a source of life outside itself. The social and political implications of this relationship surface occasionally in the text:

> Group rather than universal recognition can be a better support for both economic activity and community life ... not only is universal recognition not universally satisfying, but the ability of liberal democratic societies to establish and sustain themselves on a rational basis over the long term is open to some doubt.[61]

These implications are tentatively drawn, as they have to be to keep any semblance of congruity with Fukuyama's official views. Yet his fears for the future of liberal democracy flow directly, it should now be clear, from the underlying logic of his theory of history and find no countervailing reassurance there. They may be said to represent the deepest strand of thought in his book. In this light liberal democracy appears as an inherently precarious achievement without strong roots in the basic structure of human desires – a familiar kind of liberal nightmare. It is rather the product of quite specific historical conditions which are now in a process of dissolution. To this diagnosis Fukuyama has added what might be termed the dialectical insight that the seeds of the process lie within. The societies of radical individualism are being consumed by the very forces which made them possible in the first place. Thus the process is essentially one of self-destruction, and all the more inexorable on that account. With the surface froth removed this is a bleak vision, an announcement with elaborate theoretical backing that it really is closing time in the gardens of the West.

The Problems of Inequality

A reference was made earlier to conceptions of history which allow reason a larger role than Fukuyama envisages. The obvious case in point is that of Hegel, ultimately the dominant intellectual influence in Fukuyama's book. The issue is the subject of some of Hegel's most dramatic pronouncements, as when he affirms that history is a rational process because reason is active in it as 'substance and infinite power'.[62] It might be supposed that the most direct way to draw out the implications of this doctrine for Fukuyama's problems is through the concept of freedom. The workings of reason in history constitute the ground of Hegel's canonical description of it as 'the progress of the consciousness of freedom'. They do so in virtue of the complex dialectical relationships believed to obtain in this area, in particular the idea that self-conscious freedom *consists in* reason.[63] There are ample theoretical resources here for dealing with the suggestion that history might conceivably end in some form of collectivist authoritarianism, an outcome that would be the very antithesis of rational, self-conscious freedom. It may be more appropriate at present, however, to turn to a different aspect of the Hegelian background. For Fukuyama makes no claim to take on board the historical ontology of freedom and reason. In his conception reason is, as we have seen, either instrumental calculation or universal predicability, and freedom is the 'negative' liberty enshrined in individual rights of the classic liberal tradition. However important it might be in a full-scale discussion to examine Hegel's quite different treatment of these categories, doing so now would lead sharply away from our concerns. It is in any case more in the spirit of Hegelian critique to seek to view Fukuyama's work immanently in its own terms. What this implies in particular is that we should attend to elements in the legacy of Hegel which Fukuyama does explicitly endorse and seek to appropriate. The obvious candidate is the concept of recognition, itself the main pivot on which the intellectual structure of his book turns. The social and political dimensions of the concept are better explored here in terms of equality rather than freedom. To do so should provide an equally effective handle on the question of the viability of authoritarian capitalism. For that system is marked as much by inequality as by unfreedom, and whatever a theory of history has to say about its status and prospects can be mediated as well by the one route as the other. As we shall see, freedom will not be left entirely behind, a fact that reflects its inescapable position at the centre of the entire conceptual field.

The question of inequality arises for Fukuyama chiefly in connection with the charge 'from the Left' that 'the promise of universal, reciprocal recognition remains essentially unfulfilled in liberal societies'. It does so, the charge runs, because 'economic inequality brought about by capitalism *ipso facto* implies unequal recognition'.[64] The pages in which Fukuyama deals with this criticism are among the least coherent in his book. On the one hand we are told that the problems of inequality are 'in a certain sense, unresolvable within the context of liberalism'.[65] The implication is, presumably, that they might be resolvable within the context of some other socio-economic system. On the other hand we learn that liberal societies are progressively overcoming those inequalities which are grounded in convention rather than nature:

We may interpret Kojève's remark that post-war America had in effect achieved Marx's 'classless society' in these terms: not that all social inequality was eliminated, but that those barriers which remained were in some respect 'necessary and ineradicable', due to the nature of things rather than the will of man.[66]

In keeping with this second line of thought there is the claim that the egalitarian passions in American society exist because of, and not despite, 'the smallness of its actual remaining inequalities'.[67] In keeping with the first there is an eloquent description of 'the situation of the so-called black "underclass" in contemporary America'. It is one of a deprivation to which 'achievement of full legal equality for blacks and the opportunities provided by the US economy will not make terribly much difference'.[68] It is, that is to say, a situation in which both the pillars of Fukuyama's world-view, liberal democracy and capitalism, prove to be ineffective. Thus, in the space of a few pages, the inequalities in liberal societies are trivialized and depicted seriously, said to be unresolvable by such societies, and said to be on the way to resolution by them in so far as that is humanly possible. These conflicting tendencies may indicate some uneasiness on Fukuyama's part in meeting the charge from the left. What is wholly consistent is his resolve that, however it is to be met, it ranks in importance below the countercharge from the right that liberal democracies err in recognizing unequal people equally. This pole of criticism is, he insists, 'more powerful', 'greater and ultimately more serious', and 'more profound'.[69] It leads directly into the vein of Nietzschean, elitist speculation on the low spiritual state of the 'last men' which bulks so large towards the end of the book. Yet Fukuyama may well have good grounds for being uneasy when confronting the egalitarian case. For the rank ordering of problems he adopts in response is not endorsed or warranted by his mentors, Hegel and Kojève; nor does it accord with the character of his borrowings from them.

Following the Argument Where It Leads

This is most readily shown by returning to what is for Kojève, and following him Fukuyama, the *locus classicus* of the recognition theme, in order to expand the remarks made earlier. It is all too obvious that in the master–slave relationship there is no recognition available to the slave. The loss of humanity in that status precludes it utterly. Much more interesting is Hegel's insight that it is this very same factor which ensures that the master cannot be satisfied either. For the value of recognition derives from, and cannot transcend, its source, and recognition by a being who lacks all human worth and dignity is itself nugatory. As Hegel explains, this 'one-sided and unequal' recognition does not suffice for 'recognition proper'. The master can never achieve satisfaction, in Hegelian terms the certainty of 'the truth of himself', through the relationship with a 'dependent' consciousness.[70] This is the character of the particular contradition of desire in which the master is trapped. His plight takes on another aspect when one notes that recognition by such a consciousness must be, or must be under a fixed and vitiating presumption of being, enforced just in virtue of the fact of dependency, of the relation of subordination and dominance. As Kojève saw clearly, it is of the essence of the distinctively human desire for recognition that it is a desire 'for a desire', for what cannot by its nature be commanded from without but must arise as an inner determination of the self, that is, as something freely given. Here, as generally elsewhere, equality is not opposed to freedom but is rather a precondition of it, and freedom in its turn, it now appears, is internally linked to the ability to provide satisfactory recognition. Since these are all properties that admit of degrees the situation may be conceived in terms of a continuum. At one extreme, in the gross inequality of master and slave, there is both complete subjection of one being to another and complete absence of meaningful recognition. At the other there is the free, self-determined mutual recognition of equals, embodying what are for these purposes the very lineaments of gratified desire. In between, the quality of recognition varies inversely with the inequality of the recognizers. The point may be put more formally by saying that equality is a condition of the possibility of 'recognition proper'. To put it in this way is to offer a kind of transcendental argument for the principle of equality in the context of the human practice of giving and receiving recognition.[71] It reveals a presupposition of that practice, both a requirement of its intelligibility and a commitment that has to be taken on by anyone who engages seriously with it. Hence it is that the true meaning of the master–slave dialectic, the paradigmatic struggle for recognition, is a radical egalitarianism.

It is a meaning from which Hegel himself increasingly shrank as his thought fell into its well-known pattern of a deepening conservatism. The process is reflected in the way the recognition motif loses its force and identity in his later writings. By the time of *The Philosophy of Right*, 'recognition' itself has become simply a general term that is appropriate wherever there is any kind of 'being for another'.[72] It was precisely, however, the strong sense it bears in the *Phenomenology* that Kojève, with a deep insight, had seized on as the cornerstone of his interpretation. From it he derives the doctrine that the master–slave nexus can be dialectically overcome only in 'homogeneity'. This implies, in particular, as he makes clear, a world without 'class strife', indeed without the 'specific differences' of class.[73] The doctrine is one which he failed to maintain in a consistent or principled way. In later years, swamped by cynicism and the spirit of accommodation, it surfaces mainly in fatuous remarks such as that cited by Fukuyama about the 'classless society' of the postwar United States.[74] Yet even here a truth is being acknowledged in a degraded form and with a bad conscience. The truth is that a philosophy of history which puts the human struggle for recognition at its centre is compelled to envisage a society free from the structural inequalities of which class is the type and emblem. For recognition is, as we have seen, an essentially egalitarian concept. To take it seriously is necessarily to be confronted with a vision of a community of free and equal beings in reciprocal relations of acceptance and respect.

The transcendental character of this argument deserves further comment. It seeks to tell us where we get to in the philosophy of history if we start from recognition. As usual in such cases, it seems possible to evade the conclusion by declining the starting point, and so an independent grounding of that is needed. To try to provide it would go well beyond the limits of this discussion, though it is not difficult to see where one might look for inspiration and guidance. Most immediately there is the Hegelian system with its manifold resources and large authority. Further off there lies behind the category of recognition, as Fukuyama reminds us in tracing its ancestry, the main weight of our tradition of political theory.[75] For the centrality of the category is the distinctive contribution of that tradition to the understanding of human motivation and behaviour. It may be that Fukuyama's best achievement is to have reopened in a pressing way the theme of recognition as a subject of inquiry. He has shown here an acute feeling for what is important and fruitful to explore, even if the full consequences of doing so might not be personally acceptable to him. To justify recognition as a starting point would enable one to demonstrate, not merely to deduce transcendentally, that history cannot end in authoritarian capitalism, and that would in itself be welcome. That it cannot end in any form of class society and, *a fortiori*, of capitalism would not be at all congenial to him.

In a general way, of course, it would be difficult to think of a conclusion less in tune with the spirit of our age than one which holds that the concept of the classless society is the key to the direction and goal of history. Even those who might be sympathetic to it as an ideal are likely to be unnerved by a sense of the difficulties, in particular that of envisaging in any concretely intelligible way how we get from here to there. These are what, in different ways, overwhelmed both Hegel and Kojève, and even standing on their shoulders, things are not likely to be easier for us. Yet it would be irrational to assume in advance that the difficulties are wholly intractable. Moreover, there are those who have not been overwhelmed and will stay with us to the end in grappling with them. Such an enterprise would, however, lie still further beyond the limits of present concerns in some realm of social science. For the present it will simply have to be borne in mind when proposing our conclusion that in philosophy we are enjoined to follow the argument wherever it leads. It may be added that if even the philosophy of history cannot allow access to some larger view of our situation, we may well be cut off from such views altogether. It surely has an obligation to say whatever is revealed by its weak and flickering light even in dark times, and perhaps in them most of all.

Notes

1. Francis Fukuyama, *The End of History and the Last Man* (henceforth *EHLM*), London: Hamish Hamilton/New York: The Free Press, 1992.
2. *EHLM*, p. xii.
3. *EHLM*, p. 48.
4. *EHLM*, p. 98; cf. p. 90.
5. *EHLM*, p. 46.
6. In an earlier article I wrote of an 'exoteric' and an 'esoteric' version of Fukuyama's position. But this way of putting things makes assumptions about his intentions which cannot be justified here. Nothing will be lost by simply distinguishing between an official doctrine or doctrines and what is implied by the deeper logic of the argument, without imputing any particular degree of self-consciousness to the author. See Joseph McCarney, 'Endgame', *Radical Philosophy* 62, Autumn 1992, pp. 35–8.
7. *EHLM*, p. 334.
8. *EHLM*, p. 339.
9. *EHLM*, p. 77; cf. p. 91.
10. *EHLM*, p. 131.
11. *EHLM*, p. 109.
12. *EHLM*, p. 162.
13. Alexandre Kojève, *Introduction to the Reading of Hegel*, edited by Allan Bloom, New York: Basic Books, 1969, pp. 40, 237.
14. *EHLM*, p. xxi.
15. *EHLM*, p. 207.
16. *EHLM*, p. 202.
17. *EHLM*, p. 203.
18. *EHLM*, p. 200.
19. Leo Strauss, *On Tyranny*, edited by Victor Gourevitch and Michael S. Roth, New York: The Free Press, 1991, pp. 213–325.
20. It may be worth noting that the influences here are mediated by the person of Allan Bloom, as pupil of Strauss, editor of Kojève and teacher of Fukuyama
21. *EHLM*, p. 386n.
22. *EHLM*, p. 301; Strauss, pp. 209–10.
23. *EHLM*, p. 302; Strauss, p. 238.
24. *EHLM*, p. 304.
25. *EHLM*, p. 302; Strauss, pp. 207–8.
26. *EHLM*, p. 312; Strauss, pp. 208, 239.
27. Strauss, p. 208.
28. As Strauss complains, some twenty-five years into their correspondence; Strauss, p. 291.
29. Kojève, p. 144. Following Fukuyama, we shall not inquire how far Kojève's interpretation of Hegel is correct, but simply assume 'a new synthetic philosopher named Hegel–Kojève' (*EHLM*, p. 144). For some doubts about Kojève on Hegelian 'desire', see, however, Hans-Georg Gadamer, *Hegel's Dialectic: Five Hermeneutical Studies*, trans. P. Christopher Smith, New Haven: Yale, 1976, p. 62n.
30. Kojève, pp. 40, 58.
31. Most effectively from Perry Anderson whose epithets these are. Perry Anderson, *A Zone of Engagement*, London: Verso, 1992, p. 323. Fukuyama comes to have similar

misgivings; see below.

32. Kojève, pp. 158–9n. He later had 'a radical change of opinion on this point' as a result of a visit to Japan (Kojève, pp. 159–62n).
33. *EHLM*, p. 323.
34. *EHLM*, p. 322.
35. *EHLM*, p. 388n. At this point the fiction of 'Hegel–Kojève' has completely broken down.
36. *EHLM*, p. 323.
37. *EHLM*, p. 324.
38. *EHLM*, p. 324.
39. *EHLM*, p. 325.
40. *EHLM*, p. 242.
41. *EHLM*, p. 325.
42. *EHLM*, p. 231.
43. *EHLM*, p. 238.
44. *EHLM*, pp. 240–41. Its most prominent advocate is Lee Kuan Yew who has argued that 'a form of paternalistic authoritarianism is more in keeping with Asia's Confucian traditions' than is liberal democracy (*EHLM*, p. 241).
45. *EHLM*, p. 109.
46. *EHLM*, p. 134.
47. *EHLM*, p. 205.
48. *EHLM*, pp. 123–4, 241.
49. *EHLM*, p. 233, p. 335.
50. *EHLM*, p. 123.
51. *EHLM*, p. 123.
52. *EHLM*, pp. 41, 100–101, 124.
53. *EHLM*, pp. 242–3.
54. *EHLM*, p. 243.
55. *EHLM*, p. 242; cf. pp. 201, 266, 337.
56. *EHLM*, pp. 185, 334.
57. *EHLM*, p. 200.
58. *EHLM*, p. 238.
59. *EHLM*, p. 207.
60. *EHLM*, p. 334.
61. *EHLM*, p. 335.
62. G.W.F. Hegel, *Lectures on the Philosophy of World History*, trans. H.B. Nisbet, Cambridge: Cambridge University Press, 1980, p. 27.
63. Ibid., p. 144.
64. *EHLM*, p. 289.
65. *EHLM*, p. 289.
66. *EHLM*, p. 291.
67. *EHLM*, p. 295.
68. *EHLM*, pp. 291–2.
69. *EHLM*, pp. xxii, 299, 300.
70. G.W.F. Hegel, *Phenomenology of Spirit*, trans. A.V. Miller, Oxford: Oxford University Press, 1979, pp. 116–17.
71. For transcendental arguments generally, see Charles Taylor, 'The Validity of Transcendental Arguments', *Proceedings of the Aristotelian Society*, 1979, pp. 151–65. For Kojève

on the 'Transcendental', see Kojève, pp. 123–4.

72. I owe this formulation to Andrew Chitty. It should be noted that even in *The Philosophy of Right* Hegel treats social inequality in a more serious and principled way than does Fukuyama. In society, he insists, 'poverty immediately takes the form of a wrong done to one class (*Klasse*) by another'. It is a wrong which in spite of his best efforts he finds no way to correct and his discussion ends in a most uncharacteristically inconclusive way: 'The important question of how poverty is to be abolished is one of the most disturbing problems which agitate modern society.' *Hegel's Philosophy of Right*, trans. T.M. Knox, Oxford: Oxford University Press, 1967, pp. 277–8.

73. Kojève, pp. 90, 237. Among the specific differences to be overcome Kojève includes those of race. It would not be difficult to extend the argument to include gender also.

74. Kojève, 'Note to the Second Edition', p. 161.

75. Of all the thinkers mentioned by Fukuyama, it is perhaps Rousseau who has, before Hegel, the deepest understanding of the inner link between recognition and equality: 'It is only in relation to persons whom one values and honours as equals, Rousseau argues, that one can oneself receive that recognition and respect that is truly meaningful, that truly represents one's being honoured as a morally significant being.' N.J.H. Dent, *A Rousseau Dictionary*, Oxford: Blackwell, 1992, p. 116; cf. p. 35.

2

The Enthronement of Low Expectations: Fukuyama's Ideological Compromise for Our Time
Frank Füredi

When Max Nordau published his controversial bestseller *Degeneration* in 1895, he could count on a substantial readership to share his disdain for the prevailing vogue of *fin-de-siècle* pessimism. He could assert confidently that 'the great majority of the middle and lower classes is naturally not *fin-de-siècle*'.[1] Today, by contrast, end-of-century gloom overshadows society, enveloping even the middle and lower classes, even in the USA where a middle-class sense of well-being has always been more securely established than in Europe. Reflecting on his sixty years' experience as an observer of the American scene, Alistair Cooke writes that the 'feeling is epidemic across the country that daily life, in every sort and size of community is getting more squalid, expensive and dangerous, and that the US is going or has gone over the peak of what the Spenglers and Toynbees would call its "maturity".'[2]

Today pessimism permeates the Western world. Deep-seated scepticism about the possibility of economic growth and social progress coexists with widespread anxiety about the future. Ours is an era of nostalgia, in which the 'good old days' provide more inspiration than anything born out of the present. In this context Francis Fukuyama's triumphalist essay 'The End of History?', published in 1989, and his 1992 book of the same title seem to go against the general mood of society. But do they? Could it be that this is merely a rhetorical gesture, like President Bush's boast in his 1992 State of the Union message that the USA had won the Cold War, a boast that merely focused attention on America's anxieties about its place in the 'new world order'?[3]

The Intellectual Climate

Fukuyama's 'end of history' thesis is very much a product of our time. Ever since the Enlightenment upholders of continuity and tradition have done battle with supporters of change and progress. A consciousness of change, a belief in progress and an understanding of history as the product of human action are characteristic of *historical thinking*, an outlook that emphasizes the transience of all social arrangements. This sense of historical specificity and flux has been fiercely contested by conservative thinkers who view the past, embodied in tradition or race or culture, as the ultimate arbiter of the present. Conservative historians dismiss historical thinking as utopian; instead they have constructed History, with a capital H, as a version of the past that legitimizes the existing order of society.[4] For History, the story of the past is not one of change, but one in which fundamental values remain constant and are continuously reproduced in new circumstances.

In the late twentieth century, historical thinking has reached a low ebb. Political organizations and social movements oriented towards liberation and revolution, or even towards protest and experimentation, are in a state of deep, often terminal, decline. They have been compromised by the decay of the left, the defensiveness of social democracy and above all by the collapse of Stalinism. As a result the project of social change today appears unrealistic, even absurd, and those who pursue it attract widespread indifference or derision. Indeed because traditional left-wing programmes have been so discredited, it is widely accepted that any attempt to change society would be a greater menace to individual welfare and liberty than the failures of capitalist society. In this climate of opinion, History, with its attachments to national tradition, culture and myth, is enjoying unprecedented popularity. Thus, for example, the eruption of ethnic conflict in the former Stalinist countries is portrayed as the victory of ancient traditions over the arrogant project of social engineering. Resurgent atavistic nationalism is depicted as the triumph of History over historical thinking.

Fukuyama is fully in sympathy with the central role allocated to tradition in conservative thought. In his *The End of History*, he casts the past – in one form or another – as the main protagonist. Thus, for example, although he notes that 'in the contemporary world, it is not considered acceptable to talk about "national character": such generalizations about a people's ethical habits are said not to be measurable "scientifically", and are therefore prone to crude stereotyping and abuse', he proceeds to explain national differences by the weight of the past embodied in national culture: 'anyone who has spent time travelling or living abroad cannot help but notice that attitudes toward work are decisively influenced by national cultures.'[5] For Fukuyama, 'national culture' explains everything from the economic achievements of Jewish people to the superiority of German technology. It is as if what we are and what we do is decided in advance by our culture; human beings are reduced to acting out the role it assigns to them.

It is not surprising to find that deference to tradition goes hand in hand with a lack of respect for the role of human consciousness and action. For Fukuyama events are decided by the overwhelming power of national culture rather than by the puny efforts of reasoning human beings. He is relieved that the days when 'many reasonable people could foresee a radiant socialist future' are over. From his elitist perspective, it seems that people, especially the 'masses' can only be motivated by irrational forces: 'One is frequently struck by the weakness of both reason and politics to achieve their ends, and for human beings to "lose control" of their lives [sic].'[6] Wherever he sees crowds or masses, Fukuyama can identify only the forces of unrestrained irrationalism.[7]

The uneasy place of reason in conservative thought is clearly expressed in Fukuyama's work. As there can be no place for logical discourse in the temple of tradition, rationality must give way. Fukuyama proclaims the role of the non-rational in his endorsement of contemporary capitalism: 'Capitalist prosperity is best promoted by a strong work ethic, which in turn depends on the ghosts of dead religious beliefs, if not those beliefs themselves, or else an irrational commitment to nation or race.'[8]

In his restatement of conservative thought, Fukuyama acknowledges that social cohesion and solidarity depend upon irrational influences: 'the emergence and durability of a society embodying rational recognition appears to *require* the survival of certain forms of irrational recognition'.[9] Together with influential recent thinkers of the right, such as Allan Bloom or Friedrich Hayek, Fukuyama upholds 'dead religious beliefs' as essential for the reproduction of society.

Although Fukuyama adopts a liberal style of presentation, his work captures the conservative mood of the late twentieth century. Indeed one of the curious features of Fukuyama's work is the coexistence of a self-consciously liberal rhetoric with profoundly conservative conclusions. The worship of tradition and the rejection of the role of human beings in the making of history are the central themes of contemporary Western political theory. This tension between liberal form and conservative content particularly pervades his book *The End of History and the Last Man*. As we shall see, his approach to the present is triumphalist in *form*, but not in content.

The Sense of Terminus

The notion of the 'end of history' is in every sense representative of the dominant themes of contemporary Western culture, particularly the prevailing sense of low expectations. There are often conflicting conclusions drawn about the meaning of the end of history, but there is a consensus that fundamental social change would only make matters worse. When Fukuyama states that 'no regime' is able 'to satisfy all men in all places' his objective is to discredit the aspiration for human liberation as a utopian dream.[10] His conclusion is that a pragmatic reconciliation with the emptiness of bourgeois life is the apogee of human achievement.

In one sense it is surprising that Fukuyama's article caused such a stir. The view that history is coming to an end has been a recurrent theme in Western thought over the past century, as an intellectual response to the fear of change. This argument is often expressed as a call to preserve or to defend the status quo and as a direct negation of historical thinking. The intellectual representation of the sense of terminus is influenced by a variety of motives. While, in general, the sense of history reaching an end reflects the anxieties unleashed by rapid social *change*, since the late nineteenth century it has also increasingly come to express the perception of *decline*. The sense of decline is experienced in a number of ways: as a spiritual or moral crisis, as the weakening of racial or national vitality, as natural or cultural decadence. For such a conservative perspective, any change is problematic since it inevitably undermines tradition and leads to the attenuation of spirituality, national identity and humanity. For a conservative, the sense of loss resulting from change inevitably outweighs the gains of progress.[11]

Although 'end of history' arguments first became fashionable in the late nineteenth century, it was not until the interwar years that such notions became widely popular. In the days when Oswald Spengler's 1926 book *Decline of the West* was a talking point in European salons, Fukuyama's contribution would have gone unnoticed. The intellectual climate of the period was well summed up by the sociologist Louis Wirth in 1936, when he pointed to the 'extensive literature which speaks of the "end", the "decline", the "crisis", the "decay", or the "death" of Western civilisation'.[12] Wirth explained the gloomy interwar mood as a result of the fashion for questioning the 'norms and truths which were once believed to be absolute'. Ironically, Wirth himself became preoccupied with the potential catastrophe that 'endism' foreshadowed. He worried that the 'depreciation of the value of thought' threatened 'to exterminate what rationality and objectivity' had achieved, thus accelerating the 'deepening twilight of modern culture'. He concluded grimly that 'such a catastrophe' could be 'averted only by the most intelligent and resolute measures'.[13] For Wirth, the very questioning of reason which the sense of terminus implied threatened not only to bring history to an end, but to destroy the earlier achievements of rational human activity.

Spengler forcefully captured the sense of terminus through his theory of history as a series of cycles in which every culture rises, reaches its limit, and then decays:

> The future of the West is not a limitless tending upwards and onwards for all time towards our present ideals, but a single phenomenon of history, strictly limited and defined as to form and duration, which covers a few centuries and can be viewed and, in essentials calculated from available precedents.[14]

The inexorable decline of the West is specifically attributed to the rise of the masses, for whom Spengler has the most venomous contempt. In his view the mass 'recognises no past and possesses no future'; furthermore, it hates 'every sort of form, every distinction of rank, the orderliness of property, the orderliness of knowledge'. This rabble, lacking the proper restraint of the past, is the living negation of class society: 'the mass is the end, the radical nullity'.[15] It is apparent that, in Spengler's interpretation, 'the end' really means the end of a particular social arrangement. The threat of the masses to a particular way of life is presented as the end of human civilization in general.

It is striking that the sense of terminus is often expressed as a threat to 'Western Civilization'. Mass society is regarded as the negation of a culture and way of life defined as the achievements of a select group of superior personalities. In his wartime broadcast to Germany, T.S. Eliot was fearful for the fate of this elite culture:

> My last appeal is to the men of letters of Europe, who have a special responsibility for the preservation and transmission of our common culture ... we can at least try to save something of those goods of which we are the common trustees: the legacy of Greece, Rome and Israel, and the legacy of Europe throughout the last 2,000 years. In a world which has seen such material devastation as ours, these spiritual possessions are also in imminent peril.[16]

Although not everybody shared Eliot's fears about the imminent demise of Western culture, even those who were more sanguine about the future were convinced that the old order had come to an end. This was the viewpoint, for example, of E.H. Carr, who in 1944 noted casually that the 'old world is dead'. For Carr this was not a problem as he concluded that the 'future lies with those who can resolutely turn their back on it and face the new world with understanding, courage and imagination'.[17]

However, Carr was very much the exception. The sense of terminus was widely expressed in terms of gloom and foreboding. Writing in 1943, Arthur Koestler suggested that the period which had celebrated the 'ascendancy of reason over spirit' had come to an end, and he predicted a 'new global ferment' that would 'probably mark the end of our historical era'.[18] Others projected an end in apocalyptic, quasi-religious terms. Noting that the New Testament envisaged 'a culmination of history', the theologian Reinhold Niebuhr explained that it 'looks forward to a final judgement and a general resurrection which are at once both the fulfilment and the end of history'.[19]

There are dramatic differences between Spengler's reactionary despair and Carr's liberal optimism, and between Koestler's gloom and Niebuhr's messianism. Yet all these responses had something in common: they were all symptoms of an awareness that, with the experience of fascism and global war, Auschwitz and Hiroshima, history had reached an impasse. However, in the postwar years such views were gradually replaced by the conviction that history had escaped the more dramatic fates anticipated in the forties and had instead slowly ground to a halt in the dreary conformity of Cold War consensus society.

The sense of terminus was now conveyed in the pragmatic form of the 'end of ideology' thesis. This was the first of a succession of terms that implied that 'this is it', that historical change had reached its conclusion. As the sociologist Krishnan Kumar indicated, the prefix 'post-' came into use to suggest that the existing state of society was in some sense *beyond* what had happened in the past, and thus beyond further change:

> Thus Amitai Etzioni speaks of the 'post-modern era', George Lichtheim of the 'post-bourgeois society', Herman Kahn of 'post-economic society', Murray Bookchin of the 'post-scarcity society', Kenneth Boulding of 'post-civilised society', Daniel Bell simply of 'the post-industrial society'.[20]

To this list one could add 'post-imperialist', 'post-Fordist' and a number of other 'post-' terms.

The proliferation of 'post-' terms is another symptom of the sense of historical closure. The 'post-' terms reflect a common approach towards change, one which seeks to suppress a sense of temporality. As Brook Thomas argues, the label 'post-' 'announces that we are past the new': it implies a 'belatedness, an age in which everything has always already occurred'.[21] By means of a prefix, 'post-' terms revoke history. Fukuyama appropriately affirms the revocation of history by declaring the Western world to be 'post-historical'.[22] If history has already happened, then change is now excluded and what exists must be the end result of human development. By projecting an immutable present into the indefinite future such a revocation of history exposes its fundamentally apologetic intent. For these theories do not merely imply that history has ended, but that so also has the potential for human fulfilment.

Fukuyama continues the 'end of history' tradition but with a significant modification. The sense of terminus is represented positively: not as decline but as the high point of history. Thus, for Fukuyama, the end of history is at once the realization and vindication of the principles of liberal democracy and of the free market. Fukuyama not so much criticizes as eternalizes the present. The same apologetic intent was also evident in earlier 'end of ideology' theories. The notion that history has ended helps to eternalize the past and retrospectively legitimizes tradition: if ancient ideals have been finally realized in the present, then this confirms that they must have been sound in the first place. Writing in 1955, Edward Shils revealed the wholeheartedly traditionalist character of such theories:

> The belief that our traditional ideals have now been exhausted because of their complete fulfilment must be avoided as much as the conviction that our virtue consists in our rejection of whatever exists. We must rediscover the permanently valid element in our historical ideals – elements which must be recurrently realised without ever being definitively realisable, once and for all.[23]

The same approach permeates the writings of Daniel Bell. Bell is particularly concerned that the 'primordial elements that provide men with a common identification' such as religion have been weakened, leading to the erosion of social cohesion.[24] The recurrent celebration of traditional ideals becomes the intellectual staple of a society living through post-historical times. Fukuyama elaborates this argument by suggesting that tradition provides the 'cultural "prerequisites" for democracy' such as 'some degree of irrational love of country'.[25] Fukuyama's personal disdain for the irrational does not prevent him from advocating a political theory of democracy based on the preservation of superstition in the form of national myths.

The Fukuyama Thesis Explored

Much of the critical reaction to Fukuyama's article 'The End of History?' missed the central point of his argument. Fukuyama did not seek to imply that history had literally ended and that nothing new would ever happen again. Rather, as he explained, he used the term 'history' in the special Hegelian sense:

> 'History', for Hegel, can be understood in the narrower sense of the 'history of ideology', or the history of thought about first principles, including those governing political and social organization. The end of history then means not the end of worldly events but the end of the evolution of human thought about such first principles.[26]

In fact this conception of history, which emphasizes the role of subjectivity, approximates, albeit in an idealist form, *historical thinking*.[27]

When Fukuyama declares the end of history, he is evidently celebrating the demise of historical thinking. He excludes the possibility of any further evolution of human consciousness in terms of offering new and superior social arrangements to the existing state of society. This means the 'end of ideology' in the sense that there appear to be no ideas available to society that can credibly offer to take humanity beyond the status quo. For Fukuyama the proof of this thesis lies in the fact that liberal democracy enjoys a greater legitimacy today than at any previous time: 'This ideological consensus is neither fully universal nor automatic but exists to an arguable higher degree than at any time in the past century.'[28] The establishment of liberal democracy as the *final* form of government means the end of history. It also means that it is impossible for humanity to reach any higher level of self-knowledge than it has already attained.

Fukuyama's thesis contains one important insight: he has accurately identified the weak state of historical thinking in the late 1980s and early 1990s. But his fatalistic conclusion that human consciousness has reached its limit is not presented logically. It is simply a generalization from the empirical recognition that at present there is no ideological alternative to liberal capitalism. Indeed, this argument that the absence of new ideas means that the end has been reached has been mobilized by 'endist' theories throughout this century. The crisis of bourgeois ideas is invariably presented as conclusive evidence that it is impossible for anybody to generate new ideas. Spengler's decline thesis is paradigmatic: in the depths of interwar despondency he wrote that the 'age of theory is drawing to its end ... that of Marx is already half a century old, and it has had no successor'.[29] Following the same method, Fukuyama argues that liberal democracy has been around for a long time and yet it too has no successor: 'the ideal of liberal democracy' cannot 'be improved on'.[30] Fukuyama's rational recognition that ideas of change are currently exhausted is presented in the irrational form of the conviction that history has ended.

The 'end of history' thesis could be more appropriately labelled the 'triumph of the past'. All the proponents of 'endism' insist on the continuity of the past with the same vigour as they pronounce that history is finished. Thus Daniel Bell's main objection to 'ideologies', particularly that of Marx, was that they wanted to 'rid the present of the past'.[31] His argument that all ideology had become exhausted became a proof that a complex modern society could not be changed through the influence of ideology.

The distinctive feature of Fukuyama's 'end of history', compared with the pessimistic tone of earlier theories of historical closure, is its self-conscious triumphalism. In terms of their subjective outlook, there is apparently little in common between Fukuyama's euphoria and Spengler's deep melancholy. Even Bell, writing in the fifties, reflected the mood of 'a decade of political conservatism and cultural bewilderment', a time he characterized as 'a period of disillusionment'.[32] The subtitle of Bell's key work sums up the prevailing sentiment: *The End of Ideology: On the Exhaustion of Political Ideas in the Fifties*. By contrast, Fukuyama's celebratory rhetoric reflects the more confident right-wing intellectual offensive of the 1980s.

However, on closer inspection, Fukuyama's triumphalism seems far from convincing. Like many liberal thinkers, he finds it much easier to gloat over the failure of his opponents than to provide a full account of what the society in which history has ended has to offer its citizens. To his credit, Fukuyama did not attempt in 'The End of History?' to glorify the realities of contemporary Western capitalism. He simply presented the future as the continuation of the present, a vision of Middle America in perpetuity. But this is a society of conformity and routine, one that offers little scope for the expression of human imagination or creativity.

It is not surprising that many commentators have taken offence at Fukuyama's uninspiring picture of the future of Western capitalist society. This is how he responded to his critics:

> The idea that one should be anything other than unconditionally happy about the victory of liberalism, or that one could be bored in a society that offered perfect security and well-being, is one that has caused a certain amount of indignation, particularly among the space-travel lobby. Some of the more liberal-minded of my readers have not recognised that one can be a supporter of liberalism, believe passionately in the superiority of liberal democracy over any other alternative system, and yet be aware of certain fundamental tensions and weaknesses in liberalism.[33]

These belatedly acknowledged 'fundamental tensions and weaknesses' are the inevitable features of a society that excludes any consideration of the meaning of life and the development of human potential. They are the results of a way of life that, by excluding change, offers nothing but more of the same. In a roundabout way, Fukuyama ends up confirming the same exhaustion of ideas that preoccupied Bell thirty years earlier.

Rearming the West

It is not merely because of its underlying pessimism that Fukuyama's work should be placed firmly in the 'endist' tradition. Another common theme is the link between the notion of the 'end of history' and the concern about the 'decline of the West' vis-à-vis the rest of the world. In this schema, the ideas of liberalism and market forces are assimilated to the wider political culture of the advanced capitalist countries. In his first article, Fukuyama wrote that the 'triumph of the West, of the Western idea, is evident first of all in the total exhaustion of viable systematic alternatives to Western liberalism'.[34]

It is interesting to note that the most distinctive feature of Fukuyama's work has received the least critical comment. Although his epistemological premises and theoretical assumptions are in line with those of earlier chroniclers of Western decline, Fukuyama has reversed their conclusions and declared the West the winner. Thus, although he predicts that international tensions will take the form of conflicts among rival national cultures, Fukuyama is confident that Western civilization has seen off the challenge of the Third World.[35] History may have come to an end, but this time the West has come out on top.

Fukuyama also offers an alternative to the defensive character of Cold War 'end of ideology' theories that accept a compromise between West and East. For example, the theory of 'convergence' recognized the Soviet Union as another complex industrial society with many features in common with Western countries and acknowledged it as a permanent fixture in the modern world. Convergence theory neatly sidestepped the question of which society was more efficient and more progressive. It represented a compromise solution and a willingness to modify the claims of bourgeois values. Such defensive postures reflected the West's lack of confidence in fighting for the absolute values of bourgeois thought. Fukuyama accepts that truth is historically relative, but insists that, since history has come to an end, it is henceforth 'impossible to state a philosophical proposition that [is] both true and new'. In other words, Fukuyama is prepared to accept the relativity of truth for the past, but by closing off the possibility of further intellectual development, endows the latest truths of Western society with the character of absolutes. He justifies this closure as being necessary to prevent 'historicism from degenerating into simple relativism'.[36] In any case, he is deeply hostile to the relativism implicit in theories of convergence and related ideas.

Unlike old-style Cold War ideologues, Fukuyama has no need to compromise. He is highly critical of American pragmatists like Henry Kissinger, Jeanne Kirkpatrick and Samuel Huntington for accepting for so long the Soviet presence in international affairs.[37] Fukuyama, of course, writes with the advantage of hindsight; after Gorbachev there was no need for the 'extraordinary historical pessimism' of the end-of-ideology compromise. Cultural relativism is not for Fukuyama, who speculates that soon the 'idea of relativism may seem much stranger than it does now'.[38]

Fukuyama's reassertion of absolute values takes the form of absolutizing the present and presenting liberalism as the culmination of human development. Anxious to affirm the 'notion of progress', Fukuyama presents it in a teleological form – what he calls 'directional history' – in which all previous historical stages are inexorably driving towards the realization of this notion in the contemporary West. Fukuyama's positive defence of the West is much bolder than that of the old Cold War ideologues, as he indicates:

> The century that began full of self-confidence in the ultimate triumph of Western liberal democracy seems at its close to be returning to where it started: not to an 'end of ideology' or a convergence between capitalism and socialism, as earlier predicted, but to an unabashed victory of economic and political liberalism.[39]

Fukuyama's criticism of the intellectual heritage of the postwar compromise is unequivocal. His defence of the West contains not a hint of the defensiveness of Raymond Aron, Daniel Bell, Edward Shils and the rest.

Nevertheless, the very fact that Fukuyama is preoccupied with the West gives the game away. A more or less conscious fear about Western decline has been a consistent theme among 'endist' commentators. Writing in 1951, in one of the earliest postwar 'endist' contributions, H. Stuart Hughes accurately described the convergence of political trends in Europe as a defensive Western response to the spectre of Third World revolt raised by the Korean war. He observed that 'this time the West is at length united in a single bloc' and noted a novel development: the 'creeds of "progress" – liberalism, democracy, socialism – have made their peace with what remains of traditional conservatism'.[40] It was this tendency towards the merger or neutralization of former ideological rivals that Hughes described as the 'end of ideology'.

Four years later, Edward Shils reported some good and some bad news from a CIA-funded conference in Milan. The good news was that ideology was at an end in the West, so Cold War intellectuals could now relax their defensive posture against the Soviet menace: 'There was a very widespread feeling that there was no longer any need to justify ourselves vis-à-vis the Communist critique of our society.'[41] The bad news was that the Third World delegates were less than enthusiastic in their embrace of the bland 'end of ideology' thesis. According to Shils, during the discussion on nationalism 'the distance between the African and Asian members on the one side and the Europeans and Americans on the other became tangible.' This session demonstrated to Shils the 'danger of Western complacency at having weathered the storm of ideologies'.[42]

A similar motif is evident in Bell's classic article 'The End of Ideology in the West', the geographical limits of the title reflecting one of its chief concerns. Bell was worried that the West, far from winning the ideological battle in the

Third World, was actually losing it: 'Russia and China have become models', he warned. In the sixties and early seventies, the situation deteriorated further as the postwar economic boom came to an end, heightening the sense of decline in the West at a time when the challenge of Third World nationalism reached its height. Looking back, Fukuyama notes the close relationship between 'the decline of the moral self-confidence of European civilization' and the 'rise of the Third World'.[43]

Writing in 1984, K.D. Bracher, too, noted the parallel between the West's defensiveness and the rise of Third Worldism. He recognized the profound impact of the economic recession of the mid-seventies, which 'was interpreted by an increasing number of contemporaries – either indignant or resigned – as a crisis of Western civilization generally'.[44] This sense of internal crisis was compounded by the perception of a growing external threat from radical Third World nationalism, which Bracher characterized as a new ideology: 'That the decade of de-ideologization would not be the last word was reflected most clearly in the rise of the "Third World", in the new nationalism and socialism of the developing countries.'[45] For Bracher, the rise of the Third Word led to a 'crisis of values upon which modern western policies were based'. Yet, only five years later, a confident Fukuyama could dismiss Third Worldism as an ideology capable of competing with liberal capitalism.

The notion of Third Worldism as a coherent ideology was a myth. In reality, there was a wide variety of more or less radical nationalist regimes and liberation movements in the Third World and a parallel upsurge of a diffuse anti-imperialist sentiment among Western youth and liberal opinion. Above all, however, it was the prevailing sense of internal decay in the West that made the Third World seem such a threat. As a result the Western establishment could no longer hold the moral high ground and traditional assumptions of Western superiority could not be publicly aired. Burdened by the presentiment of decline, the ideologues of the West panicked and slipped into Spenglerian despondency about the menace of the Third World. In the late 1980s Fukuyama sought to dispose of the fears of the previous decade with a theory of history that aimed to provide the West with moral certitude.

Fukuyama justifies his pro-Western perspective by replacing the old East–West polarization with a new conception of a bipolar world. He predicts that for 'the foreseeable future, the world will be divided between the post-historical part, and a part that is still stuck in history'.[46] This new division will be according to *culture*, which serves for Fukuyama the same role that race did for Spengler. Thus, for example, he mobilizes the German sociologist Marx Weber's 'Protestant ethic' thesis to explain Western economic superiority. Pointing to India, he observes that 'there are legion of cases [sic] where religion and culture have acted as obstacles' to development. Those, whether Indians or American blacks, whom Fukuyama delicately characterizes as 'culturally hobbled in the economic competition' have only themselves to blame.[47]

Fukuyama's thesis attempts to legitimize Western intervention in the Third

World by providing a coherent moral justification for imperialism. Thus he endorses the established Western prejudice that any assertion of Third World independence is the act of an unrepresentative dictator. Fukuyama asserts that the 'end of the Cold War has allowed us to debunk the moral pretensions of Third World tyrants'.[48] In practice, 'debunking' means criminalizing and trivializing the actions of the opponent. Thus Saddam Hussein's 'challenge to the international system' is dismissed as 'nothing more than the effort of a well-armed gangster to rob the world's largest bank'.[49] Fukuyama anticipates further conflicts between the West and the Third World and he openly acknowledges that in the new post-historical world order force will still be the ultimate arbiter: 'The relationship between democracies and non-democracies will still be characterized by mutual distrust and fear, and despite a growing degree of economic interdependence, force will continue to be the *ultima ratio* in their mutual relation.'[50] Thus Fukuyama clearly draws out the military consequences of his moral rearmament of imperialism.

The more concretely Fukuyama discusses the new Western-dominated world order, the more he is obliged to abandon his universalistic rhetoric. Thus he has little time for the United Nations, since its General Assembly 'remains populated by nations that are not free', that is, Third World nations. Instead he prefers NATO, an organization 'capable of forceful action to protect its collective security from threats arising from the non-democratic world', that is, the Third World.[51] In this way, Fukuyama provides a coherent case for Western domination. The key significance of his work lies in this capacity to offer a moral justification for Western imperialism.

The new couplet of the post-historical advanced capitalist countries and the still-historical states of Eastern Europe and the Third World will be familiar to anybody acquainted with earlier 'endist' theories. The old polarization between the West and the Third World, which had so preoccupied the Cold War theorists, is now re-created in a new triumphalist form. Post-history is in fact the end of ideology with a smile.

A Failure of Imagination

It is striking that, despite its internal consistency and robust defence of the West, Fukuyama's thesis did not win widespread popular acclaim. To some extent this is because his celebratory tone jars too much with the reality of a Western world in the depths of recession. 'The triumphalist apotheosis celebrated in Fukuyama's essay '"The End of History?", was the briefest of interludes', wrote the editor of the *Times Higher Educational Supplement* in 1991.[52] Nevertheless, it is surprising that such a coherent attack on historical thinking did not gain more influence amongst the right-wing intelligentsia. Perhaps one reason for this lack of enthusiasm is the fact that Fukuyama's explicit closure of history deprives capitalist society of even a semblance of a *promise* of the future. The inevitable effect of such an eternalization of history is to encourage low expectations. This is why it is ultimately impossible to present the end-of-history thesis in an optimistic form. At the very least, as Fukuyama himself concedes, his thesis leaves unresolved all the basic questions about the meaning of life, culture and society.

In the end, Fukuyama is forced to admit that life in liberal capitalist society is life without meaning. In his vision of the future, human beings will struggle 'for the sake of struggle' out of a 'certain boredom'.[53] There is a palpable sense of nihilism pervading this 'post-historical' society. For Fukuyama the fundamental problem lies not in society but in the human condition, in the desire for recognition that can never be satisfied. The 'struggle for recognition' is one of the strongest of human passions, which 'may have required an historical march of ten thousand years or more'.[54] This is not the place to develop a critique of Fukuyama's ahistorical abstraction of the desire for recognition. Our concern here is merely to point to the apologetic content of the concept. From this perspective the manifest problems facing humanity are not attributable to capitalism or indeed to any specific form of human social organization. Rather, these problems are rooted in the foundations of human existence, and capitalism cannot be blamed for the defects of human nature. Moreover, any attempt to overcome these failings is doomed by their very human foundations. Such a pessimistic orientation serves only to devalue human consciousness and action: 'Forget it, this is it' is the simple message of Fukuyama's history.

Fukuyama's basic proposition is well summed up in his statement that today 'we have trouble imagining a world that is radically better than our own, or a future that is not essentially democratic and capitalist'.[55] In other words, liberal capitalism is not justified on its own account, but because we are apparently incapable of devising anything better. In the tradition of elitist theories of mass society, Fukuyama finds much to his distaste in contemporary capitalism. But unlike classical elitist theorists, Fukuyama is prepared to accept existing capitalist society as the best possible solution to the problem of the human condition. Thus, although he rejects the compromise of the Cold War liberals, he too speaks the language of defeat. 'This is it' for Fukuyama too, and even he cannot summon up much enthusiasm for the End of History. The obvious conclusion, that the failure of imagination invites the reconstitution of historical thinking, is not one that Fukuyama is prepared to countenance.

Notes

1. Max Nordau, *Degeneration*, London: William Heinemann, 1913, p. 2.
2. *Financial Times*, 5–6 October 1991.
3. As one journalist, Peter Jenkins, observed, 'at the moment of victory in what was a historic global contest, the stuffing has been knocked out of American self-confidence' (*Independent*, 30 January 1992).
4. History with a capital H argues that it is the authority of the past that lends legitimacy to contemporary action. The contrast between History and historical thinking

is discussed at length in Frank Füredi, *Mythical Past, Elusive Future: History and Society in an Anxious Age*, London: Pluto Press, 1992, ch. 2.

5. Francis Fukuyama, *The End of History and the Last Man* (hereafter *EHLM*), London: Hamish Hamilton/New York: The Free Press, 1992, p. 224.

6. Ibid., p. 212.

7. He suggests, for example, that the unrestrained nationalism of the masses was responsible for the instability of the interwar years in Europe. See ibid., pp. 267–8. This was one of the standard arguments of the classical elite theorists against the masses. As Nye writes: 'Later, in the half-decade of rising nationalism that preceded the First World War, collective psychologists exulted in the emotional and patriotic behaviour of the masses and noted contentedly the relative loss of influence of left-wing leadership' (See R.A. Nye, *The Anti-Democratic Sources of Elite Theory: Pareto, Mosca, Michels*, London: Sage, 1977, p. 14).

8. *EHLM*, p. 335.

9. Ibid., p. 207.

10. Ibid., p. 334.

11. Fukuyama is not in principle against change in so far as it relates to the past. But he seems to accept the conservative conviction that identifies change with spiritual impoverishment. It is worth noting Fukuyama's ambiguous relationship with Nietzsche on this point. Fukuyama seems to share Nietzsche's critique of progress while distancing himself from Nietzsche's more extreme illiberal and anti-democratic conclusions. Fukuyama notes that 'we can readily accept many of Nietzsche's acute psychological observations, even as we reject his morality' (ibid., p. 313). Since individual psychology appears to play such a crucial role in Fukuyama's schema it is not surprising that the influence of Nietzsche on *The End of History* is almost palpable.

12. Louis Wirth, 'Preface' to Karl Mannheim, *Ideology and Utopia*, London: Routledge & Kegan Paul, 1960, p. xiii.

13. Ibid., p. xxvii.

14. Oswald Spengler, *Decline of the West*, London: George Allen & Unwin, 1926, pp. 38–9.

15. Ibid., p. 358.

16. T.S. Eliot, *Notes Towards the Definition of Culture*, London: Faber & Faber, 1948, pp. 123–4.

17. E.H. Carr, *Conditions of Peace*, London: Macmillan, 1944, p. 275.

18. Arthur Koestler, *The Yogi and the Commissar and Other Essays*, London: Hutchison, 1983, pp. 103–4.

19. Rheinhold Niebuhr, *Faith and History*, London: Nisbet, 1949, p. 267.

20. Krishnan Kumar, *Prophecy and Progress*, Harmondsworth: Penguin, 1986, p. 193.

21. Brook Thomas 'The New Historicism', in H.A. Veeser, ed., *The New Historicism*, London: Routledge, 1989, p. 200.

22. See Francis Fukuyama, 'Forget Iraq – History is Dead', *Guardian*, 7 September 1990.

23. Edward Shils 'The End of Ideology?', *Encounter*, November 1955, p. 57.

24. Daniel Bell, *The Cultural Contradictions of Capitalism*, London: Heinemann, 1979, p. 155. For a discussion of the demand for tradition by Bell and other Cold War liberals, see Füredi, *Mythical Past, Elusive Future*, ch. 4.

25. *EHLM*, p. 222.

26. F. Fukuyama, 'A Reply to My Critics', *The National Interest*, Winter 1989/90, p. 22.

27. With Fukuyama this is presented in an idealist form of 'human consciousness thinking about itself and finally becoming self conscious' (see ibid.). Whilst we would agree with the stress on the self-knowledge of human reality, this can be achieved not through consciousness thinking about itself but through conscious action.
28. Ibid.
29. Spengler, *Decline of the West*, p. 454.
30. *EHLM*, p. xi.
31. Daniel Bell, *The End of Ideology: On the Exhaustion of Political Ideas in the Fifties*, New York: The Free Press, 1964, p. 370.
32. Bell, *Cultural Contradictions*, p. 41.
33. Fukuyama, 'A Reply', p. 28.
34. Francis Fukuyama, 'The End of History?', *The National Interest*, no. 16, Summer 1989, p. 3.
35. *EHLM*, pp. 234 and 338.
36. Fukuyama, 'A Reply', p. 23.
37. See Chapter 1 of *EHLM*.
38. Ibid., p. 338.
39. Fukuyama, 'The End of History?', p. 3.
40. H. Stuart Hughes 'The End of Political Ideology', *Measure*, no. 2, 1951, p. 158.
41. Shils 'The End of Ideology?' p. 54.
42. Ibid., pp. 55–6.
43. *EHLM*, p. 338.
44. K.D. Bracher, *The Age of Ideologies*, London: Weidenfeld & Nicolson, 1984, p. x.
45. Ibid., p. 202.
46. *EHLM*, p. 276.
47. Ibid., pp. 228 and 238.
48. Cited in *Independent*, 7 September 1990.
49. Ibid.
50. *EHLM*, p. 279.
51. Ibid., pp. 282–3.
52. See *Times Higher Educational Supplement*, 31 May 1991.
53. *EHLM*, p. 330.
54. Ibid., p. 207.
55. Ibid., p. 46.

3

The Cards of Confusion: Reflections on Historical Communism and the 'End of History' *
Gregory Elliott

> [I]t is well known that History is not a good bourgeois.
> ROLAND BARTHES (1957)

> An anti-Communist is a cur. I couldn't see any way out of that one, and I never will.
> JEAN-PAUL SARTRE (1961)

The contemporary topos of the 'End of History' has a distinguished pedigree, ancient and modern, rendering it a virtual cliché of intellectual culture. Eschatological and soteriological doctrines of the Final End have been around since the very beginning – Christianity, with its distinction between calendrical and providential time, being only one such.[1] Ends come and go; or, as they used to say in Eastern Europe, 'the future is certain; the past is unpredictable'.

In the twentieth century, the immediate precedent for current sightings of a cessation or culmination of history is to be found in Cold War liberalism – in particular, Daniel Bell's *The End of Ideology* (1960). The latter, published amidst the Khrushchevite switch to 'peaceful coexistence and competition' in the USSR, revolved around the postulate of a convergence between East and West: the tranquil conclusion of the contest between capitalism and socialism as a result of the postwar 'democratic social revolution', which had solved the riddle of modern history with the reconciliation of liberty and equality, efficiency and humanity, in regulated capitalism. A less exultant – indeed, bleakly pessimistic – left-wing version of the thesis was advanced concurrently, in one of the classics of Western Marxism: Herbert Marcuse's *One-Dimensional Man* (1964), which counterposed an impotent 'Great Refusal' to the omnipotence of the ubiquitous 'technocratic society'.[2]

For To End Yet Again and Other Fizzles...

The intervening social, cultural and political turbulence of the 1960s and 1970s having passed without undue perturbation of the OECD order, another variation upon the theme has emerged in the 1980s. To characterize today's cultural climate as one in which 'endism' is pandemic would doubtless be an exaggeration. And yet the efflorescence of what might be called the P-word is surely an index of something: postmodernism, post-structuralism, post-Fordism, post-industrialism...; the prefix is neither fortuitous, nor innocent. The final decade of the second millennium AD signals, according to a certain apocalyptic litany, the death of communism and socialism, the passing of the working class, the termination of the Cold War, the waning of industrial society, and – most portentously of all – the 'end of history'. *Fin de siècle, aube de siècle* – except that the contours of the new dawn are only dimly discerned, the future invariably being depicted as the eternal repetition of the transitional, untranscendable present: a future of no future, so to speak.

Considerations of time and tact prevent me saying anything very much about the cultural complex known as postmodernism. But I do want to indicate two things. First – and, I imagine, uncontroversially – propositions to the effect that the West is in passage to a post-industrial society, a post-Fordist economy, a post-socialist politics, and a post-ideological culture, wherein post-metaphysical philosophy comes into its own, are half-truths, where not outright falsehoods: symptoms of a late-twentieth-century reality systematically misrecognized, not adequately conceptualized. Second, the class of '68 which articulates (or recognizes itself in) them coincides, albeit inadvertently and in a distinct idiom, with Cold War liberalism in its assessment of the socialist legacy. 'Post-Marxism' may locate itself at the intersection of Heideggerian, Wittgensteinian and post-structuralist trends in philosophy; a neglected feature of its depreciation of historical materialism, however, is its unpremeditated antecedent in the thought of Berlin, Popper and co., who likewise contrasted the philosophico-political 'pluralism' of the liberal tradition with the 'monism' of Marxism (even if in defence of the Open Society, rather than the Democratic Revolution).[3] What Richard Rorty calls 'North Atlantic Postmodern Bourgeois Liberal Democracy' and North Atlantic Modern Bourgeois Liberal Democracy have more in common than the self-images of the age, infused with the 'narcissism of small differences', care to acknowledge.

As critics have demonstrated, postmodernist affirmations of an 'end of history' – in the shape of the 'metanarrative of emancipation' targeted by Lyotard in *The Postmodern Condition* (1979) – succumb to a series of crippling performative contradictions, which prevent them from grasping their indicated object.[4] The reconfiguration of avant-garde Anglophone theory leaves much of the left intelligentsia carolling the virtues of a meretricious miscellany which, as has been remarked, would shake all metaphysics (Marxism included) to the superflux, while leaving material structures intact (therewith replicating metaphysics in the very gesture of repudiating it). Today, to assign class an explanatory status is to invite the charge of 'classism'; to posit a social totality (never mind a global system) with organizing principles, that of 'essentialism' ('economism', should – ultimate sin – one of them be economic); to assign causal priority (misconstrued as exclusivity) to anything, that of 'reductionism'; to invoke history (unless tendentiously serviceable), that of 'historicism'; to mention science – without scare quotes – that of 'scientism'; and as for objective knowledge, well, it is known to be passé (undesirable, even were it attainable). Quite how any essay in social explanation – of necessity, selective (reductive, but not *eo ipso* reduction*ist*) – can secure acquittal on the charge of suppressing 'difference' is one of the many imponderables, given the infinite, facilely iconoclastic, spiral inherent in these premises. A little difference goes a long way... As Francis Mulhern has remarked, 'metaphysics is safe in the keeping of the disenchanted'.[5]

The intrinsic problem with this sub-Maoism of the signifier – combining, to quote Mulhern, 'a fanciful belief in subversion *ordinaire* with a knowing disdain for revolutionary ideas, in a mutant creed that might be called anarcho-reformism' – is that it flouts its own protocols. It employs reason as an instrument of illumination to denounce reason as an arm of oppression. It deploys a metanarrative – and one of the tallest, if not greatest, stories ever told – to deliver metanarrative its quietus. It constructs an expressive social totality, the entirety of whose phenomena would be exfoliations of the postmodern essence, therewith trampling pertinent differences underfoot. Disposing of history historically, of theory theoretically, of ethics ethically, of politics politically, this intellectual recidivism drafts its own indictment: *de te fabula magna narratur*.[6]

Viewed in the twilight of the idols, what is striking about Francis Fukuyama's essay 'The End of History?',[7] otherwise so consonant with the ideological *Zeitgeist*, is its avoidance of such performative contradictions. Despite following Derrida's lectures in Paris, Fukuyama reverts to the French Hegelianism – metanarratives of speculation and emancipation, *par excellence* – against which, so the standard intellectual history runs, (post-)structuralism was largely directed. Fukuyama, I want to argue, borrowing Blake's verdict on Milton,[8] is, in at least two senses, 'of the Devil's party without knowing it': a circumstance which may account for the hostility or suspicion with which his original article of 1989 was greeted on the right.

Fukuyama is of the Devil's party *analytically*, in so far as he has resurrected totalizing (and globalizing) theory as an indispensable mode of conceptualization of the 'One World' impending on the threshold of the twenty-first century. His work displays the arresting paradox of a (post-)Cold War liberal political individualism whose historicist philosophical framework, with its holism and teleologism, was anathematized by his Anglo-American predecessors as the royal 'road to serfdom'. For them, moral-political individualism entailed methodological individualism, while teleological prospects dictated 'totalitarian' results. By the norms of mainstream Anglophone philosophy, Fukuyama is culpable of the kind of dialectical metaphysics extirpated by the interwar 'analytical' (counter-)revolution.[9]

Fukuyama is of the Devil's party *politically*, in so far as he has punctured some of the historical amnesia induced by the right during the 1980s. For, truth belying comfort, Fukuyama reminds us what was at stake in the Second Cold War: a comprehensive reversal of the consequences of the Second World War in the First World (Keynesian welfare capitalism), in the Second (the existence and performance of Stalinism), and in the Third (the defeat of colonialism). As Fred Halliday has written, 'The actions of the Reagan Administration and its allies in Europe sought to reverse these consequences, using the recession, anti-communism, and historical amnesia to impose a new set of values and policies on the world.'[10] They have largely succeeded; and Fukuyama's is one, especially ambitious, endeavour to prospect the 'New World Order' arising upon the ruins of formerly existing socialism: the only actual socialism, *hélas*, that we have known.

After the Deluge

'A spectre is haunting Europe – the spectre of Communism.'[11] Overly optimistic, historically, at the moment of its composition, the opening line of the *Communist Manifesto* was, by its centennial in 1948, unduly pessimistic geographically, as accomplished or imminent revolutions in Asia compounded the postwar transplantation of Stalinism from one country to a whole geographical zone, occasioning the Cold War in concerted Western response. Some four decades (and a second Cold War) further on, the ghost has been exorcized. The spectre haunting the world today is not the end of '*prehistory*' envisaged by Marx, but the 'end of *history*' envisioned by Fukuyama: the global apotheosis – as opposed to the global abolition – of capitalism.[12] The main premiss of the *Manifesto* might be thought to have been vindicated, close to a century and a half later, while its consequent has been informed en route. The predicted global expansion of capitalism has finally transpired, but in such a way as to eliminate its principal twentieth-century impediment: 'historical Communism', tributary to the Bolshevik Revolution – 'the moment when' (according to Edmund Wilson) 'for the first time in the human exploit the key of a philosophy of history was to fit an historical lock'.[13]

For another right-Hegelian philosophy of history, capitalism has vanquished its secular antagonist – actually existing socialism – in the East, and dug the grave of its appointed gravedigger – the proletariat – in the West, allegedly rendering socialism utopian (for lack of agency and rationality as a goal), and Marxism redundant (for want of explanatory or normative purchase). The knell of socialized public property has sounded: the expropriators are expropriating.[14] Satirizing a 'scientific socialism' which certified the inevitability of the classless future, the French Communist Paul Nizan had written in 1938 of a 'world destined for great metamorphoses': great metamorphoses, the reverse of those foreseen, have supervened.[15] What, for Fukuyama, do they consist in?

In sum, the 'epic of transition' heralded by Lenin amid the 'highest stage of capitalism' has proved to be a mere *divertimento*. Sundown having fallen on the Union, Minerva's owl spreads its wings and espies the materialization of Kant's 'Universal History': 'an unabashed victory of economic and political liberalism' over its 'world-historical' competitors, portending a '"Common Marketization" of world politics', or 'liberal democracy in the political sphere combined with easy access to stereos and VCRs in the economic'. Following Hegel, then, for Fukuyama 'the History of the World is none other than the progress of the consciousness of Freedom';[16] and that consciousness has prevailed. The 'triumph of the West' – or of the 'Western *idea*', at any rate – has concluded history, not in the sense of bringing empirical events to an abrupt halt (these will continue), but in the sense of realizing a goal: 'freedom' as the 'end point of mankind's ideological evolution'. (Culmination, not cessation: to mobilize two Americanisms, 'end-times' are 'quality time'.) The end of history is the end of ideology, for the consummation of one universal ideology. History with a capital 'H' – construed as a *Kampfplatz* between competing universal ideologies, 'embodied' (so Fukuyama stipulates) 'in important social or political forces and movements ... which are therefore part of world history' – has arrived at its terminus. Contrary to Plekhanov's classical Marxist assurance that 'We, indeed, know our way and are seated in the historical train which at full speed takes us to our goal',[17] the train of history has terminated not at the Finland Station, but at the nearest hypermarket. All roads lead to Disneyland... Sartre's projected dystopia in the event of the defeat of Stalinism in postwar France has come to pass: 'the universe will be bourgeois'.[18]

Given Fukuyama's construction of 'History', the myriad malcontents of post-historical civilization, whatever their visibility or volubility, represent no challenge to his basic thesis. As he himself argued in an article on the Gulf War (baldly entitled 'Forget Iraq – History is over'), apparent discomfiture over his speculations in the event supplied substantiation of them; failing even to hegemonize Arab nationalism, Iraqi Ba'athism was scarcely a world-historical force. The 'strange thoughts occur[ring] to people in Albania or Burkina Faso' – we should now have to substitute the former Yugoslavia or India – are impotent before the march of history. The 'past' is unpredictable, the future is certain: an Americanization of the planet – a 'universal homogeneous state' of liberal capitalist democracy – from which system-threatening antagonisms (or contradictions) have been eliminated. *Contra* Hegel, the Earth forms a sphere and capitalist history is describing a circle around it.

Not that this triumph prompts a triumphalist tone. Indeed, Fukuyama's article strikes an elegiac note in conclusion: 'The end of history will be a very sad time', bereft of the 'struggle for recognition' and the audacity it elicited from human beings, and reduced to consumerism and technocracy. To conjugate the terms that provide the title of Fukuyama's book-length expansion of the prospectus, the Hegelian End of History will be inhabited by Nietzschean Last Men, wedded to their 'pitiable comfort' or (in De Tocqueville's fastidious phrase from *Democracy in America*) 'trivial and vulgar pleasures'.[19] A narcissistic culture of conspicuous self-consumption – 'Dionysus in Disneyland'?[20] – is condemned to the spiritual vices of its material benefits.

Mystical Shell and Rational Kernel

When, in a Postface to the second edition of Volume One of *Capital*, Marx sought to specify his relationship to the Hegelian dialectic, he famously contended that via its 'inversion' he had 'discover[ed] the rational kernel within the mystical shell'.[21] I want to attempt an analogous operation with the ersatz Hegelian dialectic of Fukuyama.

A first – and pervasive – objection to the thesis has been its apparent irrefutability. What evidence, if any, could refute it? Or is it, consequent upon the definition of 'History', a vacuity, immune to contradiction? This, to backtrack, is the gravamen of the critique of metanarratives *stricto sensu*. Lest anyone think that I am now praising what I had earlier damned, it should be noted that the single most influential contemporary form of Marxism – Althusserianism – was precisely based upon dissent from orthodox historical materialism, with its epic tale of the forward march of the productive forces towards an ineluctable communism, on the grounds that it was a 'materialist' inversion of Hegel's philosophy of history – starring the Ruse of Economic Reason – which secreted a mystical kernel within a technological shell.[22] As Edward Thompson memorably satirized this 'diabolical and hysterical mysterialism' in his verse on the Emperor of Ch'in: 'However many the Emperor slew/The scientific historian/(While taking note of contradiction)/Affirms productive forces grew.'

For Althusser, the abiding sin of philosophies of history reposed in their incorrigibly *narrative* structure, which plotted a story with a hero and an appointed end. Literally telling stories, even (or especially) under the guise of Marxism, these 'philosophical novels' necessarily abstracted from the complexities of the specific historical conjuncture which it was the explanatory task of an authentically historical materialism to elucidate at any given time, so as to furnish the objective knowledge of a 'concrete situation' indispensable to any responsible political practice aspiring to transform it for the better. Philosophical novelists were no more adequate a guide to action than the 'alchemists of revolution' derided by Marx. *Capital* – the 'Book in which the Second International read the fatality of the advent of socialism as if in a Bible'[23] – supplied, so Althusser maintained, the requisite corrective: the opening up of the 'continent of History' to *scientific* exploration.

Just as the founding gesture of Althusserianism was rejection of the Stalinist-Marxist prolongation of the philosophy of history in a 'right-Hegelian' version – economism as *raison d'état* – so too it refused the option of a 'left-Hegelian' variant by way of anti-Stalinist response – humanism as *raison de la révolution*.

Before Althusser was Althusser, as long ago as 1950, he declined a central postulate of the Hegelian Marxism nourished by Kojève's *Introduction to the Reading of Hegel* (1947): the notion of an end of history. Reproving Jean Hyppolite's attribution – reiterated by Fukuyama – of a Hegelian postulate to Marx, the young Althusser insisted that the latter had conceived communism as the end of 'prehistory' (historically determinate economic alienation/ exploitation) and not the end of history – some realm from which the dialectic and contradictions would have vanished, ushering in universal harmony.[24] A 'process without a subject or goal(s)', to use the specifically Althusserian category, history was not agonistic alienation – the descent from primitive communism into class society – or its irenic sublation – the realization of the classless goal present in germ at the origin. To the irreducible complexity of the historical process corresponded the constitutive complexity of any communist society which *might* arise from it. Notoriously, communism would not be marked by the end of ideology.

Althusser's critique of the philosophy of history *tout court* as (bourgeois) historicism – an Enlightenment progressivism which has no place in historical materialism – is scarcely unprecedented within the Marxist tradition. Repudiation of it is central to Walter Benjamin's 'Theses on History', which detected in social-democratic theory and practice a 'concept of the historical progress of mankind [which] cannot be sundered from the concept of its progression through a homogeneous, empty time'.[25]

The first dimension to Fukuyama's mystical shell, then, is what Althusser identified as the mystical kernel of Hegelian Marxism (and which is preserved intact in this inversion of the inversion): the very notion that History harbours goals and progressively realizes them – be they the Soviet Communism indicated by Kojève in the aftermath of Stalingrad (Comrade History), or the Western liberalism identified by Fukuyama after the deluge (Citizen – or is it Sovereign Consumer? – History). As regards the latter, it is worth remembering that Hegel, let alone Kojève, was – dialectically – *anti-liberal*, rejecting the social contractarianism and individualist pluralism of the classical liberal tradition. Trotsky had claimed that the revolutionary-socialist movement 'leads humanity from out the dark night of the circumscribed I'; for Fukuyama its eradication heralds the radiant dawn of the circumscribed I.[26]

A second area of contention concerns Fukuyama's quite non-Hegelian understanding of 'contradictions'. For him, unlike Hegel and Marx, contradictions are exogenous to systems, not endogenous to them. The relevant contradictions are *inter*-systemic (between systems), as opposed to *intra*-systemic (within systems). Hence the transition from a bipolar world system, principally structured by the antagonism between capitalism and historical Communism, to a multipolar world system, comprising competing capitalisms – a restoration, in other words, of the prewar primacy of intra-systemic contradictions – is read as an elimination of significant contradictions. A certain historical myopia construes the exception – the post-Second World War composition of capitalist differences for the pursuit of the 'great contest' – as the norm. Yet historical Communism was one product of – a response to – a capitalist ascendancy riven by antagonisms so acute as to plunge the world into two cataclysmic wars in the span of a mere quarter-century. Communism was given its chance in 1917 by liberalism (not to mention social democracy). It came into existence promising to resolve the chronic problems generated by the 'combined and uneven development' of capitalism. It manifestly bequeaths those problems – social inequality, global inequity and ecological despoliation – to liberal capitalism, which, if its immediate horizons stretch no further than 'ready access to stereos and VCRs' on a planetary scale, is doomed to exacerbate them. One competitive capitalist world, in which survival is strictly reserved for the fittest, is an unpromising formula for survival.

If Fukuyama is able to exclude systemic intra-capitalist contradictions from his panorama, it is as a result of the sleight of hand whereby Fascism is assimilated to Communism – a standard Cold War move, of course (the trope of 'totalitarianism') – and both are counterposed to capitalism.[27] This conveniently dissimulates the historical reality that, the parliamentary road to Fascism having proved considerably more fecund than that to socialism, Fascism was a general tendency of prewar capitalism. Horkheimer's dictum assumes a new urgency: those who do not wish to speak of capitalism should keep silent about Fascism – just as, I would argue, anyone who has nothing to say on the subject of imperialism is disqualified from pronouncing on Stalinism. One would not guess it from Fukuyama, but on the fiftieth anniversary of Stalingrad there is less excuse for neglecting an uncomfortable fact: namely, that Stalinism – and not liberalism, which had collapsed in the 'thirty years civil war' of 1914–45 – vanquished European Fascism, therewith, paradoxically, laying the foundations for the revival of liberalism after 1945.[28] 'Progress,' to quote Freud, 'allied itself with barbarism' on the Eastern Front, where the Red Army eventually halted – and then broke – the hitherto invincible Wehrmacht.

Fukuyama may be an unreliable guide to the past; most criticisms of him centre on the present, however. And it is here – in Fukuyama's reading of contemporary history – that the rational kernel of his thesis is to be found. Setting aside the discursive alchemy whereby, capitalism supposedly no longer being capitalism, it cannot be said to have triumphed, we may attend to the converse consolation: namely, that formerly existing socialism not having been socialism, the latter cannot be claimed to have suffered a setback – indeed, can only benefit from a termination of a travesty and tragedy in the East.

Regrettably, this line of critique seems to me seriously misplaced. It is true that the Second World was not, nor had ever been, socialist, and would have failed the most cursory inspection of its credentials by Marx and Engels. Moreover, contemporary capitalism might appear to furnish – in the classical Marxist schema – the material and social preconditions for international socialism (thus permitting a Hegelian-Marxist philosophy of history to construe it as returning to the main line after a secular detour via peripheral tracks). It may be supposed also that, quite the reverse of being utopian, the vision of a global socialist order is the new realism dictated by the immense challenges besetting humanity, so that the alternative lies between a renovated socialism or a resurgent barbarism. If, in all these respects, the collapse of historical Communism removes the Stalinist incubus – the calamitous descent of socialism *into* barbarism in the twentieth century – which has functioned as one of the main impediments to the struggle for human emancipation, nevertheless, notwithstanding all this, in the current conjuncture that collapse constitutes a decisive defeat for socialism, which may be the abstract order of the day, but which is nowhere on the concrete agenda. Why?

First we may note the efficacious propagation of the Cold War equation: Socialism = Stalinism = (optimally) Penury + Tyranny – an imposture sufficiently credible, in the foreseeable future, to inoculate not only those recently liberated from the 'prison of peoples', but many more besides, against the socialist plague. Its prosperity derives not solely from the depradations of Stalinism, but from the palpable absence of any feasible and desirable alternative to it as a non-capitalist societal future. For the disappearance of the international Communist movement has not redounded to the benefit of social democracy, whose own crisis has rather been accentuated by it. Having long ago renounced its vocation – the 'democratic-socialist' resolution of the problems that induced the birth of Communism – social democracy has defaulted on its pledge of a humanization of capitalism: good for little more than winning elections, it is no longer good at that. Thus, what has occurred in the 1980s is the extinction or exhaustion of the two central traditions of socialist politics in the twentieth century – without anything plausible emerging to fill the vacuum.[29] And capitalist nature abhors a vacuum.

Alternatives to Communism and social democracy – futures for socialism that could clear its name, rehabilitate its reputation – have come and gone with alarming regularity. Restricting the focus to contemporary history, the spectacular promise of '1968' – the global return of the revolutionary repressed in punctual refutation of Marcuse's prognosis – was flagrantly breached. A conjuncture marked by the triple crisis of imperialism in the Third World (the Vietnamese Tet), of Stalinism in the Second (the Prague Spring), and of capitalism in the First (the Parisian May), seemingly resynchronized dialectical theory and the historical dialectic. The harvest of May dissevered them once more. In the East the Soviet invasion of Czechoslovakia brutally arrested de-Stalinization, irremediably disfiguring 'socialism with a human face'. In the West an unexpectedly resilient liberal capitalism surmounted yet another 'terminal' crisis, condemning the Fourth International(s), renascent in these years, to a protracted death-agony, once the Spanish transition and Portuguese Revolution had incorporated the Iberian Peninsula into Western Europe. Among the bitterest fruits for the revolutionary class of '68 was the failure of elective Third Worldist alternatives to the Soviet model: the exposure of the Chinese Cultural Revolution as a virulent Oriental compound of *Zhdanovschina* and

Yezhovschina, prior to its replacement by Dengist market Stalinism; the involution of the Cuban regime in the aftermath of Guevara's ill-fated Bolivian expedition and the failure of the '10 million tons' campaign in 1970; the murderous dispensation of the Khmers Rouges in Kampuchea Year Zero; Vietnam's embroilment, courtesy of Cambodian incursions and Chinese invasion, in wars with two 'fraternal countries' within years of the liberation of Saigon.

The imitation, rather than the supersession, of the Soviet experience – amounting, in some cases, to the repetition of history as worse tragedy – could, in every instance, only discredit (as well as demoralize) those who had hitched their socialism to the red star over Peking, Havana or Hanoi. With the passing of such reveries, the Soviet experience appeared exemplary, not aberrant – the 'totalitarian' corollary of 'totalizing' politics: in E.M. Forster's cheering liberal rendition, 'programmes mean pogroms'. At all events, what cannot be gainsaid is the record of failure of socialism, West and East, North and South, in the twentieth century, prompting perception of it as utopian (unviable) or dystopian (undesirable). Writing in *Le Monde* in October 1991, the Spanish ex-Communist Jorge Semprun suggested that 'today we are confronted with this reality: the society in which we live is an untranscendable horizon'. Wittingly or not, his terms echoed a slogan with which the 1960s had opened – Sartre's celebrated characterization of Marxism as 'the untranscendable philosophy of our time' – while reversing its verdict: the adventures of the dialectic vindicate 'dialectical' theory *à la* Fukuyama, not *à la* Sartre.[30]

What, however, of the post-Marxist intelligentsia who would point to the 'new social movements', rather than the old socialist movement, as the bearer(s) of an emancipatory politics? Granted, it might be said, that socialism as traditionally conceived is dead, but what of its recasting, for example, as one moment of a more capacious project for a 'radical and plural democracy' – a goal involving the extension of the liberty and equality borne by the 'democratic revolution' of 1789 to other sets of social relations (economic, sexual, ethnic, and so on), and a concomitant pluralization of political agency, beyond the (diminishing) ranks of the industrial working class, to other social forces?[31] The answer is simple: lacking the requisite agency, organization and strategy, these are not – and are not set to become – (counter-)hegemonic forces of the kind required to refute the Fukuyama thesis. In the absence of articulation and mobilization of the anti-capitalist 'general interest' to which their concerns ultimately point, hegemony will be endured, not forged.[32] Moreover, those on the left who detect a silver lining in acid-rain clouds, drawing solace from the putative fatality inscribed in capitalist accumulation (*viz*. its destruction of the ecological preconditions for its own reproduction), overlook the fact that 'environmentalism' precisely possesses no necessary class belonging. In and through its very 'universalism', it is *socially* indeterminate – compatible, in the medium term at any rate, with a grotesquely inegalitarian and authoritarian global capitalist order.

Not least among the reasons for a certain scepticism about the 'new social movements' as a contestant of the new order is their own manifest crisis (invariably neglected by those who harp on the crisis of the labour movement) and eclipse by some very old social movements: the furies of communalism, fundamentalism, nationalism, and so on, their militantly particularist dystopias stamped with the mark of exclusion. And yet, if the prominence of regressive social movements on the current world scene contributes to the disconsolation of socialists, does it not simultaneously discountenance Fukuyama's prospectus – the beneficent global diffusion of liberal commerce? Yes and no. Yes: the 'Common Marketization' of global politics is a fanciful projection (we need look no further than the present Maastricht imbroglio of the Common Market itself). No: for almost by definition, they are not of the requisite 'universal' character. Furthermore, the occasional rhetorical declamation notwithstanding, they are scarcely anti-capitalist, offering no alternative to the economic 'modernization' – *le dur commerce* – of whose contradictions and dislocations they are a symptom, rather than a solvent. The dialectic of Enlightenment qualifies, but does not contradict, the Fukuyama thesis.

Results and Prospects

With the destruction of actually existing socialism – the eradication of the Second World and its ongoing integration into the First – we are witnessing the elimination, possibly only temporary, of socialism as a world-historical movement. '*Die Weltgeschichte ist das Weltgericht*: world history is the final arbiter of right', Fukuyama, invoking Kojève, proclaims in his book.[33] We need not accept that economic might is political right. But it would be paradoxical, to say the least, were professed historical materialists to evade the reality that world history is the final arbiter of might – or the conclusion that, relative to the projections of classical Marxism, socialism is utopian once again: a desirable future confronting an unamenable present.

By any realistic calculation, the 'intelligence enough to conceive, courage enough to will, power enough to compel' adduced as prerequisites of socialism by William Morris are wanting today. In none of its significant embodiments has socialism succeeded in inventing a mass political organization that did not degenerate into either a simulacrum of the bourgeois-democratic state (the parties of the Second International), or a bureaucratic-centralist machine (those of the Third). In the advanced capitalist states it has not hit upon a strategy for a transition beyond welfare capitalism (and could not prevent a regression behind it); the reformist route has proved ineffectual, the revolutionary road chimerical. Where it has gained power (or office), its programmes have not realized the goal envisaged by Marx: the economic, political and cultural *supersession* of liberal capitalism. In the West, social democracy humanized capitalism, but did not abolish it; and utilized the liberal-representative state, but did not fundamentally transform it. In the East, where (as Trotsky would have it) history took the line of least resistance, Communism abolished capitalism, but substituted the command economy; and uprooted despotic states, but established authoritarian regimes. The social agent identified by socialists as possessing the requisite combination of a material interest in, and a structural capacity for, the achievement of socialism – the industrial working class – has not performed the role allotted it in the classical scripts. Notwithstanding recurrent economic militancy, and intermittent political radicalism, it has largely ceded composition of the 'poetry of the future' to the institutions of formerly existing socialism and actually existing social democracy.

The results of socialism to date, then, might be tersely summarized as 'the painful failure of revolution in the West and the almost equally painful success of revolution in the East'.[34] And yet there is more to be said about what must now be characterized as the even more painful failure of revolution in the East. For if much of the left consistently underestimated the durability and vitality of capitalism, as a result of its disastrous record from 1914 to 1945, it similarly discounted the significance of historical Communism. Not to the extent that it constituted an obstacle to socialism in the West, given its dire record in numerous respects; but in so far as it possessed, in addition to much that was simply deplorable and unforgiveable, what Lucio Magri has called 'another side':

> A historical experience is now ending in painful defeat – an experience which, both materially and in terms of ideas, served sometimes as a model and in any case as a reference point for broad movements of liberation. It is now fashionable in the West, even on the Left, to treat that connection as a thoroughly harmful product of manipulation or folly – that is, to consider the October Revolution and its sequel not as a process which degenerated in stages but as a regression *ab origine*, or a pile of rubble. But the historical reality is rather different. First Stalinism, then the authoritarian power of a bureaucratic, imperial caste, were one side of that historical process.... But for decades another side also continued to operate: the side of national independence; the spread of literacy, modernization and social protection across whole continents; the resistance to fascism and victory over it as a general tendency of capitalism; support for and actual involvement in the liberation of three-quarters of humanity from colonialism; containment of the power of the mightiest imperial state.[35]

To speak thus, controverting a certain anti-Communist commonsense on the left, is to court the charge of 'closet Stalinism'. For is it not to identify a socialism deserving of the name with formerly existing socialism; to accept the sometime Soviet Union and its satellites at their own mendacious (and now definitively repudiated) self-valuation; to deny the reality of an odious system whose crimes have besmirched the reputation of socialism the world over? One might as well come out of the closet: the unequivocal response is 'no'. It is to insist that the main alternative tradition of socialism – social democracy – had already sold the pass at the outbreak of the First World War and again at its conclusion, its derelictions marked by the social patriotism of August 1914 and the German October *manqué* of November 1918. It had proved unequal to the test of the Second World War, when it effectively disintegrated; was restricted to the advanced capitalist world (Europe and Australasia); and matched its accommodations to capitalism at home by collusion with imperialism abroad, enthusiastically prosecuting the Cold War against the Second and Third Worlds. By contrast, the record of Communism was significantly different, offering some support for Shaw's contention that 'a Bolshevik ... is nothing but a socialist who wants to do something about it.'[36]

Crudely inventoried, the existence and performance of historical Communism were positive in three crucial respects.[37] The first – as has already been indicated – was in the resistance to, and defeat of, European fascism: a fact incontrovertible by any amount of Cold War mythology and accounting for the prestige in which the Soviet model was held after 1945, Stalingrad constituting an even more potent symbol than Petrograd. Had the Swastika been run up over Moscow or Leningrad, it might still be flying over Paris or Prague.[38] The second was in the subsequent emergence of the Third World and its protection thereafter. As Noam Chomsky has argued, the rational kernel of 'deterrence theory' is to be found here: that is, in the Soviet deterrent to imperialist designs on the South.[39] Where that deterrence failed to avert US intervention, the forces confronting it prevailed only when sustained by the Second World: the tanks that entered Saigon in April 1975 were made – and where else? – in the USSR. A third – and final – merit of historical Communism was its role in precipitating the postwar compromise in the First World itself; the presence, within and without, of the 'red menace' weighed decisively in the meliorist reconstruction of Europe – countercyclical economic regulation, full employment, welfare services, universal suffrage, and so on – after Liberation.

Considerations such as these explain why it was rational, given the dilemma of *les mains sales*, to opt for Communism or, in the manner of Sartre and Merleau-Ponty, for 'anti-anti-Communism'.[40] To wash one's hands of the Communist movement was to risk dirtying them with something else – the implacable domination of capital – or to elect for political innocence at the cost of historical impotence. To the predictably adverse impact upon the reputation of socialism of any collapse of historical Communism must be added, then, a second fundamental reason for looking to a regeneration of the revolution *where* it had degenerated: the contradictory character, internally and externally, of Communism as a historical phenomenon.

Today, of course, it is fashionable to sneer that the USSR amounted to little more than an 'Upper Volta with rockets'. But we should remember that the rate of extensive, quantitative economic growth achieved by it – levels of 'stagnation' which M.S. Gorbachev would have done better to emulate at home, than impugn abroad – rendered it a potent force in the late 1950s and 1960s, when Khrushchevite de-Stalinization was underway, provoking some saturnine reflections from Harold Macmillan on the prospects for the Free World. In retrospect, the Soviet Union was clearly losing in the 'peaceful competition' with the West. And yet it imploded when apparently quite strong – in the aftermath of a wave of anti-imperialist revolutions in the Third World, in the

1970s. The USA had anxiously anticipated a domino effect in the South; the subsequent domino effect in the East was not expected by friends or foes. Sputnik ultimately gave way to Chernobyl; the latter was as much of a surprise as the former.

The last rites and ceremonies of the Cold War disclosed its systemic character: a great, but unequal, contest between opposed socio-economic and political systems, initiated by the Bolshevik Revolution. That contest has concluded, as predicted by Fukuyama, in the unqualified victory of capitalism, bringing an era – the era opened by 1917 – to a close. Sundown on the Union of Soviet Socialist Republics on Christmas Day 1991 – coda to a tragi-comic coup which hastened the denouement it vainly sought to deflect – means, for the time being at any rate, goodbye to all that, North and South. In his 'Theses on History', completed in the unrelieved gloom of spring 1940, Benjamin wrote: '*Even the dead* will not be safe from the enemy if he wins; and this enemy has not ceased to be victorious.'[41] In the intervening half-century, the enemy ceased to be victorious: but only when and where the forces contesting capitalism and imperialism mustered under, or subsequently rallied to, the banners of the international Communist movement. In winding up the Cold War journal *Problems of Communism* last year, the US State Department filed an affidavit for the counter-hegemonic role of historical Communism. It would be paradoxical, to say the least, were the post-Communist left, by traducing its memory, to sacrifice some of the dead to the enemy.

To the Watchtower

At the height of the first Cold War, in 1950, Isaac Deutscher wrote a review of *The God That Failed* which, *mutatis mutandis*, contains some salutary advice for those of us for whom the Communist movement has figured among the ties that bind:

> It seems that the only dignified attitude the intellectual ex-Communist can take is to rise *au-dessus de la mêlée*. He cannot join the Stalinist camp or the anti-Stalinist Holy Alliance without doing violence to his better self. So let him stay outside any camp. Let him try to regain critical sense and intellectual detachment. Let him overcome the cheap ambition to have a finger in the political pie. Let him be at peace with his own self at least, if the price he has to pay for phony peace with the world is self-renunciation and self-denunciation. This is not to say that the ex-Communist ... should retire into the ivory tower.... But he may withdraw into a *watchtower* instead. To watch with detachment and alertness this heaving chaos of a world, to be on a sharp lookout for what is going to emerge from it, and to interpret it *sine ira et studio*...[42]

In the spirit, but without the equanimity or eloquence, of Deutscher, I want to conclude by briefly identifying some 'ironies of history' – ironies which 'post-history' is unlikely to be spared – that dictate an ultimate reservation of judgement about the prospects for Fukuyama's thesis.

First, then, if it is the case that Stalinism rescued liberalism at the mid-point of the century, this is sufficient to indicate that, whilst a week in British party politics may be a long time, fifty years in geopolitics is shorter than we think – though not for the human beings fated to live and die in unredeemed historical time. Half a century hence, socialism might – just might – have staged as dramatic a comeback as its antagonist.[43] But one precondition of any future peripeteia is an adequate explanation of its current effacement from the global scene: the coolly realistic message conveyed by Fukuyama.

Second, the scope of the ongoing reversal of the verdicts of World War Two arguably far exceeds the humbling of Communism. In 1945 the 'Big Three' defeated the Axis Powers. But if Britain's political and economic declension was sealed in the very act of 'winning' the war, courtesy of American dollars and Soviet arms, and if the USSR, having been promoted to global 'superpower' status by its role in the conflict, has been erased, these do not entail that a Pax Americana has succeeded Cold War and Pax Britannica alike. One verdict of 1945 has been reversed with the erasure of the Eastern bloc, leaving capitalism in possession of the field. The end of that history does not, however, betoken a New World Order in which the New World, untrammelled, gives the orders. As was demonstrated to sanguinary and deterrent effect in the Gulf, the USA is the world's only military superpower. Yet its military prepotency was already implicit in the outcome of the First World War – prompting those endists *avant la lettre*, the authors of *1066 and All That*, to conclude (in a chapter entitled 'A Bad Thing'): 'America was thus clearly top nation, and History came to a .'[44] Militarily unipolar, so to speak, the contemporary world is multipolar economically. Within the inter-imperialist system that always persisted alongside the inter-systemic competition between historical Communism and capitalism, the USA is arguably no longer hegemon (as its search for subventions to finance the Gulf War attests).[45] With an impeccable sense of occasion, George Bush was laid low in Japan, as if in psychosomatic display of the anxiety that the US is set to repeat the postwar trajectory of the UK. For at its political meridian – the very moment of its 'unabashed victory' over the Evil Empire – America's economic descent – derivative, in part at least, from the 'over-extension' attendant upon prosecution of the Cold War – has been cruelly exposed to the light of day. The Soviet challenge has been met and routed; yet the means required for that end may portend the eclipse of the USA. Like Great Britain, the US may have won a war only at the cost of losing the ensuing peace – to the vanquished of 1945, with Germany at the centre of the EC trading bloc, and Japan the nodal point of the Pacific Rim. There is no success like failure…

Third, and finally, if this (or anything approximating to it) is the case, it throws into relief a possibility left unexplored by Fukuyama: that at the end of the twentieth century, the world – and not just Europe – may be reverting to something like the pre-1914 situation, when the antagonisms and rivalries mining the Belle Époque issued in the 'war to end all wars'. The 'landmines laid by the past'[46] have been detonated in the East; those being laid the world over by the present may turn out to be no less explosive. 'The future lasts a long time', de Gaulle once remarked. If so, it may be 'a very sad time' – prehistory all over again; or, alternatively, one in which, it having proved necessary to reinvent communism, an answer to barbarism may be discovered. 'In my end is my beginning'?[47] Perhaps. Meanwhile, Spinoza's injunction obtains: the point is neither to rejoice nor to deplore, but to understand. Understanding achieved, there will be all the time in the world for celebration – or lamentation.

Notes

* For Tom and Martha, divisibly.

1. See, for example, Frank Kermode, *The Sense of An Ending*, Oxford: Oxford University Press, 1967.

2. 'The critical theory of society possesses no concepts which could bridge the gap between the present and its future; holding no promise and showing no success, it remains negative. Thus it wants to remain loyal to those who, without hope, have given and give their life to the Great Refusal' (*One-Dimensional Man*, Boston: Beacon Press, 1964, p. 257).

3. Compare Karl Popper, *The Open Society and its Enemies* (two volumes, London: Routledge & Kegan Paul, 1945) and *The Poverty of Historicism* (London: Routledge & Kegan Paul, 1957) with Ernesto Laclau, *New Reflections on the Revolution of Our Time* (London: Verso, 1990). There is an excellent discussion of Cold War liberalism in Anthony Arblaster, *The Rise and Decline of Western Liberalism*, Oxford: Blackwell, 1984, ch. 18.

4. Cf., *inter alia*, Alex Callinicos, *Against Postmodernism*, Cambridge: Polity, 1990.

5. Francis Mulhern, Introduction to Francis Mulhern, ed., *Contemporary Marxist Literary Criticism*, London: Longman, 1992, p. 36. Cf. Aijaz Ahmad, *In Theory: Classes, Nations, Literatures*, London: Verso, 1992.

6. Mulhern, p. 17. The comments above should not be construed as a wholesale rejection of French philosophical modernism. There is a world of difference (for once) between the original meditations on anti-method of Foucault or Derrida and the kind of deliquescent Derridadaism or illegible Lacanglais spawned by their eclectic assimilation into the Cultural Studies departments of the Anglo-American academy. Nevertheless, some of the aporias of the former are reproduced, in exasperated form, in the latter. They might be summarized as follows: a discursive idealism, tributary to the linguistics of de Saussure, which, eliding epistemological and ontological categories, conflates the theory-dependence of knowledge of the world with the theory-dependence of the world; an epistemological relativism impaled on the traditional fork – *viz*. that if relativism in general is true, then no particular statement of it can claim to be; but if the particular statement of it is true, then that suffices to refute the generalization – and an ethical relativism subversive of the normative claims to which post-structuralism, despite itself, is prone; a perspectivism, of Nietzschean provenance, which fallaciously deduces the incommensurability of theories from their historical, social and cultural specificity; a hyperbolic anti-naturalism, which trades in biological essentialism for a nominalist culturalism. Of the many critiques of post-structuralism, see especially Peter Dews, *Logics of Disintegration*, London: Verso, 1987.

7. Originally published in *The National Interest*, no. 16, Summer 1989; reprinted in Kenneth M. Jensen, ed., *A Look at the End of History*, Washington, D.C., 1990. Among the critical literature it has provoked, I have learned most from Joseph McCarney, 'History under the Hammer', *Times Higher Educational Supplement*, 1 December 1989, and 'Endgame', *Radical Philosophy* 62, Autumn 1992; Perry Anderson, 'The Ends of History', in *A Zone of Engagement*, London: Verso, 1992; and Fred Halliday, 'An Encounter with Fukuyama', *New Left Review* 193, May–June 1992. For (some of) Fukuyama's antecedents, see Lutz Niethammer, *Posthistoire: Has History Come to an End?*, trans. Patrick Camiller, London: Verso, 1992.

8. *The Marriage of Heaven and Hell*, 'The Voice of the Devil', in William Blake, *The Complete Poems*, Harmondsworth: Penguin edition, 1977, p. 182.

9. Vices other than Communism could, of course, be deduced from the 'German ideology'. Thus in 1918 we find the 'New Liberal' philosopher, L.T. Hobhouse, having heard German aeroplanes overhead en route to their target, stating in the dedication to his *Metaphysical Theory of the State* that he had 'just witnessed the visible and tangible outcome of a false and wicked doctrine' pioneered by Hegel (quoted in Peter Clarke, *Liberals and Social Democrats*, Cambridge: Cambridge University Press, 1978, p. 193). The salience of 'English Hegelianism' at Oxford in the late nineteenth and early twentieth centuries prompted the Fabian Graham Wallas to remark that 'All bad German philosophies, when they die, go to Oxford' (quoted in ibid., p. 12). As Clarke points out, 'it is not a gibe that would have been current in Balliol', given the presence there of T.H. Green. By the 1950s, courtesy of the innoculations of 'Ordinary Language' philosophy, it is not a gibe that would have been current anywhere.

10. *The Making of the Second Cold War*, 2nd edn, London: Verso, 1986, p. 243. For the vicissitudes of the 'great contest' in the 1980s, see also Fred Halliday, *Cold War, Third World*, London: Radius, 1989.

11. *Manifesto of the Communist Party*, in Marx and Engels, *Selected Works*, Volume 1, Moscow: Progress Publishers, 1969, p. 108.

12. 'This social formation [capitalism] brings ... the prehistory of human society to a close' (Marx, Preface to *A Contribution to the Critique of Political Economy* (1859), in *Selected Works*, Volume 1, p. 504).

13. Edmund Wilson, *To the Finland Station* (1940), Harmondsworth: Penguin, 1991, p. 546. The category 'historical Communism' derives from Norberto Bobbio's obituary, 'The Upturned Utopia' (1989), reprinted in Robin Blackburn, ed., *After the Fall*, London: Verso, 1991.

14. Cf. Marx, *Capital* Volume 1, ch. 32 ('The Historical Tendency of Capitalist Accumulation'), Harmondsworth: Pelican edition, 1976, pp. 927–30.

15. 'Thank God, in November [1929], the Wall Street crash was to reassure them: they welcomed it like news of a victory. Since they tended to confuse capitalism with important people, when they saw their fathers' faces they convinced themselves that they had been quite right to stake their lives on the cards of confusion, and that they could indubitably count upon a world destined for great metamorphoses' (Paul Nizan, *The Conspiracy* (1938), trans. Quintin Hoare, London: Verso, 1988, p. 49).

16. *The Philosophy of History*, New York: Dover edition, 1956, p. 19.

17. *Socialism and the Political Struggle* (1883), quoted in Adam Westoby, *The Evolution of Communism*, Cambridge: Polity, 1989, p. ii.

18. *The Communists and Peace* (1952), trans. Irene Clephane, London: Hamish Hamilton, 1969, p. 118.

19. Such incipient 'cultural pessimism' is by no means restricted to Fukuyama, of course: for a brief but incisive communitarian diagnosis of the 'malaise of modernity', indicating its prevalence under left- and right-wing guises, see Charles Taylor, *The Ethics of Authenticity*, Cambridge, Mass.: Harvard, 1992.

20. Anderson, p. 49.

21. Marx, *Capital* Volume 1, pp. 102–3.

22. See Louis Althusser, *For Marx*, London: Allen Lane, 1969; and (with Étienne Balibar) *Reading Capital*, New Left Books, London, 1970. Cf. the retrospective in Althusser's 'autobiography', *L'avenir dure longtemps*, Paris: Stock/IMEC, 1992.

23. Althusser and Balibar, p. 120.

24. See Yann Moulier Boutang, *Louis Althusser: Une biographie. Tome 1 – La formation du mythe (1918–1956)*, Paris: Grasset, 1992, pp. 314ff., for an account of Althusser's extraordinary 72-page letter of 25 December 1949–22 January 1950 to Jean Lacroix, explaining his adhesion to Marxism and the French Communist Party. A propos of the 'end of history', it concludes (p. 33): 'And I believe that we can close this chapter on the end of history, while celebrating the fact that history continues, that Marx was not Hegel, that Stalin and Thorez are not Hyppolite.' For Fukuyama, by contrast, 'The notion of the end of history is not an original one. Its best known propagator was Karl Marx, who believed that the direction of historical development was a purposeful one determined by the interplay of material forces and would come to an end only with the achievement of a communist utopia that would finally resolve all prior contradictions. But the concept of history as a dialectical process with a beginning, a middle, and an end was borrowed by Marx from his great German predecessor, Georg Wilhelm Friedrich Hegel.' Althusser's relevance to the contemporary debate is further explored in my review article, 'Analysis Terminated, Analysis Interminable', *Economy and Society*, vol. 21, no. 2, May 1993.

25. See the 'Theses on the Philosophy of History', in Walter Benjamin, *Illuminations*, trans. Harry Zohn, London: Fontana/Collins, 1982, especially pp. 262–3. 'Nothing,' Benjamin wrote, 'has corrupted the German working class so much as the notion that it was moving with the current' (p. 260). And not just the German working class: compare the desperate optimism of Jean Jaurès on the eve of his assassination and the outbreak of the First World War – 'Les choses ne peuvent pas ne pas s'arranger' ('Things are bound to turn out all right') (quoted in James Joll, *The Second International 1889–1914*, London: Routledge & Kegan Paul, 1974, p. 169).

26. Quoted in Wilson, p. 506.

27. Hayek's unfashionable anticipation of this, as of so many other, trends is noteworthy: see especially his 1944 Philippic, *The Road to Serfdom*, dedicated 'To the Socialists of All Parties'.

28. For the requisite historical contextualization of the exterminism of Operation Barbarossa, see Arno Mayer, *Why Did the Heavens Not Darken?*, London: Verso, 1990, ch. 1.

29. As Willie Thompson has written: 'The communist parties have constituted the first (and to date only) world movement which has treated with deadly seriousness the project of transforming social relations on a planetary scale for the benefit of the world's masses – as well as appearing to achieve stunning success in terms of that objective' (*The Good Old Cause: British Communism 1920–1991*, London: Pluto Press, 1992, p. 212).

30. Semprun is quoted from *Le Monde*, 15 October 1991, by Emmanuel Terray in *Le troisième jour du communisme*, Arles: Actes Sud, – 1992, p. 92, where the echo of Sartre's Preface to the *Critique of Dialectical Reason* (1960; London: New Left Books, 1976, p.

822) is noted.

31. Cf. Ernesto Laclau and Chantal Mouffe, *Hegemony and Socialist Strategy*, London: Verso, 1985.

32. See, for example, Francis Mulhern, 'Towards 2000, or News from You-Know-Where', *New Left Review*, 148, November/December 1984, and the book of which it is a review: Raymond Williams, *Towards 2000*, London: Chatto and Windus/The Hogarth Press, 1983.

33. *The End of History and the Last Man*, London: Hamish Hamilton/New York: The Free Press, 1992, p. 137.

34. Alan Carling, 'Rational Choice Marxism', *New Left Review* 160, November–December 1986, p. 26.

35. 'The European Left Between Crisis and Refoundation', *New Left Review* 189, September–October 1991, pp. 6–7.

36. Quoted in David Caute, *The Fellow-Travellers*, London, 1977, pp. 113–14.

37. The following quasi-Deutscherite (and crypto-Pabloite?) line of analysis variously draws upon Isaac Deutscher, *The Great Contest*, Oxford: Oxford University Press, 1960; Perry Anderson, 'Trotsky's Interpretation of Stalinism', in Tariq Ali, ed., *The Stalinist Legacy*, Harmondsworth: Penguin, 1984; and Fred Halliday, 'The Ends of Cold War', in Blackburn, ed., *After the Fall*. See also Eric Hobsbawm, 'Goodbye to All That', in ibid.

38. Moreover, had the Hammer and Sickle not flown over the Reichstag, it is unlikely that the Red Flag would – metaphorically speaking – have been accorded a subaltern station, alongside the Union Jack, over the Royal Palace of Westminster. On 1 December 1942, when the Beveridge Report was being published in London, the Red Army was otherwise engaged at Stalingrad.

39. *Deterring Democracy*, London: Verso, 1991, p. 60.

40. In addition to Sartre, *The Communists and Peace* (1952–54) London: Hamish Hamilton, 1969, see Sartre, 'Merleau-Ponty' (1961), in *Situations IV*, Paris: Gallimard, 1980, and Maurice Merleau-Ponty, *Humanism and Terror* (1947), Boston: Beacon Press, 1969. For Merleau-Ponty's subsequent (auto-)critique, see *Adventures of the Dialectic* (1955), Evanston: Northwestern University Press, 1979 (especially ch. 5).

41. Benjamin, p. 257.

42. 'The Ex-Communist's Conscience', in Isaac Deutscher, *Russia in Transition*, revised edition, New York: Grove Press, 1960, p. 234.

43. For some intriguing (if semi-detached) reflections on the future prospects for socialism, see the concluding pages of Anderson's 'The Ends of History', pp. 357–75.

44. Sellar and Yeatman, *1066 and All That*, London: Macmillan, 1930, p. 113.

45. American eclipse as a consequence of geopolitical 'over-extension' is the concluding scenario of Paul Kennedy's influential *The Rise and Fall of the Great Powers*, London: Fontana, 1989. The British precedent is memorably analysed in Correlli Barnett, *The Collapse of British Power*, Gloucester: Allan Sutton; 1987 and *The Audit of War*, London: Macmillan, 1987.

46. Quoted from *Pravda* in Patrick Cockburn, *Getting Russia Wrong*, London: Verso, 1989, p. 42.

47. T.S. Eliot, 'East Coker', in *Collected Poems 1909–1962*, London: Faber & Faber, 1985, p. 204.

PART II

Marx

4

The End of History or the Beginning of Marx?
Keith Graham

An inventor – call him Ninel – announced his intention to build a flying machine. Some people said 'Such a thing is impossible.' Ninel thought it was not only possible but that he knew a quick route to its achievement. True, it would involve coercing people into helping to build it, but that was a fair price to pay for such an achievement, and they would themselves be grateful in the end.

However, those coerced felt their coercion more keenly than they did any enthusiasm for the project. Their disaffection resulted in loose bolts, inaccurate drilling, substandard parts. The launch of the flying machine ended in disaster, with many killed. The sceptics concluded 'We were right. Flying is impossible.' They were not right. But it was now harder than ever to convince them.

Introduction

Fukuyama tells us that 'it is our misfortune that few of us are familiar with Hegel's work from direct study, but only as it has been filtered through the distorting lens of Marxism'.[1] It may seem surprising, but a strong case can be made for saying exactly the same of Marx's own work. Marxism as a historical phenomenon had already begun to develop in his own lifetime in ways he wished to distance himself from. The content of his own writings suggests that he would have been even more insistent on separating himself from the brutal and oppressive regimes of Eastern Europe which came to bear his name (and not merely because they turned out to be brutal and oppressive). If he is justified in doing so, it is far from obvious that the welcome demise of those regimes constitutes an abandonment of Marx's ideas. Only what has formerly been embraced can be abandoned.

Marxism in its historically dominant form would more accurately be called Leninism. Marxism in that sense is dead. But a historically significant movement dedicated to realizing Marx's own aspirations in his favoured way has yet to be born. In this chapter I shall attempt to substantiate that claim by calling attention to Marx's specification of the nature of capitalist society and the future society, and the commitments which follow concerning the method of realizing that future society. I then examine points of similarity and difference in Fukuyama's and Marx's views on the dynamics of human history, and I consider how some of the deficiencies in Marx's account might bear on the likelihood of a movement devoted to realizing his proposed future society. Finally, I call attention to the sort of reason Marx has for holding that capitalism requires supersession in the first place – a matter which has not always been well understood.

Capitalism and the Future Society

Capitalism is identified by Marx as the form of society, and the *only* form of society, in which wealth predominantly takes the form of commodities, goods produced for the purpose of exchange. Wealth in capitalism 'appears as an "immense collection of commodities"' and 'this only happens on the basis of one particular mode of production, the capitalist one'.[2] Exchange may take place exceptionally and peripherally in many societies, for example those where wealth is produced immediately for subsistence. But although there are therefore other societies with markets, capitalism alone is identified as the market society. Here, it is standard that owners of objects and services relinquish control over them only on condition that they are the beneficiaries of a similar relinquishment on the part of others. And economic activity is standardly geared to such reciprocating relinquishment, rather than to the immediate enjoyment of objects and services by those who produce them.

Where commodities, and therefore the market, predominate, then money comes to assume an importance beyond that implied by the roles it plays in facilitating the circulation and exchange of commodities. It comes to play the role of *capital*: wealth which is advanced in order to increase wealth, rather than wealth in one form which is exchanged in order to acquire and consume wealth in some other form. According to Marx, the circulation of capital is limitless and becomes an end in itself, the *raison d'être* of the production process.[3] But this can take place only in a very particular set of conditions. Capital can emerge 'only when the owner of the means of production and subsistence finds the free worker available, on the market, as the seller of his own labour-power'.[4] Capital and wage labour are two sides of the same coin. 'Thus capital presupposes wage labour: wage labour presupposes capital. They reciprocally condition the existence of each other...'[5]

If we are to understand the profundity of Marx's rejection of capitalist society, it is of the first importance to notice that he specifies it in terms of the nature of commodities and the consequences which he holds to follow when commodities predominate in a society. Capitalism, for Marx, is not specified by any particular set of political institutions; nor does he believe that its deficiencies could be removed by some different form of control over the circulation of commodities and capital.[6] On the contrary, it is of the nature of commodities that they control human beings rather than vice versa.[7] A society based on them must take a particular shape, Marx argues. Capitalism has its own imperatives which impose themselves on human beings, whatever their own plans or aspirations might be. No one, for example, wants recessions and slumps, but these events and their consequences are unavoidable. A hiatus therefore opens up between, say, ill-housed and shabbily dressed people on the one hand, and the utilization of resources and techniques for providing them with decent housing and clothing on the other. Need is there; resources are there; but the employment of resources is not need-driven.

Marx is explicitly critical of those like Proudhon who fail to see the connected nature of these phenomena – exchange, money, wage labour and capital – and 'thereby reduce socialism to an elementary misunderstanding of the inevitable correlation existing between commodities and money'.[8] Marx himself advocates 'the abolition of wage labour, capital and their mutual relationship'[9] as well as the abolition of money, the 'abolition of buying and selling'.[10]

It takes an effort of imagination to grasp how different is the world which Marx is proposing here. It would involve people relating to one another, and to the material objects surrounding them, in ways radically distinct from any which have been visible either in the West or in Eastern Europe during the twentieth century. Whatever else we may wish to say about the regimes that have been discredited and discarded, and whatever vitally important differences there might have been between them and our own form of society, both have shared features of the order which mattered to Marx. In both, access to goods has depended on exchange through the medium of currency; in both, life has been characterized for many people by a need to sell their labour-power as a precondition of living an average life. (It is a much more complex matter, in the case both of East European regimes and of our own forms of society, to judge how Marx was right about the further character which commodity-based society must assume.) Correspondingly, neither has exhibited the positive features of the future society that Marx sponsored – a 'co-operative society based on common ownership of the means of production' where 'the producers do not exchange their products'.[11] Marx envisages a state of affairs where ownership would cease to carry the significance it has for us, and indeed at the level of the productive forces of society would cease to carry any significance at all. Ownership has significance only where there are nonowners: if productive resources come to be the common property of all, this is as good as to say that they belong to no one. Various analogies may be invoked to illustrate the point. Marx himself draws a parallel between an individual Robinson Crusoe who produces directly for his own utility and its social equivalent.[12] Crusoe cannot give himself, or exchange with himself, what he already owns: he simply uses and consumes what is already his. One might equally invoke the case of a family where all cooperate in the kitchen to produce sustenance which they then take freely of. It would be idle to ask who *in particular* the equipment and the resources in the kitchen belong to, if they belong to the family collectively. To maintain a parallel with Marx's envisaged society, however, the family would need to be both nonhierarchical and generously endowed with equipment and resources. It would also have to remain a collective. In the event of break-up and divorce, it would no longer be idle to ask who the property belonged to, and the parallel would cease to hold.

The attempt to use such homely analogies for the construction of the relation between an entire society and its resources may well be thought hopelessly utopian. We should take care, however, not to make matters appear worse than they are, so far as Marx's conception of the future society is concerned. According to Fukuyama, Marx thought history would end with a 'communist utopia that would finally resolve all prior contradictions',[13] and it is not uncommon to ascribe to Marx the view that the future society will be so harmonious as to exclude any disagreement or conflict of wills at all, that it will be a place where everyone can do exactly as they want.[14] But this is far more extreme than anything he is committed to. He sponsors the removal of contradictions 'not in the sense of individual antagonism but of an antagonism that emanates from the individuals' social conditions of existence'.[15] It is the conflict between classes, and any other conflicts flowing from that, which are to be eliminated. That leaves plenty of scope for contingent conflicts, between both individuals and groups, to be negotiated and resolved in some way or another.[16]

Ends and Means

Even if the elimination of human conflict of all kinds is not part of Marx's agenda for the future, it may be felt that it does him no particular favours to call attention to his conception of the future society and emphasize its great distance from any actually occurring social arrangements. Doing so may elicit two objections in particular. First, even if he does not envisage a world where people never disagree, it may be felt that his conception of a world devoid of ownership and exchange is so obviously utopian as to belong to the crackpot category dismissed by Fukuyama, precisely because it does not belong to those challenges 'embodied in important social and political forces and movements, and which are therefore part of world history'.[17] Second, the very conviction that this nebulous future is realizable may have been instrumental in encouraging brutal means to its supposed achievement: the sacrificing of present generations to a millenarian future instead of limited, piecemeal improvements constrained by considerations of normal political and moral decency.

On each count there is more to be said in a vein favourable to Marx. First, so far as the future is concerned it is an odd prejudice to discount ideas not (yet) embodied in actual movements. This consorts ill with the primacy which Fukuyama wishes to assign to ideas in general, and it is illegitimately conservative in its effect, since it precisely privileges those ideas already so embodied.

The ideas of grassroots trade-union opposition to a monolithic state in Poland, or of democratic impulses in the face of authoritarian structures in the former USSR, were ideas that had to begin somewhere. By the test of embodiment in significant forces, there was a time when they would have been (ill-advisedly) dismissed. Marx's conception cannot therefore be dismissed solely on the grounds of (current) nonembodiment. This is bound to seem a bizarre defence of Marx when the received view is that his ideas *have* been embodied in significant forces, and when Marx himself clearly thought that these were ideas whose time had come, so that they were already or would shortly be so embodied. But the central aim of this chapter is precisely to challenge that received view by pointing out what Marx's claims actually were and attempting to trace the commitments that those claims imply. Marx's own opinion of what commitments are implied has no special privilege: it is, in fact, enormously difficult to trace the implications of one's own theories, especially if those theories are rich and complex. I examine below the justification for believing that these were ideas whose time had come in.

As for the second objection, even if we grant that Marx's conception of the future society is both nebulous and utopian, it still has sufficient specificity to carry implications about the means to its achievement, and this is testified to by Marx's own claims. Central to them is the idea, held consistently, that the agent which alone is capable of liberating the working class from its class condition is that class itself, rather than any distinct agency from without or any subgroup of the class from within. In the *Communist Manifesto* this is expressed as the idea that the proletarian movement 'is the self-conscious, independent movement of the immense majority'.[18] Marx drafted into the Provisional Rules of the First International the requirement that 'the emancipation of the working classes must be conquered by the working classes themselves'.[19] And later, in a famous letter, he and Engels dissociated themselves from 'people who openly declare that the workers are too uneducated to free themselves'.[20]

The idea gains concrete expression in Marx's well-documented support for Chartism and the extension of the franchise. Such support ought presumably to earn Fukuyama's approval, since it appears to be support for one of the central institutions of liberal democracy. Appearances may mislead, however. Although Marx never relinquished his support for elections or his insistence on proletarian self-emancipation, his enthusiasm for the highly participatory structures of the Paris Commune indicates a much slighter attachment to specifically *parliamentary* institutions.[21] That, in its turn, ought to incur Fukuyama's displeasure if he is right in his conviction that the institutions of the liberal democratic state are the final form in which human beings are to conduct their social affairs. The aspiration to a state of affairs where tiers of revocable delegates are bound by written instructions will seem both needless and utopian.

At this point we should observe a distinction. The term 'democracy' is used in two distinct senses: both to denote a concrete set of institutions and to express an abstract set of values. When it is used in the first sense, the term is usually taken to denote a state of affairs where political parties are free to organize in order to campaign for the popular vote and form limited-term governments with powers of legislation, and so on. When it is used in the second sense, it expresses, roughly, the idea of human beings governing themselves in conditions of freedom and equality. The claim that liberal democracy has brought us to the end of history is more plausible when the term 'democracy' is construed in the second sense. Since the Renaissance, the idea of the intrinsic importance of individual human beings has gradually gained ground, and with it the idea (which would have sounded so strange at other times and places) that servitude is not a natural or acceptable condition for *any* human being. Self-rule, rather than rule by others, is a value that is widely though not universally embraced. However, agreement in endorsing that value is more easily achieved than agreement over what institutional arrangements are adequate to its realization. Indeed, at the ideological level disputes between defenders of Western democracy and erstwhile defenders of 'people's democracy' can be viewed precisely as disagreements over the answer to that question. They were at one in their view that self-rule is a fitting state for normal adult human beings, but held conflicting views on the question of what political forms did best enable such creatures to govern themselves.

The contest between their respective answers to that question is at an end. But we should not suppose that the only standard by which existing institutions can be judged is some demonstrably inferior alternative set of institutions elsewhere in the world. An equally pertinent question to ask is what set of institutions is *possible* for realizing the values in question. That will depend on many factors, including technology. The civilization that has given us VCRs has also given us the means of superseding the limited extent to which self-rule is achieved in the existing world. Marx says: 'The parliamentary regime leaves everything to the decision of majorities. Why then should the great majority outside parliament not want to make the decisions?'[22] At the time of his raising this question, it might have been a legitimate reply that no institutional provision for such decision-making was practically available. That reply could not be given today. The development of information technology and the existence of a sophisticated and highly educated populace introduce a new range of possibilities. They are, moreover, highly germane to Marx's aspirations, since they afford greater opportunities for the mass of people to influence affairs and therefore to demonstrate how far they are capable or incapable of acting so as to emancipate themselves. Those possibilities may or may not be realized, and it may be that there are strong arguments against substantially increasing the degree of participation in the decision-making process enjoyed by the mass of citizens. But a technology is available which could vastly increase input into social decisions; and that provides grounds on which the view that, *institutionally*, democracy has reached its final form can be seriously questioned.[23]

The upshot is this. The nebulousness and utopianism (if such it is) of Marx's conception of the future society do not prevent his characterization from itself indicating both why Marx can say no more than he does about the form that society must take and why he incurs a commitment to democratic values. Whatever else it may be, the future society is characterized by voluntary participation rather than coercion. It is therefore in an important sense self-defining. The particular relations and institutions which it is to exhibit will depend on what its inhabitants decide that they should be. They will not depend on coercive imposition by a minority elite, nor could they possibly depend on the decisions of an individual theorist.

The tragedy of the twentieth century has been the belief that there could ever be such a thing as a Marxist society, if that means one which could be run in accordance with any specific prescriptions to be found in Marx's writings. That belief precisely fails to take seriously his thesis of self-emancipation. Marx offers a critique of capitalism and a proposal for an alternative form of society lacking its defects but utilizing its achievements. But that proposal is not and could not be more than an outline, giving the general principles governing the alternative society. *Someone* obviously has to do much more than this. Someone has to work out a specification of the mechanisms, procedures and institutions which are practically realizable and conform to the general principles. Someone, in short, has to work out how an entire society is to function. Marx's reasonable view is that the general principles governing that society dictate that this must be the great mass of people in whose interest it will be for such a society to come into being. To that extent a capacity for self-government in some substantive sense must be acquired prior to the inception of the new society. Where better, therefore, to manifest the capacity for harmonious, voluntary co-operation than in the movement which has as its objective the founding of a whole society based on harmonious, voluntary co-operation – a movement which, according to Marx, must be self-conscious and independent?

There is little in Marx's politics to license the vanguardism traditionally associated with his name.[24] It turns out that although his aspirations are revolutionary rather than piecemeal, they are constrained in ways which come close to what I referred to earlier as those of normal political and moral decency. He becomes committed to the constraints of democracy not as a result of subscription to abstract ethical principles, but rather because the very nature of the end aimed at implies the need to accept such constraints. His commitment to democratic *values*, moreover, is consistent with (one might even say implies) a dissatisfaction with the *institutions* currently held to be the vehicle of their realization. Marx is enthusiastic about electoral mechanisms and accountability, less so about the lack of control which a representative system implies for the represented as compared with the representatives.

History and Ideas

A natural reaction at this stage is to wonder why, if my version of them is correct, Marx's own proposals should have had so little influence, and why such a deformed version of Marxism should have come to dominate world history in the twentieth century. That is a complex historical question which I have partly addressed elsewhere.[25] It is worth pointing out that if Marx himself were to attempt to answer it, he would have at his disposal more theoretical resources than Fukuyama allows, including those which Fukuyama himself regards as the most important. Fukuyama tells us that Marx 'believed that the direction of historical development was a purposeful one determined by the interplay of material forces'.[26] He suggests that our tendency to retreat into materialist explanations of political or historical phenomena is 'another unfortunate legacy of Marxism', and that 'deterministic materialism that discounts the importance of ideology and culture' is as likely to be found on the right as on the left.[27] These attributions may not be strictly incorrect, but they convey a very one-sided impression of Marx's conception of the dynamic of history, as I now explain.

It is true that Marx expresses the view that the victory of the proletariat is inevitable,[28] and that he describes the 'natural laws of capitalist production' as 'working themselves out with iron necessity'.[29] But he explicitly distances himself from the idea that history has any purpose beyond the purposes of human beings themselves. History, he says, 'is not a person apart, using man as a means for *its own* particular aims; history is *nothing but* the activity of man pursuing his aims'.[30] Similarly, the communists utilize material provided by previous generations 'without, however, imagining that it was the plan or the destiny of previous generations to give them material'.[31] Now these disclaimers are compatible with nevertheless detecting a pattern in history, separate from the intentions of human beings, a pattern whose shape depends on material factors. That certainly is Marx's position. But this still does not amount to discounting the importance of ideology and culture, as Fukuyama claims. This can be seen if we consider the pattern in its general form and in the specific form which it is supposed to take in the case of capitalism.

In the general pattern, human beings develop productive forces within some determinate set of relations of production up to the point where the relations begin to fetter the forces. At that point, social upheaval occurs and new relations of production replace those which had begun to act as fetters. The point of fettering is crucial because Marx appears to regard it as both a necessary and a sufficient condition of social transformation. 'No social order is ever destroyed *before* all the productive forces for which it is sufficient have been developed.'[32] And people 'are *obliged*, from the moment when their commerce [that is, relations of production] no longer corresponds to the productive forces acquired, to change all their traditional social forms'.[33] If history is simply a matter of human beings pursuing their aims, why should this particular pattern emerge, rather than any number of others? General considerations about the nature of human life can invest the idea with at least a degree of plausibility, and make it worthwhile to investigate empirically whether, or how often, or to what degree, the pattern is exemplified. The same considerations indicate the deficiency in Fukuyama's picture of Marx.

Human beings' materiality gives them a direct interest in developing powers of production. They have material needs which must be recurrently met, and the fact of their not living in a Garden of Eden implies that action on their part is necessary for the meeting of those needs. The more efficient is the technology with which they can produce for meeting their needs, the greater will be the time at their disposal for other human activities: for writing symphonies or playing darts, for making love or conversation. In a class-divided society this general interest will itself become differentiated. Members of a privileged, exploiting class may evade altogether the onerous business of spending time producing to meet their needs. One way of consolidating their position may be to ensure that they can extract hard work from a subordinate class with a maximally efficient technology. By contrast, the subordinate class may have a more indirect interest in the same state of affairs. They may be coerced into the appropriate behaviour and thereby acquire an interest in doing so, since any alternative is liable to be even less appealing.

So far, we have a prima facie case for thinking that development of productive forces might occur in human societies. We have as yet no grounds for expecting discontinuities of the kind postulated by Marx, nor for expecting their resolution in the way he suggests, by the transformation of relations of production. Indeed, on the prima facie case as given so far, those possibilities appear more mysterious. If a dominant, exploiting class has an interest in seeing technology develop so as to sustain its own dominance, it will equally have an interest in not allowing relations of production to change in such a way as to threaten that dominance. Why should it be thought that such a pattern of replacement of dominant classes will occur?

Plausible general considerations can again be put forward which would make a hypothesis of that kind worthy of investigation. It is reasonable to suppose that there is not infinite flexibility in the social relations of production within which a given set of productive forces can be utilized. For example, it would be impossible for a modern industrial system to be run in accordance with feudal social relations. It is equally reasonable to suppose that it may simply not be evident, when productive forces are being developed in a particular way, what the implications of their use are for relations of production. In this way a dominant class may inadvertently, rather than wittingly, oversee changes which come to threaten their own conditions of existence. The very impulse to development on which they depend may throw up possibilities that are in the interest of some other group.

Marx indicates how that possibility may be played out through the dynamics of human action. Where a technology of potential benefit to non-ruling groups is not utilized, because it is not in the interests of the ruling group, this is likely to produce frustration and a new clash of interests, distinct from the clash characteristic of the settled class relations. A class aspiring to utilize the technology 'must first conquer for itself political power in order to represent its interest in turn as the general interest'.[34] It may well succeed in that representation because it 'appears from the very start, if only because it is opposed to a *class*, not as a class but as a representative of the whole society'.[35] As a result, the aspiring class may be able to unite behind it a coalition of different groups with a real or perceived interest in social transformation, groups which have a common enemy in the dominant class, though it may be for different reasons.[36] The coalition may be sufficiently powerful to remove the dominant class, but the result may be the enthronement of a new dominant class. The transformation may be carried through on an ideology of general liberation, but general liberation may not be the result.

It should be evident from this sketch that ideas, ideology and consciousness are not a mere inert residue with no role to play in the dynamic posited by Marx. On the contrary, large-scale change in social relations relies on the convergence of appropriate material circumstances and the concerted action of social groups. It is positively required that those groups should be motivated by particular conceptions of their own behaviour, and it has been a major preoccupation of recent Marxologists to work out an interpretation of the interrelation between consciousness and material conditions which recognizes the active contribution made by consciousness while allowing due primacy to the material.[37]

What is distinctive of Marx's position, however, is his belief that the conceptions which such groups possess need not reflect accurately what they are engaged in. Just as we distinguish between 'what a man thinks and says of himself and what he really is and does',[38] so we cannot judge societies by their own conceptions. Yet even if their conceptions do not accurately *reflect* what is going on, they may *aid* that process. An ascendant group may be more galvanized if it believes it is acting for the greater glory of God rather than to further its own interests. A subordinate group may be more galvanized if it believes it is helping to secure general liberation rather than furthering the interests of the ascendant group.

With a highly significant exception, Marx treats the dynamic involved in the change from capitalism to the future society as conforming to this general pattern. For example, the failure of the proletariat to attain its own ends in earlier attempts is explained by reference to the lack of convergence between concerted action and appropriate material circumstances. The attempts failed 'owing to the then undeveloped state of the proletariat, as well as to the absence of the economic conditions for its emancipation'.[39] The success of future attempts is predicated on the assumption that the point of fettering of productive forces is reached and that the required convergence obtains. The 'material and mental conditions of the negation of wage labour and capital ... are themselves results of [capitalism's] production process'.[40]

> Beyond a certain point, the development of the powers of production becomes a barrier for capital; hence the capital relation a barrier for the development of the

productive powers of labour. When it has reached this point, capital, i.e. wage labour ... is necessary stripped off as a fetter. [41]

The exception concerns consciousness. Marx tells us that the 'proletarian movement is the *self*-conscious, independent movement of the immense majority'.[42] Whereas previous transformations required *some* consciousness for their successful achievement, and whereas it might be positively functional for that result if people had a mistaken perception of the process they were involved in, the prospective transformation involves *transparent* consciousness. People have a sound apprehension of the process they are involved in. This follows, in effect, from Marx's version of an end-of-history thesis. There is no further class for the proletariat to exploit, no new set of class relations they can bring into being, and the abolition of capitalism is the abolition of class society in general. Class conflict is finally resolved, and in that respect the future society gives the final form in which human beings can conduct their affairs. Accordingly, there is no need for ideological misperception and there is no need for the proletariat to represent its movement, either to itself or to others, as anything other than what it really is.

It is not just that there is no need for such misperception, however. There is positively no room for it. That follows from Marx's commitments concerning the nature of the future society and the means for its achievement, discussed earlier. It is a form of society whose viability depends crucially on its members having a clear understanding of their own social relations and a clear determination to co-operate voluntarily. It is literally unthinkable that people should act in this way without comprehending what they are doing. Short of a magical transformation at the threshold of the new society, we must conclude that the required perspicacity and motivation are acquired in the process which leads to the threshold.

So far I have attempted to show that ideas do not have the inert character in Marx's theory of history that Fukuyama claims. He might still object that we can legitimately lay at Marx's door the 'disinclination to believe in the *autonomous* power of ideas'[43] that he, Fukuyama, deplores. There is no doubt, after all, that the role Marx assigns to consciousness is in some sense secondary and dependent on material conditions, even if it is an active role. At this point, matters take an ironical twist. On the one hand, it is not clear why we should allow *autonomous* power to ideas, as Fukuyama requires. Marx famously remarked: 'Men make history, but not of their own free will; not under circumstances they themselves have chosen but under the given and inherited circumstances with which they are directly confronted.'[44] That is surely unexceptionable, as is his comment that individuals 'work under definite material limits, presuppositions and conditions independent of their will'.[45] The difficult question is not *whether* the power of ideas is limited by circumstances, but *how* and in what ways. Marx tries to answer the difficult question. If Fukuyama thinks it does not arise, there is little reason to agree with him. On the other hand, as I shall now attempt to show, there is a defect in Marx's theory which impels him closer to Fukuyama's position despite his own aspirations.

The defect consists in an ambiguity in the notion of fettering, as between the general context and the specific case of the transformation from capitalism. As we saw, in the general case the hypothesis is that productive developments occur which could be of benefit but cannot be utilized within existing relations, and that the perception of such non-utilization produces a coalition for changing existing relations. The problem is that Marx's own characterization of the essential nature of capitalism precludes the possibility that the hypothesis should apply in this case. The bourgeoisie, he tells us, 'cannot exist without constantly revolutionizing the instruments of production'.[46]

> The capitalist mode of production ... begets, by its anarchic system of competition, the most outrageous squandering of labour-power and of the social means of production, not to mention the creation of a vast number of functions at present indispensable, but in themselves superfluous.[47]

The problem with capitalism, therefore, appears to be the very opposite of under-utilization.

It does not follow that *no* notion of fettering applies in this case, but it is a significantly different one. Productive forces continue to be developed and used, but the need to do this is governed by the need to maximize surplus value rather than directly by considerations of human welfare. The imperatives imposed by capitalism, mentioned above, are most centrally represented by the imperative to go on producing and accumulating ever greater wealth (or more strictly, surplus value) as an end in itself, according to Marx. This is a quantitative requirement which is insensitive to qualitative considerations. So long as such accumulation occurs, it is immaterial whether it does so through a process dedicated to the production of food or the production of bombs. That is what enables us to make sense of the paradoxical remark of a former head of General Motors, that he was not in business to make cars but to make money. A system governed by this imperative is inherently liable to fail to perform optimally at the provision for human need: what human beings need may not be produced, while what they do not need may be produced in abundance, just in case the alternative to meeting such need will maximize accumulation.

Marx illustrates the subordination of human need to the requirements of capital in some comments on the effects of the Factory Acts. One such Act improved conditions of ventilation, yet at the same time it 'strikingly demonstrates that the capitalist mode of production, by its very nature, excludes all rational improvement beyond a certain point'.[48] Doctors had unanimously recommended a minimum working space of 50 cubic feet per worker, but insistence on that provision would bankrupt many small employers and

> would strike at the very roots of the capitalist mode of production, i.e. the self-valorization of capital.... Factory legislation is therefore brought to a dead halt before these 500 cubic feet of breathing space. The health officers, the industrial inquiry

commissioners, the factory inspectors, all repeat, over and over again, that it is both necessary for the workers to have these 500 cubic feet, and impossible to impose this rule on capital.[49]

It is therefore not the *use* of resources which becomes fettered in capitalism, but rather their *rational* use. That, according to Marx, is the peculiarity of capitalism. In the market society needs go unmet not because of lack of resources or contingent human inefficiency, but because of the very principle of accumulation which governs productive effort in general.

Whereas in the general case groups are required to perceive *un*used resources and act collectively in the light of their supposed interests, in the case of capitalism they must perceive *mis*used resources and act in that way. That may seem a small change; but to see something lying idle as a case of waste, and therefore inimical to one's interests, is different from seeing something in use as a waste. Accordingly, even a long run of social changes involving the former could not be used as evidence in support of a change requiring the latter. The ambiguity in the notion of fettering has the result that there is no inductive evidence for Marx's belief that capitalism will be replaced by the future society of commonly owned resources.

It might be replied that this does not matter if Marx has more direct and independent reasons for that belief; and that the prospective transformation must in any case differ in many respects from earlier ones.[50] But his independent reasons are weak, and the particular character of the prospective transformation creates more rather than fewer problems for him. Indeed, this weakness and these problems have vital implications for the nature of Marx's practical proposals and their chances of success.

Marx believes that capitalism itself produces not only the material conditions required for the future society, but also the collective action. It does so negatively by placing the proletariat in circumstances where they have reason to overthrow it; and positively by providing the organizational structures that give them the capacity to do so. Negatively, the development of industry 'nearly everywhere reduces wages to the same low level'.[51] As capital becomes concentrated and the number of capitalists diminishes, so the 'mass of misery, oppression, slavery, degradation and exploitation'[52] of the working class increases. Positively, that same development of industry 'replaces the isolation of the labourers, due to competition, by their revolutionary combination, due to association'.[53] Along with the increase in misery 'there also grows the revolt of the working class, a class constantly increasing in numbers, and trained, united and organized by the very mechanism of the capitalist process of production'.[54] Indeed, capitalism produces its negation 'with the inexorability of a natural process'.[55]

Recall now the very stringent condition of self-consciousness placed on the agency of transformation. The degree of misery endured by the working class and the fact of their combination into collective entities give very poor grounds for the conclusion that they will act, with the required perspicacity, to transform society. Those considerations might well indicate the fulfilment of conditions without which such self-conscious action would not even be possible; and this, together with Marx's account of the fulfilment of the *material* preconditions for the future society, separates him from the utopian tradition, which regards socialism as a viable project without regard to particular historical circumstances. But there is little so far to justify the confidence that capitalism produces its own gravediggers. Inductive evidence to that effect has already been precluded; and since past transformations have involved *non*-perspicacious consciousness, such evidence would be of little help in the present context in any case. Indeed, Marx himself seems to recognize the counter-influences to the growth of the required movement when he says: 'The advance of capitalist production develops a working class which by education, tradition and habit looks upon the requirements of that mode of production as self-evident natural laws.'[56]

The most that Marx's arguments can establish is that a classless society is now on the agenda in a way in which it has not been in earlier times. They do not establish that the agenda will be disposed of in any particular way. That is what brings Marx, despite himself, a step nearer to Fukuyama. If his arguments do not show that the society of common ownership will come into being, it is still open to Marx to attempt to *make* that outcome more likely. He can attempt to *foster* the revolutionary consciousness which is the remaining obstacle to the transformation, at least if Marx is correct in his claim that the development of capitalism has created the *material* preconditions. He will thereby acknowledge the critical, pivotal role of propaganda or consciousness-raising, and allow a degree more autonomy to ideas. His efforts will rest on the assumption that people may *or may not* end up viewing their own lives and the relations in which they stand in a particular light. Such a degree of 'voluntarism' may clash with some of Marx's theoretical commitments, but it does not clash with his theoretical *activity*. It would be absurd to suppose that he wrote so voluminously (or so polemically) out of a detached interest in how history and his own society worked. The point was to change the world, and his own writings, even the most abstruse, were to serve that end.[57]

What's Wrong with Capitalism?

Why does the world need changing, and in such drastic ways, in the first place? What is Marx's fundamental objection to the class relations of capitalism? This matter has not been well understood, and Fukuyama's misconceptions are widely shared, even if he adds some eccentric twists of his own. He argues that the abundance of the free market economy – 'easy access to VCRs and stereos'[58] – has resolved the contradiction between capital and labour. The 'class issue has actually been successfully resolved in the West ... the egalitarianism of modern America represents the essential achievement of the classless society envisioned by Marx'.[59] There may still be rich and poor; the gap between them may have grown. 'But the root causes of inequality do not have to do with the underlying legal and social structure of our society ... so much as with ... the historical legacy of premodern conditions.'[60]

Marx would join in the celebration of the potential for abundance which capitalism has created, since that is one of the material preconditions for a socialist society.[61] But his objection to the capital/labour relation is not based in any straightforward way on the level of poverty experienced by members of the working class. His relatively muted enthusiasm for higher wages, as contrasted with the abolition of wage labour altogether, makes that clear. Higher wages would constitute '*better payment for the slave* and would not conquer either for the worker or for labour their human status and dignity'.[62] Capitalism is 'a system of slavery, increasing in severity commensurately with the development of the social productive forces of labour, irrespective of whether the worker is then better or worse paid'.[63] As capital accumulates, 'the situation of the worker, be his payment high or low, must grow worse'.[64]

The gap between capitalist and worker matters to Marx, but it matters primarily for qualitative reasons. All human beings have lives to live, and they are enslaved to the extent that their lives are not under their own control and direction. Marx observes that a land-owning capitalist 'can behave in relation to the land just as any commodity owner can with his commodities'; 'he can spend his entire life in Constantinople, while his landed property remains in Scotland'.[65] This freedom to give one's life a chosen shape contrasts with the state of being constrained to sell one's mental and physical energies as a precondition of access to the resources necessary for fulfilling any other aspirations. The standard consequence of that state is that one must spend a large proportion of one's life at a location not determined by oneself, and engaged in activities which are similarly imposed.

The contrast between capitalist and worker is therefore one where a quantitative distinction carries qualitative consequences. A capitalist is not merely someone who is better off, but someone whose ownership of resources is so great that, far from needing to sell their energies, they sustain their position from the proceeds of employing other people's energies. A worker is not merely someone who works, but someone whose ownership of resources is so meagre that they must sell their energies if they are to live an average life.[66] Capitalists have a freedom to live a life of their own choosing, a freedom which is unavailable to workers. Or, to put it another way, the time and resources available to capitalists give them several lives of free time as compared with what is available to workers. Capitalists, moreover, have this privilege *because* workers do not. The material goods and services necessary for capitalists to live their chosen lives are collectively provided by the working class. 'In capitalist society, free time is produced for one class by the conversion of the whole lifetime of the masses into labour-time.'[67]

Marx's criticism of the class relations of capitalism is materialist, but in a sense of materialism not exhausted in an account of circumstances of material poverty or an account of the dynamic governing historical change. It is what one might call *normative* materialism. Beginning from the truism that we are material organisms whose interests are profoundly affected by our material circumstances, Marx attempts to trace the implications of this in the concrete circumstances of the market society. Since material well-being is a precondition of realizing more or less any other aspirations, Marx is entitled to stress the ubiquitous importance of material interests for the behaviour of rational agents: *whatever* life you aspire to, your class position will profoundly affect the extent to which you can realize it. Marx's exhortation is, then, to build a practically realizable, alternative form of society which liberates the mass of people from the burden they incur in the central class relation of capitalism.

Conclusion

I have not in any straightforward way attempted in this chapter to refute Fukuyama's contentions. Rather, I have suggested that Marx has a programme, a set of reasons for it, and a set of commitments which follow from it, that are distinct from those associated with his name via the historical movement which bore that name. If my suggestions are correct, there will be a crucial incompleteness in Fukuyama's position: he will have declared the end of history prematurely, having nominated liberal capitalism the sole survivor of a contest which has never yet taken place. Of course, if my suggestions are also correct about some of the flaws in Marx's reasoning, such a contest may not take place in the future either. Certainly the unjustified confidence that the society of commonly owned resources must come into being can be replaced by a determination to *make* it come into being; but if some of Marx's other theses are correct, about the power of ideology in sustaining existing social relations, that determination will encounter formidable obstacles.

Ought we, then, to conclude that liberal capitalism wins by default? The conventional wisdom would certainly say so. Human nature, it would argue, precludes the characteristics which are required, on Marx's account, both of the movement to inaugurate the future society and of the future society itself. Such a high degree of active involvement in decision-making, self-motivation and commitment strong enough to sustain social organization and coordination in the absence of coercion or economic necessity are not qualities to be expected of the great mass of average citizens. It is true that it is much easier to embrace the conventional wisdom than to establish it by compelling evidence and argument,[68] and the conventional wisdom itself is sometimes posited through an illicit move from what is, currently, the case to what must necessarily and always be the case. In attempting to combat it, however, Marx is deprived of one significant sort of evidence. Capitalism produced worldwide society for the first time and must itself be replaced by a worldwide society.[69] In consequence, he cannot establish the possibility and practicability of the future society by pointing to particular examples of its instantiation. He cannot *demonstrate* that it works, and must instead proceed on indirect evidence from existing behaviour and political movements. That is why the nature of the movement to institute the new society is so critical to his project. It provides a terrain available now on which to refute by practical example some of the alleged obstacles in the project.

Despite the formidable obstacles, Marx might reasonably regard the present historical juncture as an improvement over a state of affairs where disastrously inappropriate societies and movements are widely regarded, both by supporters and detractors, as instantiations of his aspirations. The end of Leninism at least gives a unique opportunity for a sober assessment of Marx's theories on their own merits, without the millstone of such misleading associations. It also changes the circumstances of ideological debate, as some of Fukuyama's critics have noted. It will no longer be open to apologists for existing society to defend its legitimacy by implicit or explicit comparison with the far inferior visible alternative. The existing form of society will itself be assessed on its own merits, by reference to the aspirations it encourages and the possibilities it throws up. And it may yet be found wanting. Marx himself would have to regard the last hundred years as a calamitously lost opportunity. But, given the magnitude of the changes he proposes, he might take it as a setback rather than the end of his story – much less the end of history.

Notes

This paper was written during my period as Simon Senior Research Fellow in the Department of Government at the University of Manchester. I am deeply grateful to the members of that department for providing such a friendly and intellectually stimulating environment, and especially to Norman Geras and Hillel Steiner for helpful comments.

1. Francis Fukuyama, 'The End of History?', *The National Interest*, no. 16, 1989, p. 4.
2. Karl Marx, *Capital* Volume 1, Harmondsworth: Penguin, 1976, pp.125, 273. Cf. ibid., pp. 166, 949–51.
3. Ibid., pp. 250–53. For criticism of Marx's attempt to deduce the 'reinvestment motive' from the nature of capital, see Jon Elster, *Making Sense of Marx*, Cambridge: Cambridge University Press, 1985, pp. 37–40.
4. *Capital* Volume 1, p. 274. Cf. ibid., p. 439.
5. Karl Marx, *Wage Labour and Capital*, in *Marx and Engels: Selected Writings*, London: Lawrence & Wishart, 1962, Vol. 1, p. 92. Cf. *Capital* Volume 1, p. 724.
6. He therefore stands apart from traditions in which the alternative to capitalism is some form of society in which commodities persist but the undesirable consequences of their predominance do not. See K. Graham, 'Schumpeter's Critique of Marx: A Reappraisal', *European Journal of Political Research*, vol. 23, 1992, section 3.
7. Cf. ibid., pp. 167–8.
8. Karl Marx, *Contribution to a Critique of Political Economy*, London: Lawrence & Wishart, 1971, p. 86. Cf. *Capital* Volume 1, p. 188 n1; and *Grundrisse*, Harmondsworth: Penguin 1973, pp. 153–9.

9. Karl Marx, *The Class Struggles in France*, in *Surveys from Exile*, Harmondsworth: Penguin 1973, p. 70. Cf. *Value, Price and Profit*, in *Marx and Engels: Selected Writings*, Vol. 1, London: Lawrence & Wishart, 1962, p. 446.

10. Karl Marx and Friedrich Engels, *The Communist Manifesto*, in *The Revolutions of 1848*, Harmondsworth: Penguin, 1973, p. 82.

11. Karl Marx, *Critique of the Gotha Programme*, in *The First International and After*, Harmondsworth: Penguin, 1974, p. 345.

12. Marx, *Capital* Volume 1, p. 171; cf. *Grundrisse*, pp. 172–3.

13. Fukuyama, p. 4.

14. For the entertainment of such thoughts, cf. Steven Lukes, *Marxism and Morality*, Oxford: Oxford University Press, 1985, p. 32; G. A. Cohen, 'Self-Ownership, Communism and Equality', *Supplementary Proceedings of the Aristotelian Society*, vol. 64, 1990, p. 38; and Jon Elster, *Making Sense of Marx*, Cambridge: Cambridge University Press, 1985, pp. 457–8, 526.

15. Marx, *Contribution to a Critique*, p. 21.

16. The extreme view might be thought to be attributable to Marx on the basis of the following words in the manuscript of *The German Ideology*: 'The Communists ... only strive to achieve an organisation of production and intercourse which will make possible the normal satisfaction of all needs, i.e., a satisfaction which is limited only by the needs themselves.' Aside from the fact that what is referred to here is *normal* satisfaction of *needs* rather than desires, however, this passage is in any case deleted in the manuscript! Cf. Karl Marx and Friedrich Engels, *The German Ideology*, London: Lawrence & Wishart, 1965, p. 277.

17. Fukuyama, p. 9.

18. Marx and Engels, *Manifesto*, p. 78.

19. Marx, 'Provisional Rules', in *The First International*, p. 82.

20. Marx and Engels, 'Circular letter to Bebel, Liebknecht, Bracke, et al.' in *The First International*, p. 375.

21. See *The Civil War in France*, in *The First International*, pp. 187–236.

22. Marx, *The Eighteenth Brumaire of Louis Bonaparte*, in *Surveys*, p. 190.

23. For discussion of the further possibilities for democratic participation opened up by technology, see Benjamin Barber, *Strong Democracy*, Berkeley: University of California Press, 1984, pp. 273ff; James Fishkin, *Democracy and Deliberation*, New Haven: Yale, 1991, pp. 54–64; and Bill Valinas, 'Democracy and the Silicon Chip', *Socialist Standard*, vol. 74, 1978, pp. 170–71.

24. To weigh in the scales against the repeated emphasis on self-emancipation and democratic values throughout Marx's writings, there is one passage in the *Manifesto* which, if read carefully, does not even amount to an endorsement of vanguardism. For discussion, see Keith Graham, *The Battle of Democracy*, Brighton: Wheatsheaf, 1986, pp. 206–30; and *Karl Marx Our Contemporary*, Hemel Hempstead: Harvester Wheatsheaf, 1992, p. 162 n8.

25. See ibid., pp. 130–32. I find it a useful precept for trying to understand the Leninist tradition to pay particular attention to those whom the tradition itself regards as renegades and heretics. On that occasion my source was the remarkably prescient Dutch anti-Bolshevik revolutionary Anton Pannekoek, anathematized along with many others in Lenin's *'Left-Wing' Communism, an Infantile Disorder*.

26. Fukuyama, p. 4.

27. Ibid., p. 6.

28. Marx and Engels, *Manifesto*, p. 79.

29. *Capital* Volume 1, p. 91.
30. Marx and Engels, *The Holy Family*, Moscow: Progress, 1956, p. 125; stress in original.
31. Marx and Engels, *German Ideology*, p. 87.
32. *Contribution to a Critique*, p. 21; stress added.
33. Marx, 'Letter to Annenkov', in *The Poverty of Philosophy*, third impression, London: Lawrence & Wishart, n.d., p. 173; stress added.
34. Marx and Engels, *German Ideology*, p. 45.
35. Ibid., p. 62; stress in original.
36. Marx speaks of the early stage at which the bourgeoisie 'in order to attain its own political ends, is compelled to set the whole proletariat in motion.... At this stage, therefore, the proletarians do not fight their enemies, but the enemies of their enemies, the remnants of absolute monarchy, the landowners...' (*Manifesto*, p. 75).
37. The obvious pioneering work here is G.A. Cohen, *Karl Marx's Theory of History: A Defence*, Oxford: Oxford University Press, 1978. See also his more recent *History, Labour and Freedom*, Oxford: Oxford University Press, 1988. For discussion specifically about fettering, see also Elster, *Making Sense*, pp. 258–67; Andrew Levine, Elliott Sober and Erik Olin Wright, 'Rationality and Class Struggle', *New Left Review* 162, March–April 1987; and John McMurtry, *The Structure of Marx's World View*, Princeton: Princeton University Press 1978, pp. 208–18.
38. Marx, *Eighteenth Brumaire*, p.174. Cf. *Contribution to a Critique*, p. 21.
39. Marx and Engels, *Manifesto*, p. 94.
40. Marx, *Grundrisse*, p. 749.
41. Ibid. Cf. *Capital* Volume 1, p. 929.
42. Marx and Engels, *Manifesto*, p. 78; stress added.
43. Fukuyama, p. 6; stress added.
44. Marx, *Eighteenth Brumaire*, p. 146.
45. Marx and Engels, *German Ideology*, p. 37. Cf. Marx, *Contribution to a Critique*, p. 20.
46. Marx and Engels, *Manifesto*, p. 70. Cf. *Capital* Volume 1, p. 617.
47. *Capital* Volume 1, p. 667. Cf. ibid., p. 618.
48. Ibid., p. 612.
49. Ibid.
50. Cf. Graham, *Karl Marx Our Contemporary*, pp. 134–57.
51. Marx and Engels, *Manifesto*, p. 75.
52. *Capital* Volume 1, p. 929.
53. Marx and Engels, *Manifesto*, p. 79.
54. *Capital* Volume 1, p. 929.
55. Ibid.
56. Ibid., p. 899.
57. Even in the case of *Capital*, Marx applauded its serial publication in French since 'the book will be more accessible to the working class, a consideration which to me outweighs everything else' (Preface to the 1872 French edition of *Capital* Volume 1, p. 104).
58. Fukuyama, p. 8.
59. Ibid., p. 9.
60. Ibid.
61. We should retain a decent awareness, however, that much of this still is only potential. Even in the US millions of people live below official poverty lines, and in the United Kingdom ten million employees earn less than the 'decency threshold' defined by the

Council of Europe. And many a Chinese peasant would be surprised to hear of the 'colour television sets now omnipresent throughout China' (ibid., p. 3).

62. Marx, *Economic and Philosophic Manuscripts of 1844*, London: Lawrence & Wishart, 1961, p. 81; stress in original.
63. Marx, *Critique of the Gotha Programme*, p. 352.
64. *Capital* Volume 1, p. 79.
65. Marx, *Capital* Volume 3, Harmondsworth: Penguin, 1981, pp. 753, 755.
66. There is, therefore, a limit to how high a worker's wages could go, consistent with their remaining a worker. For a more accurate specification of the capitalist and working classes, and fuller justification for ascribing these views to Marx, see Keith Graham, 'Class – A Simple View', *Inquiry*, vol. 32, 1989.
67. *Capital* Volume 1, p. 67. It should be stressed, however, that Marx explicitly dissociates himself from the idea that capitalists are to be *blamed* for this state of affairs (cf. ibid., p. 92). Their elimination, by whatever means, is not his objective. They at least act as exemplars of what a human life untrammelled by material need can be like. His aspiration is that everyone should enjoy this condition, not that no one should.
68. For a comparatively rare, and interesting, challenge to the conventional wisdom, see Joseph Carens, *Equality, Moral Incentives and the Market*, Chicago: University of Chicago Press, 1981.
69. See, for example, Marx and Engels, *German Ideology*, pp. 46–7, 75–6; *Manifesto*, pp. 71, 85.

5

On Societal and Global Historical Materialism
Paula Casal

> Un jour tout sera bien, voilà notre espérance,
> Tout est bien aujourdhui, voilà l'ilusion.
> Voltaire, *Poem on the Disaster of Lisbon*

Introduction

In the development of European thought there have been three persistent aspirations. First, to understand history as a meaningful process, rather than an arbitrary succession of events.[1] Second, to offer some reconciliation to the existence of evil; for example, by accounting for it as an unavoidable cost of greater good.[2] Third, to provide an explanation of complex social and cultural phenomena by appeal to less complex material factors, such as the natural environment.[3] Historical materialism, being a philosophy of history, a secular theodicy and a materialist doctrine, promises to satisfy jointly all these objectives. Recently G.A. Cohen has made historical materialism yet more attractive by transforming it from a speculative image of history into an analytical theory which can explain historical change by reference to general laws and a description of initial empirical conditions.

Cohen's reconstruction of the Marxist view, however, does not sacrifice any of the above-mentioned aspirations. As he puts it, first, 'Marxism sees history as a protracted process of liberation – from the scarcity imposed on humanity by nature, and from the oppression imposed by some people on others.'[4] Second, it considers '[u]nfreedom, exploitation, and indignity' as 'the price which the mass of humanity must pay for the part they play in creating the material wherewithal of human liberation'.[5] Finally, it asserts that

> The biological and geographical conditions which for Hegel were but the instruments of and opportunities for spirit's self-assertion have their autonomy restored to them. The character of man and society now depends on the character of the nature of

which society lives, both as that nature is in the beginning, and as it becomes under the transformations wrought by the process of production.[6]

If Cohen succeeded, then he would have brought us closer to the ideal of Laplace, the famous Newtonian determinist, who explained the regularities of the universe without appealing to the existence of God, and imagined that a sufficiently great intelligence, given knowledge of general laws and initial empirical conditions, could predict the future.

In *Karl Marx's Theory of History: A Defence*, Cohen formulates a theory which can provide historical explanations and predictions by reference to general laws and an account of initial empirical conditions. His critics, however, contend that the modest premises to which he appeals are insufficient to sustain his ambitious conclusions. This chapter is a critical examination of the response to such criticisms found in Cohen's most recent book, *History, Labour and Freedom*. Here he attempts to defeat his major critics' counter-arguments and to provide a novel reformulation of historical materialism which could still be true even if his original arguments failed. This second version of historical materialism has also been defended by Christopher Bertram. My contention is that these three attempts are unsuccessful.

Cohen's Technological Determinism

In Cohen's most succinct formulation, 'history is fundamentally the growth of human productive power, and forms of society rise and fall according as they enable or impede that growth.'[7] As he goes on to explain, 'productive power' is measured by the amount of working time required to satisfy the basic needs of the immediate producers, were the existing productive forces used optimally for this purpose.[8] Those productive forces include means of production (tools, machines, premises, raw materials...), and labour-power (strength, skills, knowledge...) all of which can intentionally be used to make products. According to Cohen's theory, the productive forces develop throughout history, can be owned and, most importantly, can be used to explain the relations of production. Those relations are ones of economic power among individuals or groups and involve the ownership of, or effective control over, the forces of production. The total set of relations comprises the *economic structure* of a society, which rests upon an *infrastructure* constituted by the total set of productive forces. Since the former is said to be determined or strongly conditioned by the latter, Cohen's theory has been described as a form of technological determinism. (The same form of explanation is applied to the legal and political superstructure, the function of which is to further contribute to productive development by stabilizing the economic structure.)

The following provides a simple illustration of the technological determinist pattern of explanation, in which the introduction of a technology gives rise to a technical organization, which in turn gives rise to a hierarchical structure of authority. Imagine that an army adopts a machine gun which needs to be operated by three soldiers and, therefore, organizes its artillery in three-person teams. In each team one soldier is made responsible for the team and the execution of orders. Thus, corporals are appointed. Subsequently, the army adopts more powerful but heavier cannons, which must be operated by five-persons teams, into which the artillery is then organized.[9] In such a case, a technological determinist would then say that infrastructural changes give rise to changes in the army's organization and structure of authority, and that such adaptive changes can be functionally explained by the level of technological development to which they correspond. Each structure is optimal for each level and incompatible with any other: five men for each cannon can be optimal, five for each machine gun dangerously inappropriate, and five for each rifle a complete disaster.

Cohen's historical materialism applies this pattern of explanation to the relations of production. It asserts the *Primacy Thesis*, according to which the nature of an economic structure is explained by the level of development of the productive forces. His theory defines various stages, or historical epochs, in which the prevailing social forms (feudal, capitalist...) are explained by the level of productive development to which they correspond.[10] As in the cannon illustration, historical materialism claims that each structure arises when and because it is functionally optimal for a given level of development and that it is replaced by a new one when it becomes dysfunctional.

It is, however, important to note three differences between the distinctively Marxist Primacy Thesis and the military analogy. First, in the Marxist view, a society's structure is fundamentally explained by its *quantitative* level of productive development, rather than the *qualitative* features of the technology such society uses. Second, structures are not, or not primarily, explained by their being functional for the *use* of the existing productive forces, but for those forces' *further development*. This implies a third disanalogy, namely, that the structure influences the infrastructure, as well as itself being influenced by it. Hence, not only do certain levels of development and structures exclude each other, but levels of development and structures also exert mutual influence on each other. This third feature of Marxist technological determinism is particularly important. The apparently symmetrical relationship of mutual exclusion and mutual influence between the relations and the forces must be broken in order to preserve the explanatory primacy of the productive forces. Cohen therefore defends a second proposition, termed the *Development Thesis*, which claims that the forces have an autonomous tendency to develop. That tendency is autonomous of social structures because it can be explained by facts which are not social. Note, Cohen does not attribute autonomy to the forces' development, which, as indicated, is influenced by the structures, but to the tendency itself.[11] His argument for the existence of such an autonomous tendency appeals to the following so-called Asocial Premises: human beings are rational, intelligent and live in a situation of scarcity. Hence, they have both an interest in, and the intellectual capacities for, achieving improvements in their material situation.

According to what has been termed the Rational Adaptive Practices (RAP) interpretation of Cohen's argument, agents thus described would engage in a search-and-selection process for superior productive forces, in order to improve their material situation. Development would then take place, as 'the aggregate result of those several strivings'.[12] Cohen has, however, rejected such a reading and now affirms the Choice of Relations (COR) interpretation, according to which 'being rational, people retain or reject relations of production according as the latter do or do not allow productive improvements to continue'.[13] In other words, he does not 'posit a "search-and-selection process which operates directly on the ... productive forces" but "one which operates on the relations of production, which in turn control the search-and-selection of productive forces"'.[14] This is, briefly stated, Cohen's historical materialism. I shall now proceed to criticize its various versions, beginning with the traditional version which affirms that there is an autonomous and perennial tendency to progress in *each* society.

Societal Historical Materialism

Critics of the traditional version of historical materialism have challenged it on both theoretical and empirical grounds. Since most critics of the view understood it in the RAP form stated above, the adoption of the COR form invalidated some of such challenges. It does not, however, defuse the objections that I shall discuss in this section.

The previous section emphasized the materialist aspect of Cohen's theory. It is, however, also a secular theodicy, which construes natural and social adversity as necessary costs of progress. Local and temporal suboptimalities may be part of an optimal package solution. For example, it may be necessary to accept great sacrifices in order to achieve, in the long run, even greater gains. Elster argues that such complex strategies require an intentional agent, who can plan for the future. He writes,

> [i]n Leibniz's philosophy this made perfectly good sense, since on his view the course of human history was decided by God ... the intentional agent whose goal – to create the best of all possible worlds – makes sense of the local and temporary defects of the universe ... Hegel, disastrously, retained the idea that history had a goal, yet did not invoke any intentional agent whose actions were guided by that goal.[15]

Joshua Cohen directs a similar criticism against Cohen's theory, arguing that the Asocial Premisses are by themselves unable to explain the alleged tendency to productive progress. His claim – which is weaker than Elster's – is that in the absence of a 'superintendent of history' there is no compelling reason to expect that the actions of individuals pursuing their own interests would correspond in the aggregate to the requirements of global progress.[16] The contention is that Cohen's arguments are insufficient to establish a theory of history in which progress is the central tendency, whilst still claiming, as Laplace is alleged to have said to Napoleon, 'in this theory, Sir, God is a superfluous hypothesis'.

Two of the specific difficulties which animate such criticism were already noted by Cohen in his original presentation of the Asocial Premises argument. The first is the *Competing Goals Problem*, namely, that human beings have a plurality of interests and competing goals. The interest in material improvements is only one of them, and its comparative importance is not stated by the Asocial Premises. The second is the *Collective Action Problem*, namely that the Asocial Premises alone do not exclude the possibility of a predominance of 'structural arrangements that generate undesirable outcomes from individually rational actions'.[17] There is, thirdly, a *Class Specific Rationality Problem* arising from the fact that individuals occupy certain positions in the social structure from which they may lack the interest or the capacity to bring about infrastructural or structural changes required for development. For example, it may not be rational for the exploiting classes, or possible for the exploited classes, to make such changes.[18] Joshua Cohen also refers to a number of cases in which the pursuit of material advantage does not lead to productive development, such as the formation of extractive empires, and increased extraction of surplus from dependent producers. More generally, given the persistence of economic inequality throughout history, the most direct or efficient way of improving one's material situation may be by enlarging one's share of the cake, rather than its size. Thus, he argues, 'only under *specific structural* conditions is the interest in material advantage tied to an interest in a strategy of productivity-enhancing investment.'[19]

Furthermore, these problems with the Asocial Premises argument for the Development Thesis cannot be solved by simply assuming that structures will be adequately arranged to facilitate productive development. For it would then be circular to later explain, as Cohen intends to, the prevailing structures by their productivity-enhancing nature. Thus the Development Thesis could not be used to support the Primacy Thesis. Conversely, if one does not assume that structures will be adequately arranged, then – given the above-mentioned three problems – the Asocial Premises would be insufficient to establish the Development Thesis. Thus, Joshua Cohen concludes, 'the argument appears to be stuck between circularity and enfeeblement'.[20]

G.A. Cohen, however, believes that he can meet this challenge, by adopting an intermediate strategy. It appeals to social facts, without relying on them to explain the Development Thesis. The strategy involves a further defence of the Asocial Premises argument for the Development Thesis with the help of a supplementary empirical claim, which Joshua Cohen termed the Alleged Facts, that refers to the actual frequency of progress, and rarity of regress, in history. G.A. Cohen's reply proceeds as follows.

First, in respect to the problem of competing goals, Cohen suggests that 'material constraints might ensure that people's non-material interests, though not at all secondary, tend not to conflict with their material interests in progress-defeating ways.'[21] Second, he argues that the interdependency and iteration 'imposed by material scarcity' will tend to facilitate cooperative solutions to collective action problems.[22] Third, in response to class-specific rationality problems, he constructs a hypothetical case – a society where 80 per cent of its members live off the labour of the rest – in which material conditions are such that they already contain a solution to such problems.[23] Finally, Cohen presents his own challenge to his critics in the form of a new dilemma:

> Despite the fact that economic and political structures are not unproblematically congenial to progress, the Alleged Facts entail that progress wins through. The sub-argument then presents this challenge: either accept that the asocial premisses have great explanatory power, or offer an alternative explanation of the contrast between the frequency of progress and the infrequency of regress.[24]

Cohen's reply suggests that, within the debate thus far rehearsed, there appear to be different understandings of what the Alleged Facts prove, what Joshua Cohen's challenge involves, and upon whom lies the burden of proof. I shall therefore consider once more the three objections.

First, to pre-empt misunderstanding, it is important not to overestimate how telling the Alleged Facts are. Consider, for instance, the case of a society which has a plurality of equally important goals, and a number of options which will promote development to different degrees. Such a society would quite likely take the option that best accords with its various interests, traditions, beliefs, and so on, even if such an option is productively suboptimal. Such an outcome is counter-evidence to historical materialism, yet is consistent with the Alleged Facts, since some development would still take place. Second, and more damagingly, Cohen's treatment of collective action problems is inconclusive for the following reasons. To begin with, spontaneous cooperation arises only in very specific circumstances. Iteration is only one of its conditions. Thus the existence of iteration does not make cooperation more probable than non-cooperation; it merely, as Cohen puts it, 'facilitates' cooperation. Moreover, even if cooperation does eventually emerge, nothing guarantees that its gains would outweigh the losses of past or future periods of non-cooperation. Finally, cooperation is not always a positive outcome. The achievement of a cooperative solution within certain groups may be detrimental to society.[25] This leads to the third objection, to which Cohen gives no conclusive answer. He merely replaces the unwarranted assumption that class-specific rationality problems will not arise or be solved by the equally unwarranted assumption that material conditions will be such that when these problems arise, they will be solved.

By now it should be clear that Cohen's critics need not claim that, given all the above-mentioned problems, in the absence of propitious social structures, development is always impossible. Asocially based development could take place on Robinson's island. However, to point at a logically possible scenario in which development could take place is not sufficient to establish the existence of a 'perennial' and 'by and large fulfilled' tendency to productive progress in every society.[26] Cohen must offer some plausible reasons why we should believe that, wherever the Asocial Premisses hold, the expected progressive outcome would obtain, or at least would be more likely to obtain, than any other outcome.

Cohen's reply appears to be aimed primarily at the avoidance of circularity, and to that extent it succeeds. The challenge, however, is to avoid circularity and enfeeblement at the same time, and here his argument remains too feeble. Thus Joshua Cohen's dilemma still has force, whilst G.A. Cohen's dilemma quoted above does not. For his critics it is not a genuine dilemma. The first option is not available, since we already know that the Asocial Premisses have insufficient explanatory power; and the second option is not the only one left. First, providing a superior explanation of the Alleged Facts may be a sufficient but not a necessary condition for rejecting Cohen's explanation on theoretical or empirical grounds. Second, one may argue that the productive forces developed for 'miscellaneous reasons [probably quite different ones in such distant periods and places] and not in fulfillment of any tendency'.[27] Third, one may explain the Alleged Facts by appealing to socio-economic, political or ideological factors, an option unavailable to Cohen, but not to those who do not intend to defend the Primacy Thesis. Finally, one may have a different view of the Alleged Facts. One may think, for example, that

> productive forces were largely static up to recent times, when the advent of capitalism made possible a revolutionary breakthrough. This would be consistent with the many passages where Marx stresses the conservative character of earlier modes of production.... Also, as a *rough* generalization, it might be more consistent with the historical record than the rough generalization of unbroken progress.[28]

One may also argue that this unprecedented breakthrough has been accompanied by an equally unprecedented environmental destruction, involving a sharp fall in per-capita natural resources.

As initially noted, even if most criticisms were directed against the RAP reading of the Asocial Premisses argument, the adoption of the COR view does not defuse, as G.A. Cohen admits, Joshua Cohen's central contention.[29] Moreover, the adoption of the COR view generates further difficulties, one of which I shall mention.

In *Karl Marx's Theory of History*, there is an important section entitled 'Why are Classes Necessary?' where Cohen refers to the harsh working conditions suffered by the vast majority during industrialization. He comments that for Marx 'development had to be "at the expense of the majority"', and adds: 'It certainly was at their expense.'[30] He then construes the Marxian explanation of classes on the justified assumption that (i) the producers, the vast majority, would refuse to impose such inhuman conditions on themselves. According to the COR view, however, (ii) they would search and select a structure which imposes such inhuman conditions on themselves. It is hard to see how these claims could be consistent with each other, as well as consistent with (iii) the fact that people are rational and intelligent and want to alleviate their burden. (i) and (iii) are perfectly consistent with each other; (ii) however, seems at odds with each.[31]

Finally, Societal Historical Materialism has also been challenged on empirical grounds. The number of problematic empirical cases is large and varied. There have been societies where the Asocial Premisses held and yet no infrastructural or structural changes occurred for very long periods of time, as well as societies that abandoned agriculture and returned to hunter-gathering, or that abandoned more developed and complex socio-political structures and returned to earlier simpler ones. As anthropologists know, not all adaptive changes are evolutionary in the sense of progressive.[32] Moreover, for some of historical materialism's claims, not only are counter-examples abundant, but there is no single instance in history which confirms them. There has been no society which passed through all the stages the theory expects all to go through; no society exemplifying a transition from slavery to feudalism; and no single stage through which all societies have passed (if we exclude the 'primitive' stage, which was more varied that the theory's vague description of it suggests).[33]

Societal Historical Materialism is construed around a model of what it defines as the 'normal society'. It claims that in such normal cases, the forces, like children, tend to grow. This is a telling analogy. Children have an endogenous tendency to grow, which can be explained by biological, non-social facts. Because such a tendency is autonomous, they will still grow physically (but perhaps not develop optimally, emotionally or culturally) without their parents or even on desert islands. The 'normal society' is like an island society. External factors such as wars or colonizations are considered as distorting, pathological phenomena (like rickets for children), and used to reply to counter-examples of regression.[34] Although such 'normal societies' are historically rare, there are some cases which fit this model. Unfortunately, these apparently perfect cases have been precisely the most frequently invoked counter-examples to the theory. One such model case is Tasmanian society, which was cut off from the rest of humanity at least twenty thousand years ago, at which time their level of development was that of the Middle Palaeolithic. The Tasmanians remained in that technological stage until the European arrival in the eighteenth century.[35]

Ralph Linton, who holds the opposite view of 'normality' to Cohen's, claims that there is no culture which owes more than 10 per cent of its elements to endogenously developed innovations, and that humanity would still be in the Old Stone Age had the various societies and cultures been isolated from each other.[36] This type of reflection led to an often disproportionate enthusiasm for the concept of *diffusion*, which gave rise to various diffusionist theories at the turn of the century, and was also applied to evolutionist doctrines, as the following example illustrates. The reader will be familiar with the developmental sequence, employed by museums around the world to classify their archaeological material, of Stone Age, Bronze Age and Iron Age. The sequence was constructed under the assumption that it was necessary to master the problems involved in bronze-making in order successfully to face the more difficult problems of smelting and iron-working. The Bronze Age was thus assumed to be the *functional prerequisite* of the Iron Age.[37] Apparently, such functional necessity explained why in the Near East, where iron metallurgy began, the Bronze Age preceded the Iron Age. Other societies, however, such as most of Negro Africa, skipped the Bronze Age in passing from the Stone Age to the Iron Age. A certain brand of evolutionists would have claimed that this fact does not challenge the initial sequence,[38] for the following reasons. The society where iron-working first appeared developed *isosequentially*, that is, passed through all the stages in the expected order, while other societies which skipped the bronze stage, because they were able to copy the iron technique from others, still developed *isodirectionally*, that is, passed through the stages they passed in the expected order.

This example illustrates what anthropologists know as a transition from *unilineal* to *universal* evolutionism, as well as the similarity between such a transition and that from Societal to Global Historical Materialism. The importance of cultural diversity, interaction and diffusion in history, which was overlooked by Societal Historical Materialism, now seems to be emphasized in its global version. Historical materialism, however, has its own distinctive features,[39] and therefore, besides recognizing such factors, requires a new defence. It is to one such defence that I now turn.

Global Historical Materialism

The problems discussed in the previous section suggest that societies where the Asocial Premisses hold, may still 'lack an internally generated (that is, not induced by contact with other societies) tendency to productive improvement, because of standing (for example, cultural) circumstances'.[40] Despite this, as Cohen now argues:

> As long as circumstances are not always unpropitious in all societies, progress will occur somewhere, and its fruits will be preserved. On this account, (at least) the weaker version of the Development Thesis will be true: there will be a tendency to global improvement in the world as a whole...[41]

Local improvements can be said to occur globally in the sense that they happen 'in the world'. According to this *weak* version of the Development Thesis, progress will take place in at least some societies, as a result of which aggregate progress will take place. However, Cohen argues in addition that, 'improving societies are likely, through conquest and other forms of influence, to establish hegemony over laggards', in which case one 'can predicate the improvement of a larger societal whole'. In this new scenario, there will still be 'a tendency for the productive forces to develop in every society, either for reasons internal to that society, or,... because the society will eventually be dragged into the channel of progress by societies which generate it endogenously.' This appears to be the *canonical* formulation of what one may term the Global Development Thesis. Now development becomes humanity's collective enterprise, which operates following what Ernest Gellner calls a 'torch-relay' pattern: 'having brought the forces to a certain level, an erstwhile pioneering society retires in favour of a new one,... which takes the forces further.'[42] Thus, while the advanced societies will tend to lock themselves into their once progressive structures, peripheral ones, enjoying what Veblen called 'the advantages of backwardness', will overtake them, allowing, as Lenin put it, the emancipation of the 'coloured races'.[43]

The reformulation of Cohen's theory posits two processes or tendencies. On the vertical dimension is placed the weak version of the Development Thesis, and on the horizontal dimension a further claim, which I shall refer to as the Transmission Thesis. The conjunction of these two theses is intended to support the Global Development Thesis. I shall now elucidate and criticize both.

Cohen's defence of the Global Development Thesis is partly based on the assumption that even if 'there is no universal imperative of rationality to innovate ... achieved innovations will be preserved.' Thus, 'progress will occur somewhere, and its fruits will be preserved'. This may appear to be uncontroversial and able to support the Global Development Thesis. Such appearance, however, relies on certain ambiguities in the idea of productive progress. First, either particular productive forces may undergo development or the sum total of forces may do so. Cohen refers to progress in innovation. Such a positive tendency may coexist with other negative tendencies. For example, natural resources may diminish, either somewhere or everywhere; population may also grow, somewhere or everywhere; and there may be a vertical escalation and a horizontal proliferation of destructive technology. In such cases an increase in innovation is consistent with the absence of global progress in Cohen's sense. Thus, if 'progress will occur' means that 'innovations will be made', the argument is too feeble to establish the full conclusion. If it means 'real progress all things considered will occur', then it is not an argument but a re-restatement of what has to be argued for. Furthermore, Cohen's argument for the Global Development Thesis may also, like his argument for the Societal Development Thesis, face collective action and group-specific rationality problems. For example, just as it may be globally disastrous but individually rational to have a large number of children, it may also be rational for each society to contribute to global warming. And worse still, the global structure of international relations may be organized in a way in which the interests of the dominant societies are protected, at the expense of productive progress in the rest of the world.

Turning to the Transmission Thesis, it can be understood in at least two ways. According to what one may term the Infrastructure Transmission Thesis, what is transmitted to backward societies is the infrastructure (the functional prerequisite) required to enter into a more advanced stage. According to the Structure Transmission Thesis, what is transmitted to, or imposed upon, conquered or colonized societies is an economic structure, which generates the previously absent tendency to productive progress.

Let us begin with the Infrastructure Transmission Thesis. According to Societal Historical Materialism, all societies – except a few where nature was 'too lavish' – live in a situation of natural scarcity and are therefore assumed to have similar tendencies to develop.[44] The new scenario differs in so far as it is an uneven one, with some societies being far more advanced than others, and development being generated where there is less scarcity. In the former case, societies could expand their territories and resources by conquering others.[45] This is expected to be the norm in the global scenario, within which, however, territories and resources are finite. One such uneven situation might involve the most technologically advanced societies containing only 20 per cent of the total population, yet accounting for 80 per cent of world consumption of natural resources.[46] If their resource-intensive technology cannot successfully diffuse, because such a consumption pattern is incapable of generalization, then this thesis is vulnerable to a *feasibility objection*. In addition, it is liable to an *incentive objection*, if the dominant societies have no interest in such diffusion. For the sake of clarity, I shall illustrate the two objections separately. Their force, however, is cumulative. If there was a determined will to improve the economic situation of the Third World, many material obstacles could be overcome; and conversely, if there were no practical difficulties, successful transmissions would be more likely to occur, even in the absence of such will. Both objections have been argued for by many authors.

One of E. F. Schumacher's central theses is that in conditions of great global inequality, the successful large-scale adoption by developing countries of the capital- and resource-intensive technology of the torch carriers is infeasible, and on a smaller scale has undesirable consequences.

> If we define the level of technology in terms of 'equipment cost per workplace', we can call the indigenous technology of a typical developing country … a L 1-technology, while that of the developed countries could be called a L 1,000-technology. The gap between this two technologies is so enormous that a transition from the one to the other is simply impossible. In fact, the current attempt … to infiltrate L 1,000-technology into their economies inevitably kills off the L 1-technology at an alarming rate, destroying the traditional work places much faster than modern work places can be created, and thus, leaves the poor in a more desperate and helpless position than ever before … the L 1,000 technology simply cannot spread … it cannot have a positive 'demonstration effect'; on the contrary, as can be observed all over the world, its 'demonstration effect' is wholly negative.[47]

Given such differences, as well as other differences of an environmental, social and political nature, it is groundless to assume that the torch carrier's technologies are appropriate to others, instead of, as Schumacher argues, 'unkantian', since non-universalizable. Galbraith, for example, contends that it is inadvisable to make that assumption. He writes that,

> it has been taken wholly for granted ... that intelligence in these and other matters is strongly correlated with income. A country is qualified to extend economic and other advice in accordance to the size of its Gross National Product.[48]

Thus, he adds, '[w]ere something being done in Kansas, it should be done in Gujarat ... let the gap be filled by an infusion of talent from the rich countries. There can, experience shows, be few riskier enterprises.'[49] Moreover, Susan George argues that, since

> only about 2 to 3 per cent of the world's total R&D [Research and Development] capacity is located in the Third World ... it's not surprising that ... Third World nations have little influence on the types of technology developed and that their specific needs are not served by this technology.[50]

The incentives objection hardly requires a defence, since no reason has been suggested as to why the dominant societies would have an overriding interest in performing the actions that would lead to the development, and thus empowerment, of the societies they dominate, and risk losing control of them. The above-mentioned resource and consumption distribution would be upset by a proliferation of rivals competing for the same markets and for the world's dwindling resources. Greater consumption in the periphery would mean either less consumption at the core or more pollution, resource scarcity, global warming and environmental problems in general. Susan George argues that '[i]t is ... very important for the developed world that poor countries continue to supply enough raw materials and that they be in this measure reliable trading partners. They must not, on the other hand, become rivals.'[51]

One might argue that there could be other parties, such as multinationals, with an interest in performing actions which would lead to peripheral development. It is possible that the global structure will be such that under certain circumstances, given the relative power of the various parties and their respective interests, the desired outcome would obtain. However, as indicated in the previous section, the Development Thesis is not secured merely by establishing the possibility of a scenario in which the desired outcome obtains or by taking for granted certain facts that are not asocial. One needs to avoid both circularity and enfeeblement, yet this line of argument avoids neither.

Let us now turn to the Structure Transmission Thesis. This thesis can be understood in two ways. The first option is to assume that when 'improving societies', 'through conquests and other forms of influence', 'establish hegemony over laggards', they impose their own progress-inducing structures on the latter, which will also progress as a result. This seems to be the option Cohen has in mind when he writes that:

Capitalist relations could appear in a technically backward region because it is the periphery of a more advanced centre. Whether there would remain a general tendency for relations to correspond to forces — whether, that is, the Primacy Thesis would still hold — is a moot point, and at least one commentator is confident that a globally interpreted Development Thesis, no longer performs the function of supporting the Primacy Thesis.[52]

Thus, the first version of the Structure Transmission Thesis may, as Cohen notices, pose 'fresh theoretical problems' to Global Historical Materialism. Moreover, the introduction of what one may call L 1,000 structures on L 1 economies may also face feasibility problems.

The traditional version of historical materialism was sceptical about such premature structural changes and believed that they were likely to result in failure and regression to a former stage.[53] (Allowing five soldiers for each weapon may be appropriate for an army with cannons, but disastrous when it has nothing but rifles.) According to this traditional view, it is inadvisable to export modern social structures to backward countries, to impose Stalinism among African tribes, to expect a traditional agricultural society to support a capitalist state, or make other combinations of elements the theory defined as incompatible. The view does not deny that such premature structural changes are possible — they have, after all, occurred — but asserts that the result would tend towards disaster. If this warning was well-grounded, then Global Historical Materialism becomes less plausible. In this respect, Marxists and non-Marxists seem to have swapped places. For now, while Cohen appears to be optimistic about the Transmission Theses, Galbraith, for example, argues that,

> the economic design appropriate to the later stages of development *cannot*, without waste and damage, be transferred to the early stages. Nor as regards the new countries can the design and emphasis appropriate to a country in one stage of the political, cultural, and economic sequence be applied in a later or earlier stage ... Marx ... would not have taken seriously the idea that socialism could appear ... in, say, Mozambique or Ethiopia. But the failure to see development as a process has been the prime source of error in nonsocialist thinking and advice as well.[54]

Furthermore, there are various passages in which Marx supports this view. In *The German Ideology* he argues that

> when there is nothing more to take, you have to set about producing ... it follows that the form of community adopted by the settling conquerors must correspond to the stage of development of the productive forces they find in existence; or, if this is not the case from the start, it must change according to the productive forces.[55]

It is possible, however, to formulate a different interpretation of the Structure Transmission Thesis, which may be more consistent with this passage. According to this new formulation the conquerors impose whatever economic structures are appropriate to the level of development of the conquered society, perhaps in order to maximize the surplus they can extract from it. Thus constructed, the argument would appear to avoid to a greater extent the feasibility and incentive objections. However, as Elster has argued, it cannot be taken for granted that the economic structure which maximizes the surplus that accrues to the dominant groups would also maximize the net output or the level of development. As he puts it: 'It cannot be assumed without argument that the three objectives tend to be maximized simultaneously; on the contrary, there are good reasons why, under certain conditions, they tend to diverge from one another.'[56] Thus, given such divergence and that the dominant societies have an interest in achieving the first and not the third objective, the Transmission Thesis in any of its forms appears groundless.

It could be the case that in order to maximize their gains without risking their position of dominance, colonists strip the conquered territories of their resources and use them for their own development. Employing their superior coercive power, they may also introduce regressive relations, such as slavery or other 'pre-capitalist forms of production in order to avoid the necessity of paying full subsistence wages to workers in plantations and mines'.[57] In order to preserve their advantageous position and minimize control and enforcement costs, they may maintain their dominance indirectly through, for example, supporting authoritarian regimes which suppress nationalist movements, or alliances with elites concerned with their own short-term class interests rather than with their country's long-term prospects of development.[58] Moreover, as Cohen himself notes, the dominant societies do not only establish certain structures within the dominated countries, but also 'integrate' them into 'the larger whole'. This may mean that the dominated societies are placed in a position in the world market from which it is very difficult to develop and successfully compete. It may mean that they occupy a position within the global structure or world economy whereby the core or metropolis is able to extract a surplus from the periphery or satellites,[59] in the various ways described by Wallerstein, Gunder Frank, Amin, and others. The result of this uneven relationship may be the further strengthening of the core and the increased weakening of the periphery.

Cohen, who is aware of underdevelopment theories, offers no reason for these undesirable outcomes not to occur.[60] Adam Smith had already observed that the tendency to progress could be overridden by other factors or counter-tendencies. He wrote:

> The savage injustice of the Europeans rendered an event, which ought to have been beneficial to all, ruinous and destructive to several of those unfortunate countries.... By uniting, in some measure, the most distant parts of the world, by enabling them to relieve one another's wants ... their general tendency would seem to be beneficial. To the natives, however, both of the East and West Indies, all the commercial benefits which can have resulted from those events have been sunk and lost in the dreadful misfortunes which they have occasioned.... What benefits, or what misfortunes to mankind may hereafter result from those great events, no human wisdom can foresee.[61]

Once more, Cohen's arguments are insufficient to establish his conclusions. This, however, is not the only respect in which little progress has been made by abandoning Societal Historical Materialism.

One would think that the model of island-societies of the former version of the theory would have been abandoned with the move to the new scenario of war, conquest, colonization, global integration and prolonged interaction between societies. Indeed, Cohen refers to authors for whom underdevelopment is not an endogenous property of island-societies, but is instead induced and perpetuated by the relationship between core and periphery. One would also imagine that the new version of the theory would grant an overdue recognition to the importance of external factors and to the mixed effects of integration, considering, for example, the damaging as well as the beneficial effects upon the conquered, and the transfers from them to the conquerors, and not merely vice versa. Instead, it appears that differences in development are still to be explained by internal structural differences,[62] while the role of factors external to a society's structure remains, as in the former version, restricted to that of a card up the sleeve, reserved to deal with potential counterexamples which lack an endogenous tendency to progress. The global view apparently amounts to a mere addition to the former island-society model of an optimistic assumption about the purely beneficial effects of societies that independently developed upon those that independently did not. In doing so it disregards the potentially detrimental implications of global interaction, offering only a partial rather than a truly global theory of world development.

There are at least two examples of such implications which cast doubt upon Cohen's account. The first is the conquest of the New World. Recent research indicates that at the time of conquest the American population was much larger than the European – some authors estimate around 90 million for America and 50 million for Europe. The conquest reduced the American population by 90 per cent. Reduction also happened in other parts of the New World, such as: Hawaii, where the population was reduced by 80 per cent, seventy-five years after Cook's arrival; New Zealand, where it was reduced by over 60 per cent in fifty years; Australia and certainly Tasmania, where nobody survived.[63] Thus, the most important event in the process of integration that Cohen attempts to explain contradicts – if such data is to some degree correct – the canonical formulation of the Global Development Thesis. For, whatever the effects on natural productive forces, it is not true that conquest always drags conquered societies 'into the channel of progress'. It may, instead, drag them towards extinction.

The second example concerns the culmination of the globalization process. Cohen supposes that capitalism will destroy itself because of its internal contradictions, to be replaced by a world socialist society. In both books, Cohen refers to such contradictions and in particular to capitalism's unlimited exploitation of limited resources. He writes: 'The dynamic of advanced capitalism ... upsets the equilibrium of physical nature ... The pollution/resources impasse, present or future, is the unequivocal answer it gets from the elements.'[64] In the new scenario, however, if the leading capitalist societies are able to dominate the others, they may also be able to ensure a continuous supply of resources from the periphery and to export back the industrial waste resulting from the use of such resources. They may also reduce non-exportable pollution and diminish its effects by technical means. Thus, even if the system, when confined to the limits of one society, had entropic tendencies, its 'internal contradictions' may not lead to self-destruction if they can be 'externalized'. Even if this process cannot continue indefinitely, the problem remains whether at the end of it humanity would find itself in a situation of sustainable global abundance, or if 'the sacrifice of the mass of humanity' was in vain.

Finally, whatever the course of world history, the following theoretical difficulty stems from Cohen's reliance upon interaction. If the structures of societies other than the leading ones are to be explained not by their productive forces but by the fact that they have been imposed by the latter, then such an explanation departs from historical materialism in so far as it does not secure the primacy of the productive forces any more than, for example, the primacy of political and military power. Cohen himself, at the end of his defence of the global version, doubts the consistency of 'the potent role which it assigns to war ... with the emphasis of historical materialism'.[65] There is, however, a possible response to some of these difficulties in Bertram's defence, within which the importance of military competition is yet more explicit.

Darwinian Historical Materialism

Bertram's defence of Global Historical Materialism is constructed along Darwinian lines. He draws an analogy between the way organisms compete and interact within an environment, and the way societies with different structures and levels of development compete and interact in the international arena and the world market. Countries and cultures 'engage ... in both economic competition of various kinds and in military conflict', and 'possession of a higher level of technological development increases the *chance* that a given culture or state will survive.' Societies 'may adopt social structures ... for all sorts of reasons', but those which 'fail to select structures conducive to the development of the productive forces, will either be eliminated (or assimilated) by their rivals, or will undergo a crisis that will force them to select anew their basic structures'.[66] History is thus a matter of 'chance variation' – including instances of intentional selection of structures – and 'survival of the fittest'.

Bertram's view remains historical materialist in so far as the outcomes of inter-societal conflict depend on the relative productive power of the contenders. As he acknowledges, its completion requires a subsidiary theory which will 'systematically reduce' military to economic power (rather than vice versa).[67] Yet it could be said to be 'more global' in the sense that it contemplates the negative as well as the positive effects interaction may have upon a society. And it is no objection to it that entire cultures or societies may be eliminated or greatly harmed by others. There are three further respects in which Bertram's view appears less sanguine than Cohen's.

First, Bertram may have less confidence in the Transmission Thesis. He believes that peripheral countries will be 'economically undermined by the competition from countries enjoying higher levels of productivity'. He also writes that:

> While backward countries partially integrated into the main system are the most likely sites of revolutions, it is unlikely that the adoption of a more advanced social form will compensate for the technological inferiority of the country which adopts that form.[68]

Second, regarding the Primacy Thesis, Bertram is committed only to the relative superiority of surviving relations of production rather than their functional optimality. For, in the phrase 'survival of the fittest', 'fittest' is only a threshold notion and a comparative one, meaning sufficiently fit to survive and fitter than those which became extinct. Therefore the claim that only the fittest countries or structures will survive international competition is consistent with no society having optimal relations of production. (In the land of the blind the one-eyed man may be the fittest.[69]) The latter possibility in turn is consistent with little progress ever taking place.

Third, in respect to the Development Thesis, Bertram reports it but does not explicitly endorse or defend it. Nor does pointing at a certain limited resemblance between international economic and military competition and natural selection imply that he believes in it.[70] For example, certain organisms or species may fare better than others as they compete in a declining environment, where all do worse than was previously the case. Regardless of biological analogies, Bertram does not believe that international competition always brings about progress. In fact, he thinks that it is currently driving us towards ecological disaster. He writes that:

> The pressures of international competition seem to dictate that poor countries must industrialize rapidly if they are to relieve their present condition; and the environmental consequences of their doing so are awful to contemplate. Liberal-democratic capitalism looks ill-equipped to deal with such a challenge. It would perhaps be the greatest irony of history if the mission of socialism proved not to be the rapid development of human productive power, but rather its containment well below any level that scientific and technical knowledge might render possible.[71]

It is also worth noting that even when competition is not collectively self-defeating, aggregate development may decline if the damage to losers outweighs the victors' gains. Therefore, in neither Cohen's nor Bertram's remarks is there a conclusive defence of the Development Thesis. Note, moreover, that conjoining Bertram's theory with his view of the likely sites of revolution yields a bleak conclusion about future development. If ecological catastrophe can be avoided only by socialism, which is likely to emerge only in developing countries, and survival depends on relative economic and military power, then productive progress is unlikely to continue.[72]

While granting what has been said so far, Bertram might claim that competition produces development under specific circumstances, consequently perhaps limiting the periods of history to which his theory applies. For example, he might limit its scope to epochs during which some other relevant factor was present, such as a specific degree of interaction. Too little interaction between societies might allow stagnant structures to remain unchanged, while, if interaction is too intense, new superior structures may be weeded out before they had the opportunity to generate development. Even if Bertram employed such a defence, to be complete it would still require a subsidiary theory systematically reducing capacity to survive military conflict to productive efficiency. We do not, so far, have such a theory. Instead we have the following reasons to doubt that a systematic correspondence will obtain among productive efficiency, economic power, military power and survival capacity.

First, economic power depends on factors other than having functional structures, such as raw materials, territory and population sizes. For example, suppose that a society adopts an optimal economic structure, perhaps the best that ever existed. If by chance this society is small or has an unfortunate history, then no matter how progressive is the new structure, it could still be defeated by a larger neighbour, even if the latter's structure is no longer superior. Even if there were no large differences in size or history, the best structure may be threatened since it will emerge before it has had time to develop the forces, or may not succeed in so doing because of the hostile response of other societies.

Second, irrespective of economic power, societies might have very different military budgets for historical reasons. Moreover, societies may specialize in developing productive or destructive forces, since, as Joshua Cohen indicated, the former is not the only way of enhancing material well-being. Producing and stealing are two adaptive responses or survival strategies. For instance, one can think of productively inefficient societies periodically raiding more peaceful agricultural ones, with reliance on raiding both compensating for, and perpetuating, productive deficiencies.

Third, the outcome of a conflict may depend on a large variety of factors such as timing, alliances, strategy, determination, location, capacity to withstand casualties, and so on. Returning to the conquest of the New World, for example, many historians agree that a very large number of natives were killed by the sword, enslavement and overwork. Those natives, however, as well as others the conquerors never met, were already reduced and weakened by the diseases of the invaders, which travelled faster than them and were indiscriminate in respect of productive efficiency.[73]

These remarks suggest that Bertram's view shares with G.A. Cohen's the latter's main problem, namely the possibility of countertendencies frustrating an asserted progressive tendency. As it affects Bertram's view, the problem's structure can be stated as follows. Grant his claim that if a society has an efficient technology then its survival is more probable than if it does not. Grant also that he may legitimately eschew the deterministic, and empirically implausible, claim that efficient societies always survive and inefficient ones perish, but may instead couch his theory in probabilistic terms. Even so, if Bertram's theory is to possess substance, then it requires more than the uncontroversial *ceteris paribus* claim granted initially. It requires at least the stronger, yet still probabilistic, claim that the survival of efficient societies is more probable than the survival of inefficient societies. The problem arises because Bertram has not established this stronger claim, which is not entailed by the weaker *ceteris paribus* claim. For as suggested above, other things may be unequal, and the competitive advantage conferred by technological efficiency may be outweighed by disadvantages originating in a variety of contingencies. Yet Bertram provides no further grounds for the stronger claim, without which his theory lacks substance.

Finally, in Bertram's version – as in Cohen's – the theory's conditions of falsifiability are unclear.[74] This is not simply because, since there is only one world development, there are not many instances against which the theory's predictions can be tested – a problem he addresses at the end of his defence. Rather than the scarcity of instances, the problem is the abundance and vagueness of its predictions. Recall that the Societal formulation predicted that structures would arise when and because they are functionally optimal; that they, consequently, will be functionally optimal or disintegrate after a short period. By contrast, Bertram grants that structures may arise 'for all sorts of reasons', possess any degree of efficiency, and last in any case indeterminate periods of time. Stressing that the theory's assertions are probabilistic claims of unspecified likelihood, whilst defusing particular counterexamples, worsens this latter difficulty.[75]

Conclusion

Even in the attractive formulations here discussed – their many merits notwithstanding – historical materialism continues to lack a conclusive defence. It is unclear, however, whether socialists should regret this. Cohen himself remarks that 'scepticism about historical materialism should leave the socialist project more or less where it would otherwise be.'[76] Belief in historical materialism has often been attributed to wishful thinking. Yet, it is unclear why, at a time in which confidence in socialism's productive superiority has been eroded, socialists should still wish that structures which foster the greatest increase in productivity rather than, for example, diminish exploitation or injustice, win the historical battle. In this respect it is interesting to notice that both as a theory of development and as a philosophy of history, historical materialism resembles its conservative counterparts, including that of Fukuyama, elsewhere discussed in this volume.[77]

Notes

I am extremely grateful to G.A. Cohen and Andrew Williams for their very helpful advice, discussions and comments on earlier drafts of this paper. I also thank José Luís García, Michael Otsuka, the Nuffield Political Theory Discussion Group, and both editors.

1. It is a commonplace overstatement to deny the Greeks any historical consciousness. There is counter-evidence to this view in the thought of Plato, Pindaro, Thucydides, the Sophists and Polybius. It was, however, within the Judaeo-Christian tradition that the great visions of history as a global process with a direction and a pattern were developed. These include the views of Augustine, Vico and Hegel, which influenced respectively those of Bossuet, Spengler and Marx, and of others such as Voltaire and Comte. See, for example, J. Ferrater Mora, *Cuatro visiones de la historia universal*, Madrid: Alianza, 1984.

2. Some Christian views of history, such as those of Kant, Leibniz or Hegel are explicitly theodicies. Theodicies, however, were also developed in Greece, and apparently Leibniz, for example, copied his arguments from Chrysippus and Plotinus. See F. Billicsich, *Das Problems des Übels in der Philosophie des Abendlandes*, Vol. 1, Vienna: Sexl Verlag, 1955, p. 172 ff; and A. Domènech, *De la Ética a la Política*, Barcelona: Crítica, 1989, p. 38.

3. This is also a very long tradition, which includes Plato's and Montesquieu's explanations of, respectively, political and religious forms by reference to climate. It extends to the varieties of functional ecology, techno-ecological determinism and cultural materialism we know today. Their evolutionist varieties, such as those of Leslie White or Julian Stewart, bear even greater resemblance to the theory here discussed.

4. G.A. Cohen, *History, Labour and Freedom* (henceforth *HLF*), Oxford: Oxford University Press, 1988, p. vii.

5. Ibid.

6. G.A. Cohen, *Karl Marx's Theory of History: A Defence* (henceforth *KMTH*), Oxford: Oxford University Press, 1978, pp. 22–3. Historical Materialism, like many other theories, can be taken in its ambitious, distinctive, interesting form, or in its diluted version, which is none of these things. I am concerned with the former, and this is one of the reasons why I focus on Cohen's impressive defence, which aims at increasing the theory's plausibility without trivializing.

7. *KMTH*, p. x.

8. See *KMTH*, pp. 56ff, and *HLF*, p. 5.

9. See *KMTH*, p. 166. Note that nothing has been said here about how the transition arises. In the example, changes may be introduced by, for instance, the army's superintendent.

10. See *KMTH*, pp. 197ff., and *HLF*, pp. 155 ff.

11. See *HLF*, p. 90; and W. Shaw, 'Historical Materialism and the Development Thesis', *Philosophy of the Social Sciences*, vol. 16, no. 2, 1986, p. 198.

12. *HLF*, pp. 87–88; see also pp. 89–91. The expression RAP was coined by A. Levine and E. O. Wright in 'Rationality and Class Struggle', *New Left Review* 123, September–October 1980.

13. Cohen, 'Reply to Four Critics', *Analyse und Kritik* 5, 1983, p. 198. The expression 'COR' was coined by John Torrance in 'Reproduction and Development: A Case for a Darwinian Mechanism in Marx's Theory of History', *Political Studies* 33, 1985.

14. See Cohen, ibid., or *HLF*, p. 24 and p. 91. In the passage, he quotes Philippe Van Parijs's formulation. See the latter's contributions to *Analyse und Kritik* 4, 1982, and 5,

1983; 'Functionalist Marxism Rehabilitated. A Comment on Elster', *Theory and Society* 11, 1982, esp. section 2; and 'Marxism's Central Puzzle', in T. Ball and J. Farr, eds. *After Marx*, Cambridge: Cambridge University Press, 1984, p. 96.

15. J. Elster, *Making Sense of Marx*, Cambridge: Cambridge University Press, 1985, p. 109.

16. J. Cohen, 'Review of *KMTH*', *The Journal of Philosophy*, vol. 79, no. 5, 1982, pp. 256–7.

17. Ibid., p. 257. See also *KMTH*, p. 153.

18. See Levine and Wright, 'Rationality and Class Struggle'; R. Brenner, 'The Social Basis of Economic Development', in J. Roemer, ed., *Analytical Marxism*, Cambridge: Cambridge University Press, 1986, esp. p. 31. See also a relevantly similar argument in D. McKenzie and J. Wajcman, eds., *The Social Shaping of Technology*, Milton Keynes: Open University Press, 1985, esp. p. 17; and an interesting example in A. Bhaduri, 'A Study in Agricultural Backwardness under Semi-Feudalism', *Economic Journal* 83, 1973. In addition, see A. Carling, *Social Division*, London: Verso, 1991.

19. J. Cohen, 'Review of *KMTH*', p. 268, his italics.

20. Ibid., p. 265.

21. *HLF*, p. 103. G.A. Cohen's response to J. Cohen in *HLF*, ch. 5 reproduces an article that he wrote with Will Kymlicka.

22. *HLF*, p. 102.

23. For Cohen assumes that the very high productivity level such a society has to have, 'would have liberating consequences for the political capacity of the exploited' minority (ibid.).

24. Ibid.

25. As Axelrod observes, 'one should bear in mind that cooperation is not always socially desirable. There are times when public policy is best served by the prevention of cooperation as in the need for regulatory action to prevent collusion between oligopolistic business enterprises.' (R. Axelrod, 'The Emergence of Cooperation among Egoists', *The American Political Science Review* 75, 1981, p. 308). Moreover, Cohen appears to take for granted that the negative consequences of aggregation and non-cooperation would be more or less immediately felt by the non-cooperative actors. This need not be the case, for example, with many environmental problems such as deforestation, global warming or nuclear waste.

26. *KMTH*, pp. 153–5, and *HLF*, p. 87, respectively.

27. Ibid.

28. J. Elster, 'Review of *KMTH*', *Political Studies*, vol. 28, no. 1, 1980, p. 124, his stress.

29. *HLF*, pp. 97-8, where Cohen writes: 'Recourse to the political superstructure merely expands the circle.... For asocial premises cannot explain why rationality problems do not arise at the political level, and they therefore do not explain how they are overcome at the economic level.'

30. *KMTH*, p. 214. See also p. 111ff.

31. Alternatively, one may argue that the chosen relations do not have to benefit all or even the majority, but this option would not yield the desired tendency to progress.

32. See R.L. Carneiro, 'The Four Faces of Evolution', in J.J. Honigmann, ed., *Handbook of Social and Cultural Anthropology*, Chicago: Rand McNally Anthropology Series, 1973. Some frequently invoked counter-examples are the Roman Empire, Ming and Ch'ing China, Eastern Europe (from the Middle Ages to the eighteenth century, as well

as the indigenous societies of Australia, New Guinea, many Pacific Islands and many tribal societies in different continents. See, for example, Kai Nielsen, 'On Taking Historical Materialism Seriously', *Dialogue* 22, 1983; and J. Cohen, 'Review of *KMTH*'. There is also anthropological counter-evidence to the assumption that societies try to maximize productivity. See M. Sahlins, *Culture and Practical Reason*, Chicago: University of Chicago Press, 1976; M. Douglas, 'The Lele: Resistance to Change', in P. Bohannan and G. Dalton, *Markets in Africa*, Evanston: Northwestern University Press, 1962; and L. R. Sharp, 'Iron Axes for Australians of the Stone Age', *Human Organization* 11, 1952.

33. See, for example, Yu. I. Semenov, 'The Theory of Socio-Economic Formations and World History', in E. Gellner, ed., *Soviet and Western Anthropology*, London: Duckworth, 1980. See also, in the same volume, Gellner's critical review of it, 'A Russian Marxist Philosophy of History', which inspired Cohen's and Bertram's Global Historical Materialism. Gellner's piece (p. 63) also contains an amusing theatrical representation of the COR view.

34. See *KMTH*, pp.156–7.

35. R. Linton, *The Study of Man*, London: Peter Owen, 1965, p. 324ff.

36. Ibid.

37. Or *necessary presupposition*, as Edward Sapir called it in his formal treatment of this anthropological concept in 1916. *Time Perspective in Aboriginal American Culture. A Study in Method*, Canada Department of Mines, Geological Survey, Memoir 90, Anthropological Series 13.

38. Namely, universal evolutionists, who adhere to the Initial Appearance view, according to which what counts is the society that first moved into a new stage. According to the Predominance-of-Cases view, in deciding on what constitutes an evolutionary sequence, what matters is the proportion of societies which followed one order or the other. See other varieties of evolutionism in R. L. Carneiro, 'The Four faces of Evolution'. For a more critical approach to evolutionist and diffusionist theories, see, in the same volume, C. Hudson's 'The Historical Approach in Anthropology'.

39. To mention just three: (a) its claim that all the functional prerequisites are levels of development; (b) its division of history in very few stages; and (c) its notion of correspondence between infrastructure, structure and superstructure. (a) means that prerequisites are more difficult to diffuse than pieces of information, given their material and cumulative character; (b) means that gaps between stages would tend to be very large; and (c) means that certain elements are linked to others and cannot successfully diffuse independently. Note that the universal evolutionist solution is not applicable if societies enter new stages without the functional prerequisite (the required productivity level) or if there are cases of first appearance which are not isosequential (such as the Soviet Union) or cases which are not isodirectional (such as ex-socialist, capitalist societies).

40. *HLF*, p. 27. Providing a conclusive empirical assessment of Cohen's theory, which applies to the history of humanity, is neither possible nor necessary here. I shall, however, refer to some empirical data and report the views of some authors as illustration of the points made in the theoretical critique, which is not contingent on the endorsement of any of the particular empirical views mentioned.

41. *HLF*, p. 27.

42. *HLF*, p. 28. See Gellner, 'A Russian Marxist Philosophy of History'.

43. See R. Gilpin, *The Political Economy of International Relations*, Princeton: Princeton University Press, 1987, p. 273. See also J. Elster, 'Historical Materialism and Economic Backwardness', in T. Ball and J. Farr, *After Marx*; 'The Theory of Combined and Uneven

Development: A Critique', in J. Roemer, *Analytical Marxism*; and A. Brewer, *Marxist Theories of Imperialism*, London: Routledge & Kegan Paul, 1990.

44. See *KMTH*, pp. 23-4, and *HLF*, pp. 25, 126 and 152-3.

45. *KMTH*, p. 51.

46. T. Trainer, amongst others, claims that this is in fact the case. See *Developed to Death*, London: Greenprint, 1989, p. 3, 13 and 62. According to Robert McNamara such inequality is likely to persist: 'Even if the growth rate of the poor countries doubled, only 7 would close the gap with the rich nations in 100 years. Only another 9 would reach our level in 1,000 years.' Cited in A.G. Frank, 'World System in Crisis', in W.R. Thompson, ed., *Contending Approaches to World Systems Analysis*, London: Sage, 1983, p. 29.

47. E.F. Schumacher, *Small is Beautiful*, London: Abacus, 1988, p. 151. Similar arguments are presented in Trainer, *Developed to Death*. See also Elster, 'The Theory of Combined and Uneven Development', p. 63.

48. J.K. Galbraith, *The Voice of the Poor*, Cambridge, Mass.: Harvard University Press, 1983, p. 3.

49. Ibid., p. 21.

50. S. George, *Ill Fares the Land*, Harmondsworth: Penguin, 1990, p. 97. Their small purchasing power, and slight input to development decisions, as well as other important factors such as alliances between First World business and Third World elites and loans being conditional on purchasing technology, may lead to situations where Third World countries fall further in debt, paying for technologies they were better off without. In the Philippines, for example, 'the annual servicing of one project alone, the Westinghouse-built nuclear power plant (never used because its site is earthquake prone) is close to the national health budget'(*New Internationalist*, March 1990. See also 'Six Fatal Projects', in *Financing Ecological Destruction. The World Bank and the International Monetary Fund*, 1988 report produced by Greenpeace and nine other organizations).

51. S. George, *How the Other Half Dies*, Harmondsworth: Penguin, 1986, p. 96. See also T. Hayter, *The Creation of World Poverty*, London: Pluto Press, 1981, p. 66.

52. *HLF*, p. 29. The commentator Cohen refers to is W. Shaw. See Shaw, 'Historical Materialism and the Development Thesis', p. 207.

53. See, for example, *KMTH*, p. 206.

54. J. K. Galbraith, *The Voice of the Poor*, pp. 8ff.

55. *The German Ideology*, in Marx and Engels, *Collected Works*, Vol. 5, London: Lawrence & Wishart, 1976, p. 85. Cohen himself quotes this passage in *KMTH*, p. 143. See also Elster, 'Historical Materialism and Economic Backwardness', pp. 45ff.

56. Elster, *Making Sense of Marx*, pp. 241ff.

57. Hayter, *The Creation of World Poverty*, pp. 39ff. See also J. de Castro, *The Geography of Hunger*, London: Gollancz, 1952, ch. 5.

58. J. Cohen and J. Rogers, *On Democracy*, New York: Penguin, 1983, pp. 36ff.

59. Such satellites may have their own sub-satellites, which is one of the reasons why evidence of development in some of them does not by itself support Cohen's theory.

60. Cohen does, however, note that, '[a]ccording to "underdevelopment theory" ... this [the development of the periphery] is not what happens, (or not, at any rate, at first) as capitalism spreads across the world' (*HLF*, p. 27 n. 55). Given his parentheses, Cohen might reply that even if underdevelopment theory is accurate, it corresponds only to the opening scenes of a new epoch. Such a response would nevertheless be problematic. First, Cohen elsewhere suggests that such an epoch is already coming to an end because

of ecological destruction (see, for example, *HLF*, p. 122). Second, it renders the falsifiability conditions of his theory extremely unclear: alleged counterevidence can now be interpreted as a step backward, which precedes either structural change, or – after some period of unspecified duration – infrastructural development.

61. A. Smith, *Inquiry into the Nature and Causes of the Wealth of Nations*, quoted in A. G. Frank, *Dependent Accumulation and Underdevelopment*, London: Macmillan, 1982, p. 34.

62. For example, Cohen suggests that the United States may be left behind because it 'cannot readily remake its relations of production in the image of those under which Japan is currently helping to carry the torch' (*HLF*, p. 28). R. Gilpin, for example, argues that 'economic factors alone will not explain success or failure in economic development. [For as] this book emphasizes, economic forces operate within a larger political context.' (*The Political Economy of International Relations*, pp. 269–70). It is interesting to notice that this is Gilpin's non-Marxist, non-leftist critique of liberal theories.

63. See A. Crosby, *Ecological Imperialism. The Biological Expansion of Europe, 900–1900*, Cambridge: Cambridge University Press, 1986; W. Borah, *America as Model: The Demographic Impact of the European Expansion upon the non-European World*, Center for Latin American Studies, University of California, Berkeley, 1962. Populations estimates tend to be higher the more recent the publication date. See, for example, the 1990 monographic issue of *Ecología Política* (Spanish edition of James O'Connor, ed., *Capitalism, Nature, Socialism*).

64. *KMTH*, p. 307; *HLF*, pp. 121ff.

65. *HLF*, p. 29

66. C. Bertram, 'International Competition in Historical Materialism', *New Left Review* 183, September–October 1990, pp. 119–20, emphasis in original. Since Cohen's and Bertram's formulations and arguments are different, and since it is, though possible, not evident that they hold identical views, I discuss them separately, and attribute to Bertram what is explicit and central in his view, even when certain assumptions are arguably implicit in Cohen's.

67. Ibid., pp. 119 and 128.

68. Ibid., p. 124.

69. See M. Sahlins, 'Economic Anthropology and Anthropological Economics', *Social Science Information*, vol. 8, no. 5, 1969, p. 32.

70. At the end of his article Bertram replies to the 'possible objection' that his defence is 'too dependent on an analogy with biological evolution' by pointing out that 'the argument is not one from analogy' (ibid., p. 127).

71. Ibid., p. 127.

72. It is possible, though not likely, that the revolution will triumph globally. As Bertram writes, '[o]nly in exceptional circumstances – perhaps defeat in war, for example – is it likely that the shock of revolution on the periphery will give rise to revolution at the centre' (p. 124). There is also little reason to expect the core's proletariat to make common cause with the backward country's revolutionaries even if the latter won their war. Note too that Elster has discussed the unlikelihood of a revolution which requires the simultaneous satisfaction of certain subjective conditions (massive discontent) and objective conditions (high productivity) (see note 43). Bertram's view does not contain a solution to this problem, but intensifies it. The new society is, besides, supposed to be both more socially just and environmentally friendly (that is, sustainable), and have a more developed military apparatus than its rivals.

73. In fact, some believe both that some of the natives had a more efficient agriculture

and that it was the least-developed natives which best survived. Plausibly, the former's wealth and road network worsened their plight, by raising the conqueror's payoffs and facilitating penetration. See note 63.

74. See note 60.

75. Consider, for instance, the case of Rome to which Cohen refers. In *KMTH*, p. 155, he uses this remark from *The German Ideology* to dismiss counterexamples to the Societal view: 'irruptions of barbaric peoples, even ordinary wars, are sufficient to cause a country with advanced productive forces and needs to have to start right over again from the beginning.' Thus, in 'the case of Rome', he writes, 'in so far as its productive decline was due to barbarian invasion the example loses force as a challenge to historical materialism' (in its Societal version for which wars were destructive but rare). Nor can it refute the Global version (wars being now normal but progressive) if its claims are interpreted probabilistically.

76. *HLF*, p. 132.

77. See, for example, 'The End of History', *The National Interest*, Summer 1989, especially pp. 9–11; and A. Ryan's final remarks concerning Voltaire and Fukuyama's theodicy in his review of Fukuyama's book, *New York Review of Books*, 26 March 1992.

6

Marx, Moral Consciousness and History
Andrew Chitty

A widely noted feature of Francis Fukuyama's book *The End of History and the Last Man* was that it relied on a dual theory of history to reach its conclusion that liberal-democratic capitalism was the final socio-political form in history.[1] The first part of the theory we could call 'materialist', in that it relied on ordinary human economic ('material') desires as the motor of historical change. According to it, a socio-political system survives or perishes as it produces, or fails to produce, greater material abundance for its population than any feasible alternative. The reason is that human beings want material goods, and in the long term will only give their allegiance to that system which in their experience is the best at producing such goods. On this part of the theory, the explanation of the collapse of the Soviet-bloc regimes in 1989 was simply that they could no longer produce consumer goods of the quality and quantity that Western societies could.

Fukuyama relied almost exclusively on this first part of the theory in his original 1989 article 'The End of History?',[2] but in the book he argued that by itself this part was inadequate. It could explain why the final socio-political form in history should be 'capitalist' in its economic system, for no other economic system could match the rate of technological development produced by the capitalist one, at least at higher levels of technology. However, it could not explain why the final form should be 'liberal democratic' in its legal and political system. It was to explain this that the second part of the theory had to come into play. This second part was 'idealist' in that it was not based on ordinary material desires, but on a non-material 'desire for recognition' common to all human beings: the desire to be treated by one's fellows as a free agent, as a person rather than as a thing.[3] For Fukuyama this desire was the source not only of the sentiments of pride, shame, honour and guilt, but also of the sense of justice. Just as only capitalism could satisfy human beings' material desires, so only liberal democracy could satisfy their desire for recognition, by granting every individual *equal* recognition in the form of equal status as a rights-bearing citizen. According to this part of the theory, the reason for the end of the Soviet-bloc regimes was that they failed to satisfy each individual's desire for recognition. It was this second part of the theory that dominated the book, yet, as his reviewers pointed out, Fukuyama never satisfactorily integrated it with the other, 'materialist', part.

Although Fukuyama's intentions were to celebrate the demise of Marxism as the last serious alternative to liberal capitalist democracy, his own theory of history has many affinities with Marx's. Both have roots in Hegel, and Fukuyama's interpretation of Hegel comes largely from Alexandre Kojève, who was at one time routinely described as a Marxist. Like Fukuyama, Marx attempted to conceive of history as at once the development of human productive powers and the realization of human equality, a history whose end, as Trotsky put it, would be 'the increasing power of man over nature and ... the abolition of the power of man over man'.[4] Furthermore, Fukuyama's evident difficulties in integrating the two parts of his theory are matched by the difficulty which twentieth-century Marxism has encountered in finding a place in its picture of history for moral motivation – in other words, broadly, for those motivations that derive from a sense of rights, justice or fairness rather than from prudential considerations. It is this difficulty in Marx's theory of history that I shall attempt to address here. I begin by outlining the problem, and then suggest an interpretation of Marx's theory of history which may provide a way of resolving it. Finally, I briefly consider the relationship of Marx's theory, so interpreted, to Fukuyama's.

The Problem with Moral Motivation

Following the summary formulations of the 1859 Preface to the *Contribution to the Critique of Political Economy*, Marx's theory of history is standardly seen as centred on the growth of human productive powers, and as explaining the rise and fall of socio-political systems by their tendency to develop or prevent the development of these productive powers.[5] Accordingly, in so far as an explanatory appeal is made to the motivations of individual human beings, these individuals are typically seen as motivated 'economically' by the desire to benefit individually from the wealth created by such powers. All this matches the 'materialist' part of Fukuyama's theory rather closely.[6]

Yet when it comes to the transition from capitalism to socialism, it becomes difficult to claim that the Marx's *justification* for making the transition is simply that capitalism comes to 'fetter', that is, prevent the development of, human productive powers. For in many passages Marx (and Marxists) appear to condemn capitalism on moral grounds, for its exploitation and oppression.[7] In so far as these condemnations are addressed to the working class, and are intended to make a contribution to the transition to socialism, to engage in them seems to presuppose that workers can bring about that transition at least in part through moral motivations.

Now this seems to contradict the general tenets of the theory of history. For if the explanation of the replacement of one social system by another is that the old system has ceased to be propitious for the development of human productive powers, and if the means of the transition is a class struggle, then the natural way to elaborate the explanation is to say that the fact that the old system is no longer propitious, and that an alternative is available which *is* propitious, eventually becomes obvious to everyone in the society.[8] Individuals realize that the further development of the productive powers possible under this alternative system would make society as a whole, and thus all or most of its members, materially richer. This realization weakens the motivations of the class that sustains the old system, strengthens those of the class that is struggling to institute a new system, and leads other classes to switch their allegiance from the former to the latter. Thus the elaboration works by showing how the fact that the old system is now fettering the productive powers can make a difference to individuals' economic motivations, rather than to their moral motivations. In the case of the transition from capitalism to communism, it is then the widespread realization that capitalism has become a fetter on economic development, not the realization that it is unjust, that will provide the working class, and other classes which are its potential allies, with the necessary motivation to overthrow it.

It might seem that in principle the theory could supplement this natural elaboration with one which operates by showing how the fact of fettering makes a difference to the moral, as well as to the economic, motivations of individuals. Yet this modification is not so easy. An individual's economic motivations for supporting or opposing the replacement of a social system can be altered by that system coming to fetter the productive powers, so that its replacement would be economically beneficial for the whole society and thus for at least the majority of individuals in it. All that is needed is for the individual to realize that this is the case and to believe that he or she would belong to the majority in question. But it is not obvious how the fact of fettering could alter an individual's *moral* motivations on the matter.

It might be said that workers' feeling for the interests of their fellow workers counts as a moral reason for overthrowing capitalism, and that this provides a motivation which will become stronger as workers become more convinced that an alternative system would serve the interests of workers in general better than the present one, and thus as capitalism comes to fetter the development of the productive powers. It might also be said that concern for the well-being of members of society as a whole provides a moral reason for overthrowing a system which has come to fetter development. However, I would deny that reasons of collective interest in members either of a class or of society as a whole count as moral reasons. They are, rather, collective prudential reasons.[9]

The difficulty can be illustrated by looking at a passage in Engels's *Anti-*

Dühring in which he suggests that 'so long as a mode of production is still in the rising stage of its development, it is enthusiastically welcomed even by those who come off worst from its corresponding mode of distribution'. It is only when the mode of production has entered its 'declining phase' that its 'constantly increasing inequality appears as unjust'.[10] The difficulty here is that there is no reason why the mere fact that the system is in its 'declining phase', if this means simply that it has begun to fetter human productive powers, should lead workers to consider it more unjust than they did previously. For justice is a distributive matter, and the presence or absence of economic development as such says nothing about the distribution of goods. It would only be if the fact of fettering had a tendency to produce absolute impoverishment on the part of one class, or increasing inequality between different classes, that it could be expected to lead to an increase in workers' sense of injustice. Yet although Marx and Engels sometimes suggest that capitalism leads to an absolute immiseration of the working class,[11] they do not provide an argument to show why in general the fact that a social system has come to fetter human productive powers should lead either to such absolute impoverishment or to increasing inequality.[12]

What is more, even if there were some general mechanism whereby a social system's coming to fetter the development of the productive powers led to the appearance, or activation, in an individual of convictions that condemn the system as morally unacceptable, then the recognition by the individual that these convictions had been brought about by this fact, a fact that is irrelevant to the truth of the convictions, must undermine their strength.

A response to this argument might be to say, contradicting Engels, that a social system (or at least every social system with a class division) *always* appears unjust to the workers under it, those who have to work for the benefit of other classes. Thus capitalism always appears unjust to workers, and they always have a moral motivation for overthrowing it, a motivation whose strength is independent of whether or not capitalism is fettering the productive forces. Yet this motivation is never strong enough to lead to the overthrow of capitalism by itself. For that, it must be joined by an economic motivation of a certain strength. The fettering of the productive powers progressively strengthens workers' economic motivations for overthrowing capitalism, to the point where moral and economic motivations together are sufficiently strong to ensure that workers do overthrow capitalism. But it never makes economic motivations so strong that they could bring about that overthrow by themselves. Moral motivations would then be necessary for overthrowing capitalism, but the explanation of the survival of capitalism while it did not fetter the productive powers, and its overthrow once it came to fetter them, would be that this fettering made a difference to workers' economic motivations.

This manoeuvre enables the theory to allow workers' moral motivations play a role in overthrowing social systems. However, even on this view such motivations constitute no more than a background condition for the overthrow of such a system. The theory continues to look to changes in economic motivations, rather than in moral motivations, to explain why a system is overthrown when it is. To the extent that the timing of the overthrow of a social system is affected by a rise in the strength of workers' moral motivations, the theory cannot explain that timing. For the theory explains by reference to the presence or absence of fettering, and such a rise in the strength of workers' moral motivations will have occurred independently of the presence or absence of fettering.

So Marx's apparent moral condemnations of capitalism pose a problem for the standard interpretation of his theory of history. They imply a project to awaken moral motivations in the working class for overthrowing capitalism, yet to the extent that such an awakening makes a difference to whether and when capitalism is overthrown, the occurrence (or at least the timing) of the overthrow will become inexplicable in terms of the theory.

One solution to the difficulty in reconciling Marx's apparent moral condemnations of capitalism with the standard interpretation of Marx's theory of history would be to claim that Marx did not in fact condemn capitalism as unjust in his own voice (and correspondingly that Marxists do not need to). For example, the suggestion might be that he himself was motivated to support the overthrow of capitalism for the sake of the development of the productive powers, and he then used moral language to whip up moral feeling in the working class in order to get them to act. Furthermore, this view can be supported independently by pointing to Marx's repeated characterizations of the ideas of justice, rights and morality as artefacts of bourgeois ideology.[13] However, as was pointed out in the debate amongst analytical Marxists in the 1980s on Marx and justice, Marx's assertions that capitalism is a disguised form of slavery, in which the capitalists coerce workers into giving them a portion of their labour power for nothing, are too widespread and central to be dismissed as being not in his own voice, or else as purely personal opinions extraneous to his work as a socialist theoretician. As a result the problem of reconciliation remains unsolved.[14]

This problem of reconciliation recurs in the work of the analytical Marxists over the last fifteen years, who have typically combined the standard interpretation of Marx's theory of history (specifically as set out by G.A. Cohen) with a condemnation of capitalism as unjust (specifically by standards of distributive fairness). As I have tried to argue, there are real difficulties in the way of such a synthesis.[15]

The Worker's Sense of Self

I take it as undeniable that Marx's works provide a textual basis for the standard interpretation of his theory of history. However, I now propose to argue that there is also a strand of Marx's thought that suggests a different view of the process of historical change, one which attributes a greater role to moral motivation and which is accordingly more compatible with Marx's moral condemnations of capitalism.

I begin with a passage from the *Grundrisse* in which Marx clearly seems to make moral convictions the source of historical change. Marx contrasts 'living labour' (the activity of labour) to 'labour capacity' (the worker) and says that under capitalism 'living labour itself appears as *alien* to living labour capacity, whose labour it is, whose own life-expression it is'. That is, labour capacity experiences its own labour, as well as the materials and instrument of production which it uses, as not belonging to it. As a result, it also experiences the product of its labour as not its own: 'the product appears to it as a combination of alien material, alien instrument and alien labour – as *alien property*', as something 'not belonging to it' [*nicht ihm Gehörigen*]'. Marx continues:

> The recognition [*Erkennung*] of the products as its own, and the judgement that its separation from the conditions of its realisation is improper [*ungehörigen*], coercively [imposed] – is an enormous consciousness, itself the product of the mode of production resting on capital, and as much the knell to its doom as, with the slave's consciousness that he cannot be the property of another, with his consciousness of himself as a person, slavery is reduced to a merely artificial, vegetative existence, and ceases to be able to prevail as the basis of production.[16]

Marx reproduced this whole passage almost verbatim in the 1861–63 manuscript *On the Critique of Political Economy*, but for the words 'improper, coercively imposed' he substituted 'a wrong [*ein Unrecht*], a coercive relationship [*Zwangsverhältnis*]'.[17]

The passage, in its two versions, is one of those which has been used as evidence that Marx thought that capitalism was unjust.[18] Yet if this means that Marx is appealing here to a transhistorical, absolute standard of justice, and describing a process whereby the worker comes to recognize the validity of this standard, then it appears inconsistent with Marx's derisory references to 'eternal justice' and 'natural justice' as standards by which to condemn capitalism.[19]

Instead I suggest that what Marx says about the change in consciousness of the modern worker in this passage must be interpreted in the light of the parallel which he draws there with the change in consciousness of the slave. Marx identifies the slave's consciousness 'that he cannot be the property of another' with his 'consciousness of himself as a person', that is (following Hegel's usage of the term 'person'), as a self-determining individual who is free to do what he chooses with his own body and with some part of the external world which is his property. For someone to think of himself as a person is for him to see the possession of this kind of freedom as part of his own nature. So it is to find conditions in which he is denied this freedom intolerable, not because they frustrate any of his ordinary desires, but because they contradict his sense of what he is. Thus to see oneself as a person is necessarily to be motivated in a new way. A being which sees itself as a person is a being which in view of its self-conception cannot but will its own freedom.

Marx's account of personhood and its incompatibility with slavery here matches point for point that of Hegel in the *Philosophy of Right*. For Hegel, a being which sees itself as a person is the simplest form of what he calls 'a free will which wills the free will'.[20] Such a will is the ground of 'abstract right', that is, of individual rights over person and property. To think of oneself as a person is to demand for oneself recognition from others as having exclusive rights over one's own self and over some part of the natural world, and to be willing to recognize others as having similar rights. For it is only in this way that the individual that thinks of itself as a person can realize the freedom which it sees as being essential to its own nature.[21] Thus the 'reality' of individual rights over person and property, the fact that individuals are motivated to demand them on the one hand and to respect them on the other, derives from the way in which those individuals conceive themselves, and specifically from the fact that they conceive themselves as free.[22] In particular, consciousness of oneself as a person is incompatible with slavery. For to be a slave is to be treated by one's master, and to treat oneself as something capable of being made into the property of another human being, and thus as a thing (*Sache*), or as a 'natural being' (*Naturwesen*), and this is to deny one's own freedom.[23] Accordingly, for Hegel, once individuals' consciousness of themselves as persons becomes widespread, slavery becomes impossible to sustain.[24]

If we now turn to the modern worker, Marx's choice of words in the two versions of the passage I have quoted suggests that he conceives the transformation of the consciousness of this worker as akin to that of the slave who first begins to think of himself as a person. If the motivational source for demanding and respecting the individual rights of the person is the sense of oneself as free, then the paradigmatic case of a wrong (*ein Unrecht*), a violation of such rights, would be coercion, the direct denial of freedom.[25] It is in exactly the same terms that Marx describes the modern worker as coming to experience his condition: as a condition of wrong and coercion. So by his wording Marx implicitly suggests that, as in the case of the slave, it is through coming to see himself as free in a new way that the modern worker comes to experience his conditions as coercive, in that they contradict this freedom, and so as a wrong. At the root of the change, he implies, is a change in the worker's self-conception, a change that involves coming to see the self as intrinsically free in a more demanding sense of 'freedom' than that associated with the conception of the self as a person: a sense such that the condition of wage labour is a direct denial of that freedom, and so contradicts the worker's sense of self, just as the condition of enslavement contradicts the slave's sense of himself as a person.[26]

As what kind of being, exactly, does the modern worker come to see himself, or herself, in this picture? One obvious suggestion might be that it is as a 'self-owner', meaning someone who is free to do what he wants with himself and with all the products of his labour. The 'wrong' which violates this freedom would then consist in wresting control of these products from the worker. Yet if this was the case, it would most naturally move the worker to overthrow capitalism not in favour of communism, but rather in favour of a society of 'petty commodity production' in which people individually owned or hired the raw materials and means of their own production, with which they produced goods for sale on the market; and this was a prospect which Marx repeatedly scorned.[27] I therefore suggest the following alternative: the worker comes to see himself as a being that is free to organize its own productive activity, in other words, as a 'person' in a qualitatively new sense, a sense that stands in contradiction to the worker's lack of control over the entire process of production in which he is engaged.

On the understanding that production means production for others, this is a control that can only be exercised collectively, by all the producers in an economy. Individual workers engaged in petty commodity production would still find themselves dictated to, in their decisions as to what and how to produce, by the impersonal forces of the market economy. The freedom to organize one's own productive activity could only be realized by producers collectively taking control of the means of production and deciding how and what to produce – a nutshell description of Marx's communism.[28]

My suggestion, then, is this: in the passage under discussion Marx is asserting that the consciousness on the part of slaves of themselves as persons in a minimal sense (I shall say, as 'private persons') led to the overthrow of slavery, and that the sense on the part of modern workers of themselves as persons in a fuller sense (I shall say, as 'social persons') must similarly lead to the overthrow of capitalism.[29] Furthermore, in each case this sense of 'what one is' incorporates freedom as an essential attribute of the self, and is expressed in a sense that certain conditions, conditions which contradict this freedom, constitute a 'wrong', an *Unrecht*. To change these conditions becomes a necessity if individuals are to be able to remove this contradiction between what they feel themselves to be and the life they lead.

Furthermore, the idea that the motivation for revolution comes from a contradiction between workers' sense of what they are and the form of the life that they have to lead is not unique to the above quotation. In *The German Ideology* (1845–46) Marx and Engels say:

> If millions of proletarians feel by no means contented with their living conditions, if their 'being' [*Sein*] does not in the least correspond to their 'essence' [*Wesen*], then, according to [Feuerbach], this is an unavoidable misfortune, which must be borne quietly. These millions of proletarians or communists, however, think quite differently and will prove this in time, when they bring their 'being' into harmony with their 'essence' in a practical way, by means of a revolution. (*CW5* 58; *MEW3* 42)

In spite of the ironic tone, the idea recurs here that it is a sense of what they are that is crucial to workers' motivations for overthrowing capitalism.[30]

The Personal and the Contingent

How can such an account of the motivations for the overthrow of social systems be squared with Marx's account of history as the growth of human productive powers? With regard to the overthrow of slavery I do not have an answer to this question, but with regard to the overthrow of capitalism I believe that one can be given. The starting point is the connection between the passage from the *Grundrisse* and the discussion by Marx and Engels of the emergence of a contradiction between the 'personal' and the 'contingent' in *The German Ideology*.

In this work, Marx and Engels describe human societies as structured by the ownership of property. Human beings, as owners of property in means of production and in their own or others' labour power, produce for each other. They fall into a division of labour: a division of society into classes which are distinguished from each other by the kind of property which they own and therefore the kind of work which they have to do in order to earn a living.[31]

The division of labour has arisen without any collective conscious plan and presents itself to individuals as something which is impervious to any efforts they may make to change it, as 'thinglike' (*sachlich*). The process whereby it arises, from the piecemeal adjustments of individual human beings to each other's actions, is a process whereby a system of human activity 'becomes independent' (*sich verselbständigt*) with respect to the individual actors in it. It forces each individual within it to continue with the kind of work that corresponds to the kind of property which that individual owns.[32]

As a result of the way in which the division of labour dictates the class position of each, 'there appears a difference between the life of each individual [*Individuum*] in so far as it is personal [*persönlich*] and in so far as it is subsumed under some branch of the division of labour and the conditions pertaining to it' (*CW5* 78; *MEW3* 76). This is essentially a divide between two aspects of the self. On the one hand there is the self considered as the owner of a certain kind of property, and accordingly as occupying a certain role in the division of labour, working with a certain kind of means of production (the 'conditions' of that individual's labour) and engaged in a certain kind of economic interchange (a certain 'form of intercourse'), with other individuals similarly defined by their property ownership. This is the self as a 'class' individual. On the other hand there is the self considered in abstraction from such ownership and such intercourse. This is the self as a 'personal' individual. When the two come apart, then it will be the latter which is experienced as the 'real self'.

Under tribal and feudal forms of property this division is 'as yet concealed' (ibid.), because an individual's class status remains with him throughout his life, so that he thinks of it as an essential property of his individual self: '[A] nobleman always remains a nobleman, a commoner is always a commoner, a quality inseparable from his individuality [*Individualität*] irrespective of his other relations' (ibid.). However, with the emergence of a capitalist class on the one hand and a class of wage-labourers selling their own labour power to capitalists on the open market on the other, the division becomes explicit for the latter. In particular, the wage-labourer comes to experience his class status as 'contingent' to his real self, his 'personality'. At the same time he experiences his external conditions as similarly contingent:

> The difference between the personal individual and the class individual, the contingency [*Zufälligkeit*] of the conditions of life for the individual, appears only with the emergence of the class which is itself a product of the bourgeoisie. Competition and the struggle of individuals among themselves first create and develop this contingency as such. (ibid.)[33]

From here on I shall concentrate on the 'contingency' of external conditions. The development of this 'contingency' needs to be separated into two stages, which Marx and Engels tend to elide, and to which correspond weak and strong senses of 'contingency'. In the first stage, the worker comes to 'disentangle' his sense of self from the particular work he does. He comes to see his work and its conditions as an inessential feature of his existence, something which just 'happens' to be attached to the self, but might as well not have been. Here work and conditions become contingent in the sense of *inessential* to the self. This is the weak sense of 'contingency'.

For Marx, this disentanglement of the self from its particular economic role is part and parcel of the emergence of the opposing classes of capitalists and wage-labourers themselves from the middle ages. Its key component is the process, mentioned in *The German Ideology* and extensively treated in Marx's later works, whereby workers are separated from (that is, lose their property rights in) their means of production, as an indirect result of the expansion of the market.[34] The peasant loses his land, and the urban craftsmen his workshop and tools, and both are forced instead to sell their labour power to capitalists who have gained control of such means of production.[35] The worker's relationship to the particular means of production with which he works is now precarious, and can end as soon as the capitalist, himself subject to constant market pressures, decides to terminate the contract. So the worker is forced to become mobile between different employers and even different kinds of work. Hence he inevitably comes to see the particular kind of work he is doing at any one time as 'contingent' to his self, in the sense of inessential to it. The same becomes true for the form of economic intercourse in which he engages with others: 'With money, every form of intercourse, and intercourse itself, becomes contingent for the individuals' (*CW5* 85; *MEW3* 66).

In the second stage, the worker comes to see his work not just as inessential to his self, but as a positive imposition, preventing him from engaging in 'self-activity', that is, in activity which is consonant with and expressive of his own nature as he conceives it. Furthermore, this applies not just to the particular kind of labour in which he is engaged, but to *labour as such*, where 'labour', following Marx and Engels, means productive activity performed under the compulsions established by an autonomous division of labour.[36] To experience one's productive activity in this way is to be in the condition described in the passage from the *Grundrisse* with which I began. Here work and conditions become contingent in the sense of *incompatible* with the self. This is this strong sense of contingency. It is this strong sense that is in play when Marx and Engels say that for the proletarians:

> their condition of life, labour, and with it all the conditions of existence of modern society, have become something contingent for them, something over which particular [*einzelnen*] proletarians have no control and over which no *social* organisation can give them control, and the contradiction between the personhood [*Persönlichkeit*] of the particular proletarian and the condition of life forced upon him, labour, becomes evident to him... (*CW5* 79; *MEW3* 77).

Contingency and the Productive Powers

I have suggested a way in which the development of wage-labour makes an individual's work contingent in the weak sense of inessential. However, it is Marx's account of the historical development of contingency in the strong sense that is of interest here. For it is contingency in this sense that characterizes the worker in the passage from the *Grundrisse*, and it is his presumed role in overthrowing the social system under which he lives that has to be squared with an explanation of the historical change by the development of the productive powers.

What Marx and Engels say about the development of contingency in the strong sense is that normally in the course of history 'the conditions under which individuals have intercourse with each other ... are conditions belonging to their individuality, in no way external to them'. They are 'conditions of their self-activity and are produced by this self-activity' (*CW5* 82; *MEW3* 71–2). That is, normally individuals do not find their form of intercourse – the relations of economic interchange in which they engage on the basis of the current property structure and that Marx later calls their 'social relations of production' – contingent in either the weak or the strong sense. They then go on to say that, at a certain point in historical development, a given form of intercourse comes to be experienced by individuals no longer as a 'condition of self-activity', but as a 'contingent fetter [*zufällige Fessel*]' (ibid.), which must mean, as contingent in the strong sense of incompatible with the self.

To explain the appearance of this 'contingency', Marx and Engels invoke the development of human productive powers, specifically the fact that these productive powers have developed to the point where the existing form of intercourse no longer 'corresponds' to but is in 'contradiction' with them.[37] It has become a fetter on the productive powers, apparently in the sense defined earlier of preventing their further development, and this fettering is expressed in the individuals' experience of their conditions as what Marx and Engels call a 'contingent fetter', as incompatible with the self. To distinguish the two senses of fettering in play here, I shall refer to the first as 'real fettering' and the second as 'ideal fettering'. Accordingly I interpolate 'real' or 'ideal' in the explanation which Marx and Engels give of how the latter arises:

> These various conditions, which appear first as conditions of self-activity, later as [ideal] fetters upon it, form in the whole development of history a coherent series of forms of intercourse, the coherence of which consists in this: an earlier form of intercourse, which has become a [real] fetter, is replaced by a new one corresponding to more developed productive powers and, hence, to the advanced mode of self-activity of the individuals – a form which in its turn becomes a [real] fetter and is then replaced by another. Since these conditions correspond to the simultaneous development of the productive powers, their history is at the same time the history of the evolving productive powers taken over by each new generation, and is therefore the history of the development of the powers of the individuals themselves. (*CW5* 82; *MEW3* 72)

This attempt at an explanation is inadequate as it stands. If ideal fettering, the experience of one's conditions as inimical to one's sense of self, is to be explained by an independently defined real fettering (and this is the only really consistent reading of this passage), then some reason has be given why real fettering should lead to ideal fettering. Instead of doing this, Marx and Engels try to suggest that somehow the two are simply the same thing.[38]

There seems to be an unsuccessful effort here on the part of the authors of *The German Ideology* to unite two different strands in Marx's thinking on history: specifically, to assimilate a 'phenomenological' strand, which I have been tracing in this article, into a 'functionalist' strand, which forms the basis of the standard interpretation of Marx's theory. For the phenomenological strand, what brings about the overthrow of a form of intercourse, or a form of society, is the incompatibility of the form of intercourse with the worker's sense of self. For the functionalist strand, what brings about this overthrow is the incompatibility of the form of intercourse with the further development of the productive powers. Stretching the word 'fettering' so as to make it cover both kinds of incompatibility cannot bridge the gap between them.[39]

Instead what the phenomenological model requires, if it is to base itself in the development of human productive powers, is to show how this development can lead to the contradiction as the phenomenological model conceives it.[40] In the case of capitalism, it needs to show how that development can create in individuals a conception of the self, and of what counts as the activity of the self, which is inherently incompatible with the capital/wage-labour 'form of intercourse', creating a situation in which those individuals must attempt to overthrow this form of intercourse, not so as to increase the rate of development of the productive powers, but so as to 'be what they are'. In other words, the model needs to show how the development of the productive powers leads to a sense of the self as a 'social person', as an individual free to organize its own productive activity in conjunction with others, and thus as a being whose existence is incompatible with the wage relationship as such, regardless of the economic development which that relationship may foster.

How can the development of the productive powers lead to such a result? An answer in the spirit of Marx's thought on the 'civilizing' effects of capitalism can be sketched as follows. Capitalism, because of the drive to accumulate profits that is built into it, constantly increases the education and the scientific outlook of workers.[41] This is the central way in which it develops human productive powers. At the same time it also ceaselessly widens the range of workers' needs and interdependencies.[42] The wider workers' range of both knowledge and interdependence, the broader their outlook must become, and the more they are likely to think it natural that they, indeed that human beings in general, should freely organize their own productive activity: the more, therefore, a system of production in which they are forced to sell their labour power to employers in order to live must come to seem constraining and incompatible with their sense of themselves, and with the freedom that it seems natural for them to assume. Eventually they must come to find that system as intolerable as the system of slavery. To the extent that this happens, it becomes true that the relations of capitalism are 'fettering' the productive powers of humanity – whatever the growth rate of the economy may be. For fetters, in English as in German, are the chains that bind slaves.

The Self and Right

On the interpretation I have offered here, Marx sees the essential development that leads from capitalism to the threshold of communism as a development in the way that human beings, and first of all the working class, conceive themselves. It is a development that leads from an 'individual' conception of personhood and freedom that is entirely compatible with capitalist relations of production, to a 'social' conception that is incompatible with them.

Thus, I claim, Marx grounds the revolutionary motivations of the worker, just as Kant and Hegel ground the moral motivations of the individual, in more or less explicit reflection on the nature of the self, and specifically on its nature as essentially free.[43] However, there is a major difference. For Marx the modern worker must contend with a *double* conception of the self. There is the conception of the self as abstracted from the property relations of his society, in Marx's terms the 'personal individual'. My suggestion is that the content of this conception is of that of the self as a 'social person'. Yet there is also the conception of the self as defined by its ownership of property and its corresponding position in the system of economic interaction, in Marx's terms the 'class individual'. In the case of capitalism, the content of this conception is that of the self as 'private person', specifically as a private property owner engaged in competitive exchange with others in civil, that is capitalist, society.[44] As Marx describes such a person in 'On the Jewish Question' (1843), he sees 'in other men not the *realisation* of his own freedom but the *barrier* to it' (*CW3* 163;

MEW1 365), must therefore act egoistically and think of himself as an egoist, and yet is also incorporated into a state which is necessary in order to provide the public goods that members of civil society cannot provide themselves. While, as I have suggested, the sense of the self as a 'social person' develops along with the productive powers, the sense of the self as a 'private person' is reinforced by the economic relationships of capitalist society.

In turn Marx suggests that it is this latter conception of the self that generates the ideas of right and morality that dominate the existing world.[45] This conception is itself dual. The individual is reduced 'on the one hand, to a member of civil society, to an *egoistic, independent* individual, and on the other hand to a *citizen*, a moral [*moralische*] person' (*CW3* 168; *MEW1* 370). On the one hand, the rights of man 'are nothing but the rights of a *member of civil society*, i.e. the rights of egoistic man, of man separated from other men and from the community' (*CW3* 162; *MEW1* 364); on the other hand morality is nothing but the morality of the individual who abstracts from everything particular about himself and thinks as a citizen, and as nothing else. Human motivation is bifurcated into private self-interest and public self-sacrifice.[46] Furthermore, because the content of ideas about right and morality is dictated by the necessities of a social process of production that is out of anyone's control, people systematically misattribute a metaphysical reality and an autonomous power to those ideas, a mistake that Marx and Engels call (with respect to right) the 'juridical illusion'.[47]

I suggest that Marx largely avoided using the explicit language of morality and right in describing (and articulating) workers' motivations for overthrowing capitalism, so as to avoid confusion with the ideas of morality and right generated by the relationships of capitalist society, with respect to both their content and their metaphysical connotations. Nevertheless these motivations can be thought of, from Marx's point of view, as the successors of conventional moral motivations: similar to them in deriving their source from a certain sense of self rather than from prudential thinking, although unlike them because of the different character, above all the social character, of that sense of self.

On this account, we can reconcile Marx's 'moral' condemnations of capitalism with his conception of historical change, at least on the 'phenomenological' understanding of that conception. For if that understanding is accepted then it is plausible to assume that Marx saw his role as a socialist theoretician as that of articulating workers' own developing understanding of the world, and of their own nature. This was an understanding that for him would be immediately practical in its implications, since, as I have argued, a conception of what one is can directly entail the necessity to act in certain ways.[48] Since the historical movement of transition from capitalism to communism is essentially a matter of the working class coming to a certain kind of consciousness, Marx could see his own work as part and parcel of that movement without contradiction. With regard to an understanding of the world, his explication of exploitation in *Capital* can be seen as an extended effort to overcome the ways in which the wage relationship disguises itself as a relation of exchange between equals. With regard to an understanding of workers' own nature, his characterizations of the wage system as a form of slavery can be seen as expressions of that self-conception for which wage-labour is as intolerable as slavery is for the slave who first thinks of himself as a person.[49]

Marx's essential view of right would then be parallel to Feuerbach's view of religion: that it expressed, in an alienated and unselfconscious form, a truth about our own nature.[50] Accordingly he looked on the arguments of early socialists who appealed to the right to the full product of one's labour as initial expressions of the self-conception he expected to see develop among workers: expressions which are still couched in the concepts associated with the conception of the self as a private property owner (where the property in this case is one's own labour), but which at the same time play a role in articulating a different conception of the self. The proletarians arrive at unity: 'only through a long process of development, in which the appeal to their right also plays a part. Incidentally, this appeal to their right is only a means of making them take shape as a "they", as a revolutionary, united mass' (*The German Ideology*, CW5 323; MEW3 305). Once workers realize, though, what it is that they had been expressing with the language of right, that language becomes superfluous. Marx's own resort to the language of right in his condemnations of capitalism should be seen in the same light.[51]

Given such views, it is intelligible that Marx should have simultaneously derided the contemporary language of morality and right and yet appealed to notions that look recognizably moral in his condemnations of capitalism. More importantly for the present purpose, we can see how he need have seen no contradiction between those condemnations and his conception of historical change, if that conception is understood as a 'phenomenological' one. For in making those condemnations he would simply have been articulating, in the only language available, the sense of self which he saw anyway emerging amongst workers as a result of the development of the productive powers under capitalism, and so facilitating that emergence.

Marx and Fukuyama

From the perspective of this interpretation of Marx, it is possible to look back briefly at Fukuyama's theory of history. I have already noticed the resemblances between the standard interpretation of Marx's theory of history and the first part of Fukuyama's theory. In a similar way, the alternative, 'phenomenological' interpretation of Marx which I have suggested here bears some resemblance to the second part of Fukuyama's theory. In both, social systems decline when they fail to match individuals' self-conceptions, and in both these self-conceptions are expressed in broadly moral language. However, for Fukuyama all humans have a single, if sometimes dormant, conception of themselves as free self-determining individual agents, and this is expressed in a desire to be recognized as such beings, a desire which is a fixed part of the human inheritance. A social system is incompatible with this self-conception if it fails to provide individuals with such recognition. By contrast, for Marx, this particular self-conception is characteristic of capitalist social relations, while the development of human productive powers under capitalism at the same time leads to the development of another self-conception. Capitalism is incompatible with the latter conception because it prevents individuals from exercising the form of freedom which is intrinsic to that conception.

Behind these differences there is a more fundamental one, between a picture of human beings as passive bearers of a self-conception who demand to *be treated* in a certain way, and one of human beings as active producers (albeit inadvertently and indirectly) of a self-conception, who demand to *act* in a certain way. The underlying picture of human beings as active and plastic rather than passive and fixed in their nature is what makes it possible, I suggest, for Marx to integrate moral motivations, in a broad sense, into an account of historical change based on the development of human productive powers. For that picture makes it possible to see how the conception of the self that underlies such motivations could itself be a product of the development of human productive activity. If Marx himself failed to carry through this integration, hindered, as I have suggested, by his simultaneous commitment to a 'functionalist' model of historical change, it could yet be carried through today; and if Fukuyama's work provides a spur for such a project, he will have performed a valuable service for Marxism.

Notes

I am grateful to Chris Bertram, G.A. Cohen, and Joe McCarney for comments on earlier drafts of this article.

1. Francis Fukuyama, *The End of History and the Last Man*, London: Hamish Hamilton/New York: The Free Press, 1992.
2. Francis Fukuyama, 'The End of History?', *The National Interest* no. 16, Summer 1989.
3. Fukuyama contrasts 'materialist' and 'idealist' theories of history in 'The End of History?', pp. 5–8, while failing to see that his theory straddles the divide.
4. Leon Trotsky, 'Their Morals and Ours', in *Their Morals and Ours: Marxist versus Liberal Views on Morality*, New York: Pathfinder Press, 1969, p. 36, cited by Steven Lukes, *Marxism and Morality*, 4th edn, Oxford: Oxford University Press, 1985, p. 24.
5. I have generally translated Marx's *Produktivkräfte* as 'productive powers' rather than the usual 'productive forces', in order to emphasise that they should be seen first and foremost as human capacities rather than masses of tools or machinery.
6. Fukuyama's theory includes a Darwinian element, in that it implicitly imagines socio-political systems being thrown up for more or less arbitrary reasons in different parts of the globe and then competing with each other for the allegiance of their respective populations, leading to the 'survival of the most productive'. Such an element is

absent in the standard interpretation of Marx's theory of history, of which the canonical version has become G.A. Cohen's *Karl Marx's Theory of History: A Defence* (Oxford: Oxford University Press, 1978), but it is a feature of recent attempts to reformulate the theory so as to avoid some of its difficulties. See for example: John Torrance, 'Reproduction and Development: A Case For a "Darwinian" Mechanism in Marx's Theory of History', *Political Studies* 33, 1985; Christopher Bertram, 'International Competition in Historical Materialism', *New Left Review* 183, September–October 1990; G.A. Cohen, *History Labour and Freedom*, Oxford: Oxford University Press, 1988, ch. 1; and Paula Casal, 'On Social And Global Historical Materialism', Chapter 5 in this volume.

7. For citations of Marx's texts, see Norman Geras, 'The Controversy About Marx And Justice', *New Left Review* 150, March–April 1985.

8. To simplify the argument, I assume that the theory's position is that whenever a social system comes to fetter the productive powers, such an alternative is in fact available.

9. I neglect reasons of concern for future generations here.

10. Frederick Engels, *Anti-Dühring*, London: Lawrence and Wishart, 1975, part 2, ch. 1, p. 180. This passage was pointed out to me by G.A. Cohen.

11. Engels makes such a suggestion himself a few pages after the passage from which I have quoted, at *Anti-Dühring* pp. 188–9.

12. Fettering might produce an economic motivation which would lead workers to become such a threat to the social system that the ruling class had to impose a draconian political regime to contain their revolt. Workers might then experience their political regime for the first time as unjust. But by assumption the political regime is distinct from the social system, and it is not clear why workers should transfer their perception of injustice from the political regime to the social system that it supports.

13. See Lukes, *Marxism and Morality*, pp. 5–8, for some examples.

14. In fact, when Marx's condemnations are taken as being in his own voice, they stand in need of reconciliation with his theory of morality as ideology, as well as with his theory of history, as both are standardly interpreted. The first problem of reconciliation has figured centrally in the above-mentioned debate, while it is the second that I am concerned with here, although I believe that both are susceptible to a similar treatment. For surveys of the debate, see Lukes, *Marxism and Morality*, ch. 4, and Geras 'The Controversy about Marx and Justice'.

15. As Alasdair Macintyre asserted in 1958: 'One cannot revive the moral content within Marxism simply by taking a Stalinist view of historical development and adding a liberal morality to it' ('Notes From the Moral Wilderness', *New Reasoner*, no. 7, Winter 1958–59, p. 93). The problem is visible, for example, in John Roemer's attempt to marry Cohen's theory of history with a characterization of capitalism as unjust and exploitative, in chs. 8 and 9 of his *Free to Lose* (London: Century Hutchinson, 1988). Although he endorses the view that socio-political forms are retained and abandoned as they encourage or fetter the development of the productive forces (pp. 108–12), Roemer arbitrarily asserts that resulting historical succession of socio-political forms will be such that each can be derived from the previous one by eliminating from it the form of exploitation which was the major source of inequality in it (pp. 131–47, esp. 144). So the succession dictated by the demands of economic development happily coincides with the succession dictated by the successive elimination of inequality, and the question of whether it is economic motivations (as he suggests on p. 124) or moral motivations (as he suggests on p. 3) that are crucial in bringing about change can be fudged. For a partial exposition of the difficulties in Roemer's account, see Ellen Meiksins Wood, 'Rational Choice Marxism: Is

The Game Worth the Candle?', *New Left Review* 177, September–October 1989, sections 3–4.

16. Karl Marx, *Grundrisse*, Harmondsworth: Penguin, 1973, pp. 462–3; *Grundrisse der Kritik der Politischen Ökonomie*, Berlin: Dietz, 1953, pp. 366–7. I have modified this and other translations from Marx, Engels, Hegel and Feuerbach.

17. *Marx Engels Gesamtausagabe* (*MEGA*), Berlin: Dietz, 1982, ll 3.6 pp. 2284–7.

18. See, for example, Ziyad Husami, 'Marx on Distributive Justice', in Marshall Cohen, Thomas Nagel and Thomas Scanlon, eds., *Marx, Justice and History*, Princeton: Princeton University Press, 1980, pp. 53–4; Jon Elster, *Making Sense of Marx*, Cambridge: Cambridge University Press, 1985, pp. 106, 219; and Lukes, *Marxism and Morality*, p. 51. *Ein Unrecht* can in fact be translated as 'an injustice' as well as 'a wrong', although this is misleading if it implies that an idea of distributive justice is involved.

19. On eternal justice (*justice eternelle*) see *The Poverty of Philosophy* in Karl Marx and Frederick Engels, *Collected Works*, London: Lawrence and Wishart, 1975– (hereafter *CW*) Volume 6, pp. 127, 144; and *Capital* Volume 1, p. 179n. On natural justice (*natürliche Gerechtigkeit*) see *Capital* Volume 3, Harmondsworth: Penguin, 1981, pp. 460–61; *Marx Engels Werke*, Berlin: Dietz, 1956– (hereafter *MEW*) Volume 25, pp. 351–2. Cf. note 13 above.

20. G.W.F. Hegel, *Elements of the Philosophy of Right*, edited by Allen Wood, trans. H.B. Nisbet, Cambridge: Cambridge University Press, 1991 (hereafter *PR*) §27; in references to the *Philosophy of Right*, 'R' indicates the remark to a paragraph and 'A' the addition to a paragraph.

21. *PR* §§34–44, §57, §71R.

22. Thus it can be said, for abstract right at least, that 'right is any existence [*Dasein*] in general which is an existence of the free will' (*PR* §29).

23. See, respectively, *PR* §57, §57R. On the notion of a thing [*Sache*], see §§42–44.

24. Hegel calls the idea that a human being is intrinsically free, and so cannot be another's property, the principle of 'subjectivity' or of 'subjective freedom' (*PR* §124R, §185R). In the Encyclopedia *Philosophy of Mind* (Oxford: Clarendon Press, 1971), he describes it as a historical force of 'unconquerable strength' introduced into the world by Christianity. When men became 'aware of freedom as their essence, aim and object', as something 'not which they *have*, but which as men they *are*', then they could no longer be slaves: 'Christianity in its adherents has realized an ever-present sense that they are not and cannot be slaves' (§482). Cf. *Philosophy of History*, New York: Dover, 1956, p. 334: 'under Christianity, slavery is impossible'.

25. In fact Hegel names coercion (*Zwang*) as the culminating form of wrong in the *Philosophy of Right*: 'Force [*Gewalt*] or coercion, taken in the abstract, is therefore *wrong* [*unrechtlich*]' (*PR* §92).

26. Again, Hegel provides a model here, since he sees the person, its freedom, and the abstract right that realizes that freedom as providing only initial conceptions of the self, of freedom, and of right respectively. They are successively superseded by more adequate and inclusive conceptions in the course of the *Philosophy of Right*. Abstract right is only 'right in the strict sense' (*PR* §§ 30R, 104, 106A, 141A), whereas right in the broad sense, the sense of the title of the book, includes the whole range of what is now called the moral. For evidence that Marx also associated a particular idea of freedom with a particular idea of the nature of the self, see his and Engels' description of 'materialist freedom' in *The Holy Family*: 'If man is [free] in the materialist sense, i.e. is free not through the negative power to avoid this or that, but through the positive power to assert

his true individuality ... each man must be given social scope for the vital manifestation of his essence [*für seine wesentliche Lebensäusserung*]', *CW4* 131; *MEW2* 138.

27. See, for example, his attack on Proudhon at *Grundrisse*, pp. 247–9.

28. It might be said that if producers organize their production collectively then each is still 'dictated to' by a collective decision over which he has minimal individual control. But if the decision-making process is one in which each has an individual veto, then none can be said to be dictated to, and if it approximates as closely as is practicable to including such a veto (for example, through incorporating a process of public rational debate) then there will be no more such 'dictating' than that minimum which is at present practically ineliminable.

29. A possibility that I have not considered is that in the quotation Marx claims only that these psychological transformations are epiphenomenal signs of the coming overthrow of the respective social systems, rather than that they are causes of it. Such an interpretation of the passage would be a strained one, however.

30. In the earlier *Holy Family* Marx and Engels make a similar point: 'It is not a question of what this or that proletarian, or even the whole proletariat, at the moment *regards* as its aim. It is a question of *what the proletariat is*, and what, in accordance with this being [*Sein*], it will historically be compelled to do' (*CW4* 37; *MEW2* 38).

31. As has been pointed out by Ali Rattansi (*Marx and the Division of Labour*, London: Macmillan, 1982), Marx did not distinguish the division of labour in society from the division of ownership (i.e. of classes) until his later works.

32. See *CW5* 47, 77–8, 86.

33. I have consistently translated *zufällig* and *Zufälligkeit* as 'contingent' and 'contingency'. English translations of *The German Ideology* render the former variously as 'contingent', 'accidental', and 'extraneous', and the latter variously as 'contingency', 'accidental quality' and 'chance'. The personal–contingent contrast appears in Marx's *Comments on James Mill* (1844), *CW3* 220. However, its immediate source in *The German Ideology* appears to be Max Stirner's objection in his 1845 *The Ego and Its Own* (London: Rebel Press, 1982, pp. 261–4), to the fact that success in competition depends on the possession of things (chiefly, money), something contingent to the self, rather than on personal powers. 'The *means* for competing are not at every one's command, because they are not taken from personality, but from contingency' (p. 264). See Marx and Engels' commentary on this passage of Stirner's book in *The German Ideology*, *CW5* 375–6. The section of *The German Ideology* in which they develop their own version of the contrast (*CW5* 63–93) was originally written as a digression from their critique of Stirner (see the editors' notes at *CW5* 588).

34. See especially the section on 'primitive accumulation' in *Capital* Volume 1, pp. 873–940.

35. For a discussion of this process of separation as described by Marx, see G.A. Cohen, 'The Dialectic of Labour in Marx', in *History, Labour and Freedom*, sections 2–4. For some doubts about the capacity of the market to bring about such changes, see Robert Brenner, 'The social basis of economic development', in John Roemer, ed., *Analytical Marxism*, Cambridge: Cambridge University Press, 1986.

36. 'Labour' is tacitly defined in this way when Marx and Engels equate it with 'the subsumption of the individual under the division of labour, under a determinate activity forced upon him'. (*CW5* 64; *MEW3* 50). See also *CW5* 45, 52, 77; and Chris Arthur, *Dialectics of Labour*, Oxford: Basil Blackwell, 1986, pp. 12–19. In his later writings Marx ceases to confine the term 'labour' to productive activity in class societies and speaks of

labour in communist society.

37. See *CW5* 81–2; *MEW3* 71–2.

38. Thus 'the relation of the productive powers to the form of intercourse is the relation of the form of intercourse to the occupation or activity of the individuals' (*CW5* 82; *MEW3* 71).

39. For the two to be identified, 'self-activity' – activity that is consonant with the worker's sense of his own nature – would have to be a productive activity which becomes ever more productive, or at least which is part of a social totality of such activities that becomes ever more productive as a whole. I do not investigate this possibility here.

40. I leave aside the question of what it is that brings about the development of the productive powers themselves, for Marx. The suggestion made in the last footnote provides one possible answer to this question.

41. *Grundrisse*, pp. 408–10, 541–2.

42. Ibid. pp. 156–62, 287, 527–8; *Communist Manifesto*, *CW6* 488.

43. Kant, *Groundwork of the Metaphysic of Morals*, in *The Moral Law*, edited by H.J. Paton, London: Hutchinson, 1948, ch. 3, esp. pp. 107–9 (Prussian Academy pagination: pp. 446–8); Hegel, *The Philosophy of Right*, Introduction. John Rawls in *A Theory of Justice* (Oxford: Oxford University Press, 1972) provides a contemporary variant of such a view when he says that 'the desire to express our nature as free and equal rational beings can be fulfilled only by acting on the principles of right and justice' (p. 574). Cf. pp. 252–3, 561, 575.

44. In commodity exchange, 'individuals recognize each other reciprocally as owners [*Eigentümer*], as persons, whose will penetrates their commodities. Accordingly the juridical moment of the person first enters here, and that of freedom, in so far as it is contained in it' (*Grundrisse* p. 243; Berlin edn, p. 155). Cf. *Capital* Volume 1, p. 178; and *PR* §40.

45. I understand 'right' (*Recht*) here to mean either individual rights (Hegel's abstract right; what Marx usually calls 'private right', *Privatrecht*) or else the 'right' by which the state and its organs act (Hegel's 'constitutional right', *Staatsrecht*; what Marx usually calls 'public right', *öffentlich Recht*).

46. This theme is taken up a number of times in *The German Ideology*, e.g. *CW5* 46–7, 213, 245–8, 439. It echoes Hegel's criticism of both 'abstract right' and formal morality (*Moralität*) as equally one-sided abstractions from 'ethical life', that form of motivation associated with a sense of the individual as at once a social individual. See *PR* §141R,A.

47. *The German Ideology*, *CW5* 91, 330, 362–3.

48. For a similar view on the practical import of Marx's theory, see Joseph McCarney, *Social Theory and the Crisis of Marxism*, London: Verso, 1990, ch. 6.

49. I assume that Marx thought that this later self-conception was more objectively true or adequate than the earlier one.

50. Hence Marx's early parallel between his own 'critique of right' and Feuerbach's critique of religion: 'Thus the critique of heaven turns into the critique of the earth, the criticism of religion into the criticism of right' ('Contribution to the Critique of Hegel's Philosophy of Right: Introduction', *CW3* 176).

51. By the *Critique of the Gotha Programme* (1875) Marx's view was that ideas of 'equal right' and 'just [*gerechter*] distribution' were 'ideas which in a certain period had some meaning but have now become obsolete verbal rubbish', Karl Marx and Frederick Engels, *Selected Works in Three Volumes*, Moscow: Progress, 1970, p. 17. Again, this parallels Feuerbach's theory of religion. For Feuerbach, men could become conscious of their

essence in the first instance only by conceiving that essence in the alienated form of a God. Subsequently that religious expression could be, and had to be, discarded. '[R]eligion is man's first and also indirect form of self-consciousness ... Man initially locates his essence outside himself, before he finds it in himself,' *The Essence of Christianity*, tr. George Eliot, New York: Harper and Row, 1957, p.13; *Feuerbach: Sämmtliche Werke*, Stuttgart: Frommann Verlag, 1903–10, vol. 6, p. 16.

PART III

Modernity

7

The End of History and the Metastructure of Modernity
Jacques Bidet

The fascination provoked by Francis Fukuyama's well-known essay 'The End of History?' does not just stem from its naive simplicity as a waking dream, from its ideological perfection, but also from the fact that it touched the raw nerve of a picture of history that – at least in its crude form – tended to situate 'socialism' *beyond* the present configuration of the world. What we need to reconsider is Marx's central claim that capitalism can only be abolished through the abolition of its basis: the market relation itself. According to this claim socialism has to be understood as a whole new historical era, as a *post*-market era. Marx, it seems to me, was unable to set out a general form of the modern world and the system of which it consists that is more extensive than the one he conceived of under the name 'capital'. No doubt this task is easier to accomplish today than it was a century and a half ago, and hence it is easier to understand that a 'socialist' revolution can only come about within the framework and according to the rules and limitations of this modernity.

It is also of the greatest importance that we think beyond modernity, which means conceiving of and trying to achieve what Marx called the higher phase of 'communism'. But it is specifically this that can be done only if we have first marked the boundaries of the system that is the modern world. To do this we might once again explore the theme of 'two phases' that Marx sketched in the *Critique of the Gotha Programme* and which is often known in terms of the socialism–communism sequence and which still has much left of interest for us today. According to the interpretation of that sequence that I put forward here, we have first a revolutionary process that remains within the limits of modernity and then a process that breaks out of those limits. I am concerned here mainly with the first of these stages, the prelude to everything that follows.

The theory of modernity that I put forward in a recent book sought to start again from the beginning.[1] It did not propose to put forward *another* theory to rival Marx's but rather to broaden the question by situating it in a larger space, and through this also within another temporality, within a historicity that is understood first and foremost as the circle of a present. I aim to provide what Marx was unable to produce adequately: the *dialectical* structure of modernity. Through that I seek to address a problem that Marx did know how to deal with correctly: that of the relationship between *principles of right* and domination in modern society. In other words, I aim to do something that Marxism has never known how to achieve: to insert within the analytical and critical theory of society the principles of a *political* theory.

The Renewal of Marxian Theory in Terms of the Metastructure

The metastructure is not the market, but the articulation of three dimensions of contractuality-domination

Marx begins his exposition of the theory of capitalism with market relations, which he treats not as a historical stage but as a *systemic presupposition* of capitalism. His aim is to show that market relations carry capitalism along with them. His demonstration of this is a powerful one, in that he establishes that the link between the two is neither external nor contingent, but rather that they form a systemic unity. It follows that the dream of getting rid of capitalism whilst holding onto the market – pursued by French socialists such as Proudhon – comes up against formidable theoretical difficulties. I should like to show that Marx's demonstration is nevertheless incomplete, and to complete it. In other words, I should like to give an adequate description of the systemic presupposition: in its 'abstraction' of the first moment, as Marx would understand it, it is not constituted solely by the market relationship of 'interindividuality', linking together atoms according to the market network, but it is rather, according to me, a form that is at once *interindividual, centred* and *associative* – three dimensions that shape the (meta)system. In my terminology, the matrix derived from these three elements constitutes the 'metastructure' of modernity, in other words, its presupposition.

If we set out, then, from the Marxian starting point (understood as a theoretical, not a historical beginning), that of production based on exchange, we must also understand that such a relation of production could neither be established nor maintained unless there existed a centre that in some manner ensured the following of such a rule. There would be no market sphere even in embryo (bearing in mind that this is not an aspect of its historical origins but a systemic one) without a centre as the source of the social forces of that sphere and as possessor of the relative monopoly of a more or less legitimate violence. Now such a centre, as guarantor and in this sense underlying principle of order, is able to will an order, a form of social organization *other* than that of the market: this might involve privilege, forecasting, regulation and perhaps even the near total administration of economic life. The *interindividuality* of the market relation cannot exist without a *centricity* – the epicentre of social forces – which opens it to question from the outset. An abstract and partial theory of the state is thus implied from the first moment of theoretical elaboration. But we need to add at once that these two dimensions – *interindividuality* and *centricity* – imply a further third dimension (*associativity*) that joins them together. The centre is not formed as the arena of atomic but rather of social forces. In order to clarify this point I should add that the 'metastructure' unfolds in the form of particular 'structures'. By 'structures' I mean the specific class relations of modern societies. The system of modernity is thus the unity of this metastructure with the structures, where the former is the 'posited presupposition' of the latter. I shall return to each of these points.

Contractuality and domination

This general matrix of modern society expresses itself simultaneously in terms of contractuality and domination, in terms of relationships based on rights and relationships based on force. It is the matrix for a class relation that is distinctively modern and which is brought into being through a contractuality that is also a permanently critical and subversive principle of that same domination. The particular form that domination takes can nevertheless only emerge at the more concrete level of analysis because it is only given within the mode of appropriation which is revealed solely when we look at the 'structural' configurations, the forms taken by class relations. It would therefore appear that the metastructure expresses itself first of all in contractual terms and that the 'metastructural theory' partakes of the fashion of the moment. I ask the reader to resist temptation and to wait and see.

In fact we need to complete the metastructural matrix in the following fashion: individuals who contract one with another in the market can also contract as a group; in other words, they can form associations. It is easy to understand that they do this according to their interests. In particular they have an interest in acting on the statist centre which is not itself an association but rules the whole by right *and through force* as the representative of the public in the face of private relationships whether interindividual or associative. We see from this that the third term – associativity – cannot be introduced without reference to the relation of forces.

At this stage of the exposition there is a great deal left to do so far as the explanation of the modern relation between principles of right and domination goes: specifically, to show that we cannot make sense of this relation without linking the metastructure to the structures (or class relations). I should like first of all to make clear that this is a purely 'abstract' sketch in the Hegelian sense of an abstraction of the very beginning of the exposition, similar to the outline concerning commodities that Marx puts forward at the beginning of *Capital*. My account, it will be seen, differs from his only in claiming that one cannot conceive of the commodity relation in an isolated fashion as a point of theoretical departure. Marx tries to move 'dialectically' to capitalism by taking into account the peculiar commodity that is labour power: from that point on, the concrete complexity that is the modern capitalist relation is set out. Such a way of proceeding is perfectly sound. It is not only legitimate but epistemologically necessary to begin with the commodity relation without which the distinctively capitalist relation that is based precisely on the commodification of labour power cannot be explicated. But this development is too limited because it sets out from an incomplete beginning, and this incompleteness harms the entire exposition (even if we can discern throughout the entire work corrections which implicitly refer to this necessary complete beginning). The initial abstraction in all its completeness is not the market relation alone, because that relation is only conceivable when provided with a centre that guarantees it; this centre, the contested terrain of associations, can will something other than the market, in other words, it can will and implement the opposite of the market. This is what I denote by the term 'metastructure', in the sense of general presupposition of modernity. Since it consists in a (meta)systemic relation, the market dimension cannot there enjoy any epistemic primacy over the two others.

This metastructure includes a radical antinomy; whatever is assigned to be determined by the centre – for example when the centre decides that exchange must conform to this or that condition, or that a share of resources is to be centrally administered – is withdrawn from interindividual market control. At least this is so on first examination. This antinomy is revealed in the fact that the movement from the metastructure to the structures can occur in different ways; in other words, in a manner that is more complex than the movement that Marx anticipated as a movement from the commodity (or money) to capital. The metastructure actually allows for two antinomic structural forms, two polar-opposite forms of class structure, which, within the system that they constitute, typify modernity. On the one hand, as Marx showed, according to the logic of the market, individual appropriation of the means of production opens the way to capitalism. On the other hand – as a number of theoreticians beginning with Weber have seen – collective appropriation by the managers of the centre, according to the logic of the plan (in the general sense of central determination) opens the way to statist communism.

The 'practical' intersection of interindividuality and centricity

This market–plan distinction is banal and, in a sense, widely held today. It only escapes from banality and yields its conceptual dividend (both scientifically and politically) if it is inserted into the conceptual framework of the metastructure which can alone provide the key to the relationships that obtain between the two forms of society and to mixed entities to which these give rise.

It is indeed possible, following Weber, to understand modernity in terms of the emergence of rationality. Even more precisely, it is possible to do as economists now do and distinguish between two principles of economic rationality, corresponding respectively to market and organization, with 'transaction costs' giving us a rational criterion for choosing between the two. But the unity of the two can only be provided by reference to practical reason: it is as forms of contractuality that they form a dialectical pair; in other words, they constitute themselves in their distinction through a relation of identity. The theory of transaction costs can determine that in this case or that the market is more rational than the organization or vice versa. It can allow us to compare the benefits of each according to the circumstances. But according to this way of looking at things the relationship remains an external one, one between alternatives. The thing that links these two ways of rationally arranging large-scale collective action (the level beyond mere interpersonal relations), the plan and the market – the principle underlying communication between the two – is that each refers to the other through the question – that is immanent in each – of the agreement which they are understood to give rise to. The market, as a contractual relationship between individuals, asserted to be a relation of non-dependence, refers to a universal principle of non-dependence of which the positive expression can only be a central (statist) contractual relationship opening the path to a substantive will that orders its ends and its means according to a plan. The plan, as a rational scheme, presupposes the agreement of agents to the principle of the plan, that is to say, the non-subjugation of agents during its implementation: an explanation is owed for any limitation that is imposed on the right that individuals have to contract freely amongst themselves. The cognitive dimension allows us to conceive of a complementarity and arrangement of plan and market. Only the practical, that is to say, ethical and political, dimension allows us to grasp their internal relation, the fact that the possibility of the one presupposes the possibility of the other, and also to see how the antinomy between them develops in the form of an antinomy between alternative class structures that are nonetheless dialectically linked together within modernity.

The posited presupposition

We can now return to the notion of the 'metastructure' as a posited presupposition. I have coined this word (and set up the metastructure–structure pairing) in order to designate the most general, abstract and comprehensive form in modernity. This form has the same role here that the market relation plays in the theory that Marx sets out in *Capital*, that of a posited presupposition. We are not here dealing with a historical presupposition but rather with a systemic one that is 'posited', produced by the development of the system itself. It is only in setting out from the character of the *system* that we can pose the question of its historical origin, just as Marx did in his study of primitive accumulation. Marx demonstrates very well that capitalism *presupposes* the market, but also that it alone *posits* it to its full extent. I take up the same idea but at the same time enlarge its scope in two directions. The presupposition is no longer just the market but a politico-economic form that is interindividual, centred and associative. This presupposition is the presupposition of modern societies however they differ in their 'structural' forms: it is this that gives rise in the course of their development to the capitalist structure (or class system), but also to the statist communist one and all the intermediate forms (the so-called 'Western democracies'). And it is from this starting point that we can grasp the antinomy between the forms taken by these modern societies and the movement (transition) from one to another that is at the heart of this highly provisional end of history. It is thus in the positing of this presupposition that a particular structure is confronted by the ensemble of ultimate metastructural determinations, and therefore against that which puts its very existence in question.

The Circle of Class Societies

The concept of metastructure allows us to reflect upon the cyclical nature of the modern world which makes it appear like an end to history, although for the same reason it is not. The historical sequence that advances through irreversible 'structural' processes is at the same time subject to the conditions of a metastructural circle. Thus we can think beyond Marx at the same time as thinking with him. But I should like to re-emphasize that the reflections just put forward concerning the metastructure (and more generally all theorization of the metastructure) do not aim to replace structural theory as I understand it – that is to say, in this context the theory of capitalism as such with all its developments since Marx up to and including those put forward by the Regulation School or the world-system theorists. Rather, the aim is to achieve a grasp of the more general framework in which the structure evolves.

Capitalism

Our point of departure is the analysis of capitalism put forward by Marx, and its most general element, namely the primary determination through which he makes the transition from the market to the capital relation: the transformation of labour power into a commodity, the principle of capitalist accumulation. Let us accept his analysis of the formation of two antagonistic classes on the basis of this relation. At the same time we are aware that so far as he is concerned this is just a blueprint, albeit one without which the more detailed, concrete, diverse, contrasting and contradictory relations that form the fabric of actual societies cannot be addressed. Let us also accept all the developments that can be related to this blueprint and which constitute the Marxian theory of capitalist society. But let us focus on the relation from which the remainder of analysis is developed, the wage relation as such, to show how it always already has its place within a *metastructural* framework that is much broader than that of the structure of capitalism, and how this fact appears in Marx's discourse (although in the form of a linear and teleological intrusion that involves in advance the denial of the circularity of the metastructure).

This commodification takes the form of the incorporation of labour power within the exchange relation, a fact that typifies the modern workforce. It is a relationship within which the employee is at one and the same time the agent that enters into exchange and – at least from the point of view of his labour power – the object of exchange. The decisive step in Marx's analysis comes when he shows that it is not labour but labour power that is the object of exchange. It is labour power that is put at the disposition of the employer, and the exploitation of the worker – who produces more than he receives – is thereby realized. This conception of labour power as a commodity is thus essential to Marx's theoretical account. But it seems to me that we can only make sense of what Marx from this point on describes as the class struggle in the light of the (metastructural) consideration that the wage relation is – in the sense defined above – 'centred' and 'associative'. The 'commodity' labour power – and we must now use inverted commas because we are approaching the theoretical step when that designation becomes metaphorical – is also a contractual-dominational subject, in other words, an agent who at the same instant as he engages in exchange, as he hires out his labour power for a wage, is placed within a centred and associative relation. 'Free labour', to use Weber's term, the modern ability of the worker to contract with someone else who employs him, is inseparable from his ability to associate together with other workers to put pressure on the centre – particularly to ensure that this right of association – an *essential* dimension of free contractuality – becomes effective. But from this very centre, as soon as its impact (their impact) is felt, there develops a relation that cannot be called an exclusively market relationship (in the sense where the 'law of the market' sets the value of commodities) because we are now dealing with a relationship within which the spontaneity of market relations is placed in doubt. The capitalist commodity space, in bringing forth a statist centricity which is the object of the associated social forces, becomes an arena of class struggle.

In a sense Marx demonstrates all this quite clearly when he describes the struggle of the workers for factory and employment legislation, for the democratization of political institutions, and so on. What seems to me to be missing from Marx's analysis – a deficiency which goes together with a global deficiency, which has affected the communist movement that it has constantly inspired – is a recognition of the metastructural mechanism that forms the background to and is the key element of that struggle. The power of the workers' movement, the potential gravedigger of capitalism, is mainly explained – within Marxist orthodoxy – on the basis of the development of the productive forces within capitalism, by the fact that capitalist production calls into being and develops a labour force that is simultaneously more and more exploited but also more numerous, concentrated, skilled and united by the concentration of production itself. This marks the victory of the Hegelian servant (*Knecht*) – who is put to work, becomes a worker, and is formed in all his potency through the effect of the labour process itself, within which he henceforth establishes his proficiency – over the master, who has become virtually useless. In other words, we have the rise in power of the 'proletariat' as a consequence of instrumental rationality, of the technical and social instrumentality of productive reason. All this is effectively essential. It is clearly in relation to determinate economic conditions that this *rise in power* of a class and a working-class centrality comes into being. But unless we are prepared to understand this as a counter-instrumentality, we are led to recognize the link between this power and the ability that the workers have to contract associatively. Such an ability cannot be separated from the general one of contracting interindividually and centrally. The power of the modern wage-labourer, not that of the mass-individual (considered outside of the process of his politico-juridical individuation) but rather that of the individual who is a worker and a citizen – fully recognized as such or not – who at a given moment, together with others, takes charge of himself and takes his risks, risks that he alone can take because they are his, his life, his skin and his loves, this power is inseparable from the fact that he can, in principle, and in the unequal and uncertain conditions that are those of class relations, 'change his master'. As Marx explains, this is a crucial difference with the premodern worker. This ability to 'change his master' is only given on the basis of the class struggle waged by the workers, but it rests upon unavoidable relation between the three basic dimensions of contractuality. It forms precisely one aspect of the process in which the 'presupposition' is posited.

To summarize, capitalist relations of production are always caught up in general and implicit contradictory relations by which they are always already subject to a critique. On this basis we can trace in outline the history of the workers' movement – a process that is markedly historical but is incorporated in the circle that shapes a historical epoch. The workers' movement, as we know, has so conceived of its task that, when the centre is given its direction by the associated producers, the universal contractual will that is there affirmed cannot be just that of fixing the boundaries to the regime of capitalist appropriation but must rather be a substantive general will, capable of setting its goals democratically and of organizing production in a rational manner through a harmonization of means. Driven by a range of considerations, which cannot be taken into account here but among which must be included a tradition of analysis derived from Marx, with the building of 'actually existing socialisms' we reach a limit case: once the market relation has been rejected as being indissociable from capitalism, there only remains the other means of large-scale rational organization, the plan, the general planning of productive activity.

Statist communism

Yet it turns out that this system, no more transparent by nature than the commodity relation, carries with itself the same predisposition to the appropriation of the product and to social control by a new dominant class. This happens through the scheme of contractuality-domination whilst this time originating with centricity itself. It is not possible to give a full analysis of this process here. But we can underline its strikingly modern nature, in the sense that reference is made to the idea that public politico-economic matters are everyone's business – except for those who will not listen to reason; something that is guaranteed by a constitution which affirms (subject to qualifications that are sufficient to render them largely inoperable) rights of democratic participation. Modern liberty is formally affirmed by the immanent social discourse by which the institutions define themselves. Political and economic life is supposed to be everyone's business and the institution repeats this on a daily basis – with this qualification: that the exclusive choice of the plan, and therefore of a comprehensively social contractuality refracted at and from the centre, carries with it the virtual extinction of interindividual contractuality. It is not that this disappears completely: thus the labour market, the choice by each of his profession and employment, and hence the contractual relation of the individual in a particular social situation, remains the rule. This fact can seem to disappear under the weight of various exceptions, but even though the exceptions may be large scale it remains just that, an exception. Without this liberty in the labour market – affirmed in principle, however limited and partially formal it may be – the founding discourse, which stipulates that the social order rests on the general will and therefore upon institutions put in place by the citizenry in the entirety and defining free and equal relations, would be unable to constitute itself. The sovereign is indirectly accountable to a subject that has been immersed in this discourse of modernity. This accountability is rigged, to be sure, a fact that enables the exercise of power by a new ruling class which the division of the management – political, economic and ideological – of the social process places above society. Its capacity to reproduce itself by incorporating itself into the fabric of the single party is tied to the functionality of the party for the single and hierarchized scheme of comprehensive (or would-be comprehensive) planning. The sole party allows the kind of mental homogeneity that is required for a planning centre – supposedly the repository of the general will – to set the social organism in motion. It ensures central control of supervision, of a largely asymmetrical ideological medium, which nevertheless permits a certain management of tensions. Its paradoxical character, in which the basic contradiction of this society is summarized, lies in the fact that whilst as a party it is just a private association, as the single party it parallels all the levels of public institutions, representing within them the dominant class as such. Thus the constitutional state, which presupposes a civic order that is accessible to each person and under the control of all, tends to be extinguished and the arbitrary power that is characteristic of premodern societies seems at the end of the day to get the upper hand.

But this never happens completely, because this modern planned social order cannot operate without constantly referring to the discursive constitution of the general will which is supposed in principle to occur, to the fact that each and every person without exception and on the same basis is called upon to take responsibility for public affairs. It is a formality of modern rationality that is nonetheless recalled in even the most cynical of electoral rituals. But it is at work throughout society in an underground fashion since once one claims to represent the general will one can only persuade and mobilize on the basis of a claim to legitimacy that is itself *open to criticism*. This formality of the modern juridical relation – which I have pointed to in the conjunction of the three dimensions of contractuality – is present in statist communist society. And official discourse, presiding over the rites of society, cannot but awaken a sublimated memory of this when it brings to mind the founding myth of radical emancipation. This formality remains formal in the same sense as certain freedoms remain formal within capitalism. But it is active and decisive in the emergence of the new gravedigger, of this new and immense class of workers, incomparably better gathered together by the planned economy with its giant industrial complexes, its economic machines in which the smallest jammed cog stops the whole thing. This class has to reclaim what it has been denied, the immediate use of its freedom to contract, to engage with others only on a voluntary basis. It can only turn against the class that has hitherto ruled over it and conceive of the project of destroying that which had been the basis of that class's power: the framework of a planned society under the guidance of the party. (It should nevertheless be mentioned that the party was also a venue for the playing out of social contradictions and for the marginal and confused expression of alternative points of view.) Once planning has been rejected, there remains the other means of organizing productive activity on a large scale, the market, in the established form of capitalism, of invading foreign capital, which comes rushing in. This forebodes the rising of a new association of workers in rebellion against this ascendancy who throw themselves into the arena of the circle of modernity demanding that their voice is heard at the centre, that measures are taken to ensure a substantial 'good life'.

The Transformation into Opposites

Such a (meta)structural circularity seems to contain and to condemn any emancipatory project. My claim is that if we wish to break out of this circle the strategic point to consider is none other than the linkage, characteristic of modern societies, between contractuality and domination. To do this I shall base myself on the Marxian theme of transformation into opposites.[2]

The priority of contractuality, contract as promise

One objection that has been raised – by André Tosel – against the metastructural theory of modernity is that although the theory brings together contract and domination it nevertheless gives precedence to the former, in such a way that the latter necessarily appears simply as an accident, just a perversion of the contract form which is thus picked out in the final analysis as the paradigm of modernity itself. Such an 'ordering of reasons' would inevitably give rise to an idyllic picture of modern societies. It might be more appropriate, it is suggested, to adopt a realist way of looking at the problem which would first examine the relations of domination that constitute our societies before going on to examine the pseudo-contractual forms in which they present themselves, the real forms of contractuality that another relationship of forces could more or less impose on them, or better those which a revolutionary subversion could substitute for them.

I should like to reply to this objection and justify my sequential ordering, by seeking to give a rigorous sense to the idea put forward by Marx of 'the transformation into opposites'. It is not accidental that he follows such an order in *Capital*. It is just that, as we have seen, the starting point of his analysis remains one-sided and so he describes this inversion inadequately. My thesis is that contractuality 'changes itself into its opposite' in so far as the metastructure develops into class structures. This does not occur according to a historical sequence, because the metastructure is only posited in the structures themselves, but rather in the systemic constitutive process of modernity. At this primordial level, the correct theoretical progression cannot thus consist in first setting out an existent order of domination and then an ideological form which is its mask, even if approaches of this type are justified at some later stage of analysis. First of all one must set forth the contractual (metastructural) form; the class relation which posits it can only be conceived of as its 'inversion'. Modern society posits itself through inverting the principle which it posits: in other words, it is built on a broken promise, on a covenant that is repressed.

The form of the promise

We can readdress the problem by looking at the problem of *property* in the modern era. The commodity relation presupposes reciprocal recognition by each of the property of the other. But this mutual recognition of property can only take place on the basis of a 'contractual' recognition of the conditions of appropriation. As Kant tells us, property is only provisional in nature so long as the social contract is not made, by the social contract it becomes 'peremptory'.[3] As a good liberal he can imagine only that the social contract can do nothing other than ratify the market order of exchange. But the centre defined by the social contract can, as I have said, will democratically and hence legitimately something other than the basic market relation. It can for example decide that certain types of exchange, those giving rise to profit, shall be liable to taxation, or that certain activities (of which we cannot draw up an exhaustive list *a priori*) shall be democratically managed from the centre. It is the market relation itself that *wills* this in its metastructural relationship to a democratic statist relation. It is here that we can see both how far-sighted Tocqueville was when he stressed the affinity between market relations and democracy and how shortsighted he was not to notice that democracy can will quite the opposite of the market relation. It is actually in this *critical connection* between the two relations – the interindividual and the statist – an interconnection through which they find themselves in the situation of mutual self-criticism – that modern society proclaims that it is not an order subject to *laws* (those of the market or of rational administration) but is rather capable of giving *rules* to itself. In this manner the market relation, in so far as it is metastructurally linked to the relation of centricity, defines property by an essential weakening of possession in that it introduces a reference to democratic legitimation. More exactly, modern property as metastructurally defined is vulnerable to social criticism. It is nothing but a criticizable pretension to property. And correlatively, the same goes for collective appropriation from the centre which must *give an account for* any limitation placed upon free contractuality between individuals. It is neither accidental nor simply fraudulent that modern constitutions *affirm* democratic principles. And the violence of revolutions feeds upon the disappointment engendered by a broken promise.

It still has to be demonstrated that if there is contractuality only through the *conflict between* the generalized interindividual relation and the relation of centricity, that is to say at the moment when each is subject to the criticism of the other, this criticism itself presupposes the intervention of the third metastructural dimension, associativity. This is also to say that this criticism only becomes actual through a class struggle. But for the moment let us stay with the form of the promise, which is that of contractuality.

The inversion

The inversion of contractuality into its opposite takes place in the very transition from the metastructure to the structures. This inversion is in no way one that occurs later in time, because it is only structures that posit the metastructure. But *there is* an inversion, and it is not the structures which invert themselves into the metastructure. The inversion is the failure to keep the metastructural promise. Because the social contract has a forward-looking form: it is a covenant. And its content is the promise of a congruence between interindividual contractuality and the contractuality of the centre. The inversion takes place in the autonomization of those relations. This autonomization, by distancing each of these relations from the other, from their reciprocal critique, leads them to take on a natural character. Capitalist commodity property tends to promote a central order which treats the rules governing the market as laws of nature, which makes relations of production appear as relations of exchange and the market as a natural-rational order. Collective appropriation by the bureaucratic class represents the alternative naturalistic thesis, that of planned administration. In different ways these two effects are mixed together in Western societies. The inversion is nothing other than the autonomization of the polar opposite forms of productive social reason, an autonomization through which they take on an apparently natural character and through which their rationality becomes instrumentalized. From being the basis of rules, they become the basis of laws. The instrumentality of the market gives proprietors the ability to contract using the full power of their property and through this to exploit and accumulate. The instrumentality of the plan deploys in an unlimited fashion a network that knows only means and ends, where work itself tends to be nothing but the means to its end, and the worker the means to his work. In this sense, if market and plan are *antinomic* (in that they constitute two alternative rules) and if the choice between the two has stamped societies which have defined themselves as mutually *antagonistic*, they are for all that not in the least bit *contradictory*. The masters of the market are perfectly capable of organizing themselves, and the masters of the plan or of adminstration can orient themselves in the mafia-like space of a political market (to canvass just one of the possibilities).

To refer to Habermas's analysis, I would say that it is the 'steering media' themselves – or at least what he understands as such – that form the basis for class relations.[4] I mean by this that it is their basic disjunction (which does not exclude a secondary connection, that is to say their combination) that is the foundation of the inversion. When the market proclaims itself as a 'law', a law of economics, it rejects at the same time as it presupposes the central ground of its legitimation which alone could legitimize the rule according to which the totality of production relations are to be handled according to contractuality between possessive individuals. It rejects this by subordinating it to the natural character of a 'law' which as such, as supposedly natural, can provide no legitimation. It is in the separation of the polar forms that they become instrumentalized, through which they become the governing principles of class societies. In their separation, these forms proclaim themselves uncritically as being natural-rational in character. It is only in their *intersection* that their property of being a claim that is open to criticism, of being a pact and a promise, becomes clear.

The association as subject

But this 'critical' intersection is not to be understood as a simple *combination* of market and plan. Whether we understand this as a manifestation of productive rationality or as the articulation of class relations, it does not amount to an inversion. And it is now to the third term, the association, that the analysis must turn.

It is no accident that all revolutionary thought has turned to the search for an 'association of workers'. It seems as if the conditions for an overturning of the 'transformation of freedom into its opposite' could only emerge from the association of the exploited in a struggle against exploitation and domination. It is the associated power of the modern working class – the slow development of civil society coupled with outbreaks of mass action – that has been able under capitalism, to a certain extent and necessitating certain compromises, to put in question the 'law' of the market, to make it appear like the rule of a game that one can choose to accept or not, that one can modify and modify again in the conditions of its application, and that one can in principle fit into a scheme that is wider than the market itself and defines objectives, stages, and means. Only the power of the association can effectively articulate plan and market in a critical manner and by doing this install some authentically contractual element.

It nonetheless remains to be clarified why, within which limits, and in what relationship with the real movement of modern society, the 'association', understood in its most general sense (and exemplified by self-management and direct democracy) constitutes the model for an alternative. In other words, under what conditions can the associative logic of the workers' movement be taken up, rectified and enlarged.

My suggestion is that one cannot answer this question unless one understands that the association is not a special type of contractuality but a *moment* of contractuality.[5] Contractuality cannot in fact be thought of as a *genus* of relation, which can be decomposed into three *species*, which would be interindividuality, associativity and centricity. It is rather the contradictory articulation of these three moments, which are metastructural, hence also structural, operators. The association, which is only one dimension of the contractuality-domination complex, cannot be understood as a superior form of contract.

The association is thus not innocence incarnate. Not only does it take its place in the framework of global society, and therefore of the double polarity of its rational order (market and plan); not only can it be mobilized in the service of the dominant interests who enjoy the same ability to associate as anyone else; but even from the standpoint of those who associate in struggle against the effect of domination or exploitation inherent in market or centralized social forms, the limitations of association soon become apparent. As soon as it reaches a certain level, it calls on the same polar forms found in large-scale organization: the associated persons come to an organic division of tasks and to the internalization of market norms. If one considers that the stakes of social life are of ever greater dimensions, one grasps the weaknesses and contradictions that are attached to the form of associativity.

The goal of socialism cannot be to substitute the association for the forms of interindividual and central contractuality, those of the market and plan, for these are demanded by the complexity of large-scale social life. Rather, it must be to submit these forms to the critique of the associated multitudes. It is all very well to develop forms such as 'self management' and 'direct democracy' as far as possible, but this must be done in full consciousness of the intimate relations that obtain between the three forms of contractuality and the forms of domination that are attached to them.

But what, then, is the secret of the association and why has it been, under whatever name, the privileged reference point of revolutionary thought? The explanation can only be found in the fact that it defines itself – at least so long as it is open to all without disbarment – in the promise to remain within the immediate realm of dialogue; that is to say, it pledges to exclude by definition the development-inversion inherent in the two other forms, by which the contractual relation is transformed into an antagonistic and stratified relation of property and power.

The basis of a social discourse that claims no authority beyond itself is nothing other than that which can give it social coherence, in other words the reasoned agreement of those who communicate. But this discourse can only form the basis for an effective practice if, at the same time as it argues over particular situations, it defines the principles according to which discussion ceases and action begins. Discourse ethics cannot but refer back to a theory of principles.

It remains to be seen what a theory of principles has to be like to be a political theory. If we define it by the contractual reference point, by what is acceptable according to the relevant parties, its horizon is that of the *present*. It cannot take the form of a utopia, as ultimately happens in Rawls's theory, which seeks a final coherence in the assurance of an equilibrium, in the ability of a 'well-ordered society' to reproduce itself as such, because it generates in each person a disposition to support it. The objective of a contractual theory cannot be the definition of an ideal point which others – who are not around today to debate and contract with us – must eventually reach. Its aim is rather a transformative practice that can be demanded here and now in the light of claims that can be accepted as such by all our contemporaries. The purpose of a contractual theory is thus to formulate both the critique of actually existing forms of domination and also the *strategic* principles leading to their abolition. Far from confining action within the space of discourse, this theory conjectures that the discursive link is already broken, that the discursive relation is 'transformed into its opposite', and that the contractual relation can only be reconstituted through a breach of the established order. But this breach has to occur according to strategic principles that all can accept, which is to say, that are in themselves indisputable.

For this reason the general principle of a contractual theory takes the form of a 'principle of least difference' or of 'maximal power'; not in the Rawlsian sense of an acceptable redistribution (for this is at any rate what the other components of Rawlsian discourse tend to restrict his second principle to), but in the most general sense of the requirements for a life characterized by maximal self-realization: *no difference* (of power, wealth, income etc.) *is tolerable unless it can be shown that it is of benefit to those who have least*. By 'those who have least' is meant the mass of exploited and oppressed. The 'viewpoint' of contract theory is the viewpoint of this multitude, which it alone can formulate and which it does indeed formulate when it comes to define a genuinely transformative strategy which goes as far as it is possible to go (in other words to the point where revolutionary intention turns into impotence). To grasp that this principle is a principle of justice, it is necessary to see that there is no legitimacy for power or property outside of contractual agreement on the forms of power and property. To grasp that it is a principle of politics, it must be seen that it carries with it, immanently, an efficiency or rationality clause, which makes it into a strategic axiom (this clause must not be understood as defining Pareto optimum if serious confusion is to be avoided). It both excludes courses of action that lead to failure and defines a norm of transformative intervention.

Such a principle has no utopian content; it refers only to the present situation and to its transformation. It is the principle which constitutes the association as contractual form of the movement. It delimits the political concept of revolutionary action. One can view it as the *an-archic* principle because it defines the conditions of non-subjugation.

One last point stands in need of clarification. It has been suggested to me (by Jean-Pierre Cotten) that when I put forward the paradigm of the association together with a difference principle, one is entitled to object that, under the guise of a union of the disadvantaged, what we have is a purely moral approach to politics. The problematic of the 'proletarian outlook' had at least some sociological foundation; it was based on the characteristics of a determinate historical situation, that of heavy industry, the framework for the emergence of a social force that was certainly fragile, contradictory and ephemeral, but was empirically real. To attempt to resurrect this problematic by giving it the more general form of the viewpoint of the disadvantaged is surely just to substitute a metaphysical entity for what was once something much more definite.

I would reply to this that it is inappropriate to oppose to my idea the difference between a historical-systemic approach (such as the 'proletarian' one) and moral argument (such as the 'disadvantaged' one). For I am not putting a moral group, deduced from political principles, in the place of a social group. The 'disadvantage' of which I speak is not ordained by fate but by the dynamics of modern class structures. It is exploitation that produces the antipode of those who have least – the exploited and oppressed. The metastructural approach only seeks to provide a conception that is more general and more dialectical than the one Marx left to us. It remains to be explained why and to what degree modern societies *tend* to produce and reproduce the multitude – in constantly renewed forms – *both* as oppressed-exploited *and also* as capable of associating together for a struggle against this state of affairs (in other words, as able to make the principle stated above the maxim of its practice).

Clearly only the exploration of the forms that the production process now takes, with all its cultural, scientific, organizational, ethical, sexual and geopolitical implications – forms which entirely remodel the social sphere – is able to determine the importance and configuration of these new (potentially or actually associated) social subjects. My demonstration aims just to show the most general (and decisive) conditions of the emergence of such subjects: to establish the conceptual interdependence of social reality and right in modernity. The maxim of the association of the multitude described above represents the interconnection of a political with a socio-historical idea. Liberty-equality is something that is always already metastructurally promised to the exploited and oppressed multitude within the modern system. They are thus always already justified in demanding it, with all the potential force they have as an associated multitude, where that associativity is inseparable from the other dimensions of contractuality and is always also faced with the structural dangers (class implications) which attach to contractuality. Social forces and entities only appear as structural relations in the context of the metastructure, which implies in its terms the question of right. The movement by which the dominated-exploited constitute themselves as an associated actor can be adequately conceptualized only in light of the metastructural–structural articulation of right and power.

Beyond Modernity, State and Politics

A further point remains: we need to think beyond modernity, which also implies thinking beyond 'socialism' in the sense intended by Marx when he refers to 'communism' in the *Critique of the Gotha Programme*. The systemic and dialectical approach to modernity, which was indispensable as a preamble to this consideration, leads us in turn to situate it between two others, of which one falls short of and one goes beyond Marx's perspective. I will therefore conclude by stating schematically three considerations that have the aim of marking the limits of application of the theory here proposed.

1. The first of these concerns the inescapable emergence of a global 'superposed state',[6] a structural–metastructural form unifying human society in its entirety. There is effectively a tendency – especially marked in the case of externalities – for the processes of production to be less and less assignable to territories which particular states can lay claim to. The planetary environment cannot but gradually take on the appearance of the global inheritance of humanity, the basis for a universal contractuality-domination. The Marxist theoreticians of the *world-system* have described perfectly the formation of a global capitalist system with its linkages between centres and peripheries. But from the moment that the 'development of the productive forces' tends to establish – according to a very long-term process of which the effects are nevertheless already perceptible – a statist world 'centricity', things get complicated. It is true that the imperial powers of the centre try, and succeed, in making this their own. They thus strengthen and aggravate their domination by the seizure of a planetary institutional order whose character is genuinely *statist* in character (or better, 'superposed statist', a concept that I oppose both to 'supra-statist' and to 'super-statist', because the superposed-statist form caps rather than replaces statist forms). However, they only do this whilst entangling themselves in a dynamic that overwhelms them. For the dynamic of the 'world capitalist system' as such, that of the domination of the peripheral nation-states by those of the centre, has a *pluri-statist* basis, which the new course of development bolsters but at the same time also contradicts. In this planetary space with

a tendency towards unity we again encounter 'modern' relations, this time in their extreme manifestation: here the metastructural–structural articulation first contained within the limits of the nation-state and the world-systemic configuration is unfurled to its full extent. All the representations emerge together: pact, promise, inversion, market and bureaucratic domination, a field open for association. The projects of 'emancipation' that were products of the labour and democratic movement, swept aside at the same time as the nation-states that carried them, find there their ultimate realm. Here is what we may call 'ultra-modernity'.

2. The second thesis concerns the question of a stage beyond modernity: 'communism' beyond socialism. In the sense in which Marx conceived it, this would be a society no longer bound by the necessity of work. The question of 'communism' cannot, it seems to me, be posed except on the basis that forms the historical bedrock of the (meta)structural matrix of modernity, namely the 'work-and-labour' form, the core of the modern relation of contractuality-domination. Whilst it is proper to challenge the 'mode of production' approach, in so far as it tends to characterize each epoch primarily by an economic form, we must nonetheless recognize that it is a 'work-and-labour' form that constitutes the foundation of this modern metastructural matrix. It is certainly this that determines the constitutive plan–market link, and hence the 'structural' implications of these types in terms of appropriation and domination (the way they bring particular social classes into being). But it is also implicated in the liberatory reversals of these states of affairs. Today, there is undoubtedly a question hanging over the 'work-and-labour' form, and this problem has two aspects.

The first aspect has to do with the centrality of work in human activity. Not that work is diminishing in importance: on the contrary, its growing power to change the fate of the human race ever more quickly is manifest. But the coincidence of the growth of productivity with the necessity (imposed by the fragility of the environment) to impose limits on production means that work is losing the organizing role that it has hitherto played in human sociality. It has already become 'scarce' in the sense that whilst the means of production are more and more the object of monopolistic appropriation, the vast majority of human beings can no longer find a role in an efficient system of production. This 'modern' type of scarcity fits into a post-modern scarcity which has to do with the fact that human activity is going to have to turn to objectives other than production. From that point on, the matrix of modernity in the form of plan–market link (with all that goes along with that on the metastructural and structural levels) starts to lose its pregnancy, and all the dimensions of human sociality can start to throw off its yoke.

The second aspect concerns the fact that productive labour, in its most advanced form, which is that of scientific research, tends itself to escape from this plan–market matrix as a general scheme of rational organization. Scientific activity develops as a sphere of communication, of the inappropriable, of unforeseeable development. It calls into being a new type of associative subject.

These questions, those of post-modernity, in other words of 'communism' in the higher sense of that term, are thus already our questions. The analysis put forward here simply aims to show that they can only be correctly put if one has traversed the theory of modernity.

3. The third consideration involves going beyond politics. The paradigm of contractuality defines the sphere of political ethics and, in this sense, the sphere of politics itself. But one contracts only with one's contemporaries, and this remains so even if one conceives of contractuality as a structural given and not as tied to some particular event. Yet our action upon the world determines the ecological fate of a future humanity that is not here now to contract with us. Our practice thus finds itself confronted by a standard that is not a political one, by another imperative, which we can call that of 'morality'. Both of these elements conspire together: the political project as a project of emancipation, as a strategic project, also has its place within a long stretch of time. At the same time, like two gazes focused on different distances, they can seem to be unaware of one another's objectives, because if the temporal basis of politics is revolutionary urgency, that of morality is none other than the aspiration to the interminable. If there is nonetheless a collusion between them it is because morality contains right within it, and not vice versa. The political is not the last word in wisdom.

Notes

1. My aim is to present the general themes of my *Théorie de la modernité suivi de Marx et le marché*, Paris: Presses Universitaires de France, 1990. It should be understood that on the one hand I am here using some general formulations that are to be found in a similar form in that work and on the other that this new presentation of the ideas remains elliptical concerning points that are there given a more detailed exposition. I shall try here to improve the presentation of some important elements that were less clearly expressed in my earlier writings.

2. Toshio Yamada has provided an excellent exposition of this question in his article 'La théorie de Marx sur le renversement de la loi d'appropriation', *Economic Review* (Osaka) no. 20, 1985, pp. 39–45. The use that I make here of the concept of inversion is based on the reinterpretation of the Marxian theory of the market-capital link in *Que Faire du Capital?*, Paris: Klincksiek, 1985. It was only in my most recent book, *Théorie de la modernité* that I could give this the dialectical form that a general theory of modernity calls for.

3. Immanuel Kant, *The Metaphysical Elements of Justice*, trans. John Ladd, New York: Macmillan, 1965, p. 66.

4. For Habermas's concept of 'steering media', see his *The Theory of Communicative Action Volume 2: The Critique of Functionalist Reason*, Cambridge: Polity, 1987.

5. See my 'Pour un contractualisme révolutionnaire', in J. Bidet et J. Texier eds., *L'idée de socialisme a-t-elle un avenir?*, Paris: Presses Universitaires de France, 1992

6. See my 'Demain, le sur-Etat', in 'Ethique et politique', *Actuel Marx*, no. 11, Paris: Presses Universitaires de France, 1991.

8

Socialism and Modern Times
Alex Callinicos

The concept of modernity has been at the centre of intellectual discussion for the past decade or so. In part this has been because of the silly idea current that we live in a 'postmodern' epoch.[1] The stakes of this debate have, however, been considerably raised by the political upheavals of 1989–91 – the revolutions in Eastern Europe and the disintegration of the Soviet Union. The most widely cited interpretation of the disappearance of 'actually existing socialism' – Francis Fukuyama's 'The End of History?' – amounts to an idiosyncratic, right-Hegelian version of postmodernism, in which the triumph of liberal capitalism marks the culmination of modernity, ushering in times when the motor of change will no longer be epoch-making struggles between world-historic ideologies but differences of taste and technique. Those unwilling to accept that the best humankind has to look forward to is a global version of Orange County have, among other things, to come up with a better theory of modernity, one which captures its nature and trajectory more accurately than either Fukuyama or the postmodernists.

Paradoxically Marx has been the source of the most influential ostensive definition of modernity. In a famous passage of the *Manifesto* he writes:

> Constant revolutionizing of production, uninterrupted disturbance of all social conditions, everlasting uncertainty and agitation distinguish the bourgeois epoch from all earlier ones. All fixed, fast-frozen relations, with their train of ancient and venerable prejudices and opinions, are swept away, all new-formed ones become antiquated before they can ossify. All that is solid melts into air, all that is holy is profaned, and man is at last compelled to face with sober senses, his real conditions of life, and his relations with his kind.[2]

I say 'paradoxically' because Marx himself has no concept of modernity distinct from that of the capitalist mode of production. In the *Manifesto* passage just quoted he is seeking to characterize the 'bourgeois epoch'. Even when Marx does actually refer to modernity, he typically equates it with capitalism.[3] Perry Anderson is thus being strictly faithful to Marx when he concludes an important discussion of modernism by declaring: 'The vocation of a socialist revolution ... would be neither to prolong nor to fulfil modernity, but to abolish it.'[4] Others find this equation of capitalism and modernity less convincing. Notable among them is Jacques Bidet, who laments that 'Marx has thus deprived us of "modernity", he has rendered this nevertheless indispensable concept unthinkable'.[5] Bidet is co-editor of *Actuel Marx*, a journal which since its inception in 1987 has sought to carry on the Marxist tradition through a dialogue among socialist intellectuals in Europe and North America, and between theoretical traditions – for example that stemming from Althusser, with which some members of its editorial committee were associated, and the analytical Marxism which emerged in the English-speaking world in the late 1970s – not noted in the past for communicating much. A receptiveness to divergent intellectual currents is one striking feature of Bidet's major recent work *Théorie de la modernité*. Here he sets out to show, against Marx and Anderson, that 'revolutionary action is to take place *in* this world of modernity' (275). The account of modernity Bidet develops repays the most serious critical attention: such I seek to give it in what follows.

On Bidet's argument capitalism and communism are to be seen as variants of something more fundamental, namely modernity. Probably the most influential reason recommending such an approach is the coexistence in the contemporary world of societies sharing many properties, some of which are indisputably capitalist, others of which until recently called themselves socialist. (Bidet tends, most unfortunately, to call the latter 'communist' or 'historical communist' societies, though, as Rossana Rossanda observes, 'even the most shameless leaders didn't dare talk of "realized" communism';[6] I prefer to call the societies in question 'Stalinist', on the understanding that 'Stalinism' here refers, not to the dictatorship of a particular individual, but to a system in which economic, political and cultural power is concentrated in the hands of a narrow social layer, the *nomenklatura*, ruling through its control of the fused party-state apparatuses.) Marx's vision of a world beyond capitalist modernity seems to have gone badly awry. Should we not therefore be exploring the features societies share in common beyond the apparent differences in their relations of production?

But how are we to conceptualize modernity? Different approaches abound, but it is possible to impose some kind of classification on them. The one I use, rather to my surprise, recalls Lenin's division of the sources of Marxism into German classical philosophy, British political economy, and French socialism. There are, in the first place, *philosophical* approaches to modernity, which treat modernization as a process of rationalization. Max Weber is of course the key figure here, but we have seen in recent years Habermas's attempt to formulate a much broader conception of rationality than Weber's instrumental reason, one rooted in the communicative structures of language and realized only selectively and therefore in a distorted form under capitalism.[7] Second, there are *sociological* treatments of modernity, that seek to analyse the socio-economic structures which distinguish it from earlier phases of human history. Talcott Parsons and his followers represent the most influential variant of this approach, but over the past decade or so Anthony Giddens has sought to provide an account of the institutional structures of modernity which avoids the pitfalls of functionalism and evolutionism.[8] There are, finally, *political* theories of modernity. Thus a number of contemporary French theorists have made Tocqueville's conception of democratic individualism the leitmotiv of an analysis of modern societies. The writings of Gilles Lipovetsky are perhaps the best known of such attempts.[9]

Now Bidet explicitly aligns himself with the first of these approaches, speaking of the 'connivance' between his book and 'the *démarche* of Weber (taken up again by Habermas), which seeks to uncover a general form of modernity, a (contradictory) form at once of reason and of society' (49). But the substance of his account is in fact much closer to the (French) political school. Bidet defines modernity fundamentally in terms of 'contractuality', a concept that must be understood to refer both to 'interindividual' agreements such as the labour contract between capitalist and worker and to the social contract through which states acquire their legitimacy. Thus, if, as Bidet says, his book 'seeks its inspiration in a certain liberalism nearly as much as in Marxism' (7), it is less the liberal realism of Tocqueville than the contractualist tradition whose most important contemporary exponent is John Rawls. *Théorie de la modernité* is more than anything else a synthesis of Marx and Rawls.

The critical step in this remarkable exercise is that of conceiving modernity as a 'general matrix', 'the metastructure subjacent to historical capitalism and communism alike, as well as to intermediary figures. This metastructural form, which first appears only as the "presupposition of capitalism", reveals to analysis a larger ensemble of possibilities' (50). Modernity must be understood as 'a network of contractuality and domination' (82), organized along three dimensions – interindividuality, centricity and associativity. Interindividuality is the relationship constitutive of a market economy, where the production and distribution of goods are interwoven with contracts between individual actors. But 'there is no commercial space without a central power which protects it, which assures each partner that the others cannot escape from engagements' (52). Moreover: 'Between interindividuality and centricity arises a third determination. If one can contract with someone, one can also contract with someone else, with others. The structure of the market is as much associative as it is interindividualist' (53). Contractual relationships may thus be extended to allow the formation of associations pursuing a shared interest.

The three determinations of modernity – interindividuality, centricity and associativity – are of co-equal importance, Bidet insists. Their relationship is one of mutual implication: he thus rejects a base–superstructure model in which the first would presumably have explanatory priority over the other two (see, for example, 50). They form a '[c]oherent whole, unified by an immanent logic. But a whole which is also the general matrix of social contradiction in modernity' (50). This matrix informs 'historical communism' as much as it does capitalism. The Stalinist command economy 'produces abstract man' as the subject of the plan as surely as capitalism involves a similar conception of human nature. The existence of a labour market in the Stalinist countries is no mere 'capitalist survival', nor the democratic form of their constitutions simple hypocrisy: rather, they indicate the structural features common to capitalism and to 'historical communism' (82–94). Both are 'two figures of the same modernity', belonging '[t]o the same space, that is to say the same present, which no placing in historical perspective, [and] laying out stages and goal, can permit us to evade' (82).

Neither capitalism nor 'historical communism' is a distinct mode of production with its own contradictions and laws of motion such that one necessarily precedes the other. Both rather instantiate the same 'contradiction of modernity': 'The peculiarity of commodity relations is to suppose a centre. The peculiarity of the centre is to be liable to investment, through the mediation of associativity, by the forces implicated in the market' (79). The 'dialectic of modernity' to which this contradiction gives rise does not take the form of the kind of spiral movement projected by Hegel and Marx in which, along an albeit tortuous path, more advanced social formations replace backward ones. On the contrary, it describes a circle. Bidet outlines a cycle, in which decentralized market relations generate a state which is invested by capital; one form of associativity gives rise to another, as working-class organization develops in reaction to bourgeois domination; the pressure of the labour movement then leads to increasing state regulation of the market; the limit-point of this process is represented by communism, the abolition of the market to the benefit of another form of associativity, the *nomenklatura*; this regime in turn evokes a popular reaction, which now demands the restoration of the market; and then the cycle starts again (297–8).

Bidet is rather equivocal about the philosophical implications of this cycle. In *Théorie de la modernité* he dissociates it from a cyclical view of history, declaring: 'The circle thus described is simply that which "goes round" [*fait le tour*] the limit-conditions of modernity' (298). Elsewhere he calls it a 'fable which helps us to get rid of the progressist philosophy of history ... and which reactivates a form of cyclical thought which we have neglected too long'.[10] Whichever formulation represents Bidet's settled views, we are, I think, supposed to take the 'fable' quite seriously: it is, after all, a stylized representation of the past 150 years of European history. Its significance at the very least is that we must treat contemporary social formations as alternatives rather than as stages in a succession of modes of production. Bidet thus measures his distance from Marxism. The 'central thesis' of the 'metaMarxism' he espouses is 'to substitute for the sequence capitalism–communism ... the representation of a meta-structural field which defines the limit-conditions in which "structural" figures such as capitalism and communism can historically develop' (301).

As the term suggests, Bidet's 'metaMarxism' involves the incorporation of Marxism into 'a larger theoretical space' (30). The 'transformation' of Marxism

(237) thereby entailed goes beyond the considerable revision of Marx's theory of history outlined above. Much of the book is devoted to a detailed critique of *Capital*. Drawing on his earlier study, *Que faire du 'Capital'?*, Bidet argues that Marx, in the successive drafts of *Capital*, gropes toward without ever attaining the essential distinction between the market as part of the 'metastructure' presupposed by capitalism and the capitalist mode of production proper. I discuss this argument at length below: of principal relevance here is its implication that any feasible socialist project cannot seek to abolish the market. But Bidet does not simply wish to espouse a conventional market socialism. For him, 'market and plan are *rules*, tendentially submitted to choice. The possibility of these rules, contrary to one another, is in fact inscribed in the matrix of modernity, which defines this double polarity' (107–8). Given that this matrix necessarily combines contractuality and domination, Bidet's chief preoccupation is 'to establish under what conditions the relations proper to modernity can free themselves from this element of domination' (95).

Formulating the required 'norms of contractuality' involves giving a 'radical reading' to Rawls's two principles of justice (124–38). The first, which in Rawls's hands asserts the priority of the traditional liberal freedoms over other considerations, is transformed into Étienne Balibar's 'proposition of equaliberty', according to which the historical conditions for the establishment of both liberty and equality are identical.[11] The second, Rawls's famous Difference Principle, according to which inequalities can be justified only if they benefit the worst-off members of society, is expanded to include 'not only wealth and income, social and economic positions, but also the hierarchical element of political institutions' (130). Thus while in Rawls's original version 'the economy escaped … political jurisdiction', now, after Bidet's modifications, '[t]he economy must be subordinated to elected institutions which will assure equaliberty, and determine a plan/market articulation consistent with the second principle' (131–2). The scope of Bidet's 'metaMarxism' thus becomes clear: it consists in 'the integration of Marxism in a "social theory" of modernity and a "political philosophy" of socialism as contractualism' (300–301).

The foregoing is, of necessity, a brief and inadequate summary of a rich, complex and subtle book. Although I discuss (and even sometimes praise) parts of the book below, I should first make clear my admiration for the work as a whole. It offers a challenging and ambitious reinterpretation of both Marxism and modernity. It displays the best of what one might call the Althusserian heritage in its detailed, theoretically rigorous appreciation of *Capital* and its drafts, but is open to other intellectual traditions, notably the Frankfurt School and analytical philosophy. Much of the book is of great value irrespective of whether one regards its overall argument as valid: the exposition and critique of Habermas's theory of modernity (96–124) are especially illuminating. Admiration, however, does not imply agreement. I am not persuaded by Bidet's proposed 'metaMarxism'. In what follows I explain why. Like a good Marxist, I proceed from abstract considerations to more concrete ones.

In the first place, what precisely is this 'metastructure' of modernity which subtends specific social formations? Bidet at one point calls it 'a field of possibilities' (273); elsewhere, as we have seen, he talks of it defining the 'limit-conditions' of modern societies (e.g. 301). But how exactly does the metastructure perform this role? The closest we get to an answer is in Bidet's critical discussion of Marx's treatment in *Capital* of the relation between the market and capitalism. Bidet argues that Marx does not sufficiently appreciate the priority of the market over capitalism: 'capitalist relations logically presuppose commodity relations. Not the inverse' (162). Now whatever one thinks of Bidet's claim that the market is dissociable from capitalism, the relationship of presupposition postulated here is not especially difficult to understand. Uncontroversially capitalism involves both a labour market and competition between capitals. Since it cannot exist without them, it is easy enough to see how in this case the market sets limits to the functioning of capitalism. But how does it do so in the case of other kinds of modern societies where, Bidet concedes, the market may play a much smaller part? More generally, how can the metastructure, as a 'matrix of possibilities', constrain actual societies? One does not have to share Quine's nominalist zeal for banning any talk of possible worlds to be puzzled about how a set of possibilities can have causal powers. In seeking to generalize from a (corrected) account of Marx's treatment of the relationship between commodity and capitalist relations, Bidet does not seem sufficiently to have attended to the problems involved in transforming definite social structures into an etiolated matrix of possibilities.

My first criticism, then, concerns the status of Bidet's conception of modernity. The second focuses on its content. Bidet's is a contractualist theory of modernity. The 'interindividual' relationships created by the contracts struck between private actors on the market are constitutive of modernity; these relationships then generate (logically at any rate) the state as the centre required for the functioning of any contractual order and the dense network of associations involved in civil society. Now there seems to be a good case for having some kind of theory of modernity encompassing a larger class of societies than those falling under the concept of the capitalist mode of production. Quite aside from whatever we have to say about no-longer-existing socialism, it seems to me that even a society which fully meets Marx's requirements for the higher state of communism would nevertheless have in common with capitalist societies features differentiating them from all earlier social formations. To that extent, Bidet's complaint against Marx that he 'historicizes the very structure of modernity' (293) by equating it with capitalism is valid. What puzzles me is why contractualism should be thought of as the best way of conceptualizing the features common to all modern societies.

Let me develop this point by invoking another very recent treatment of modernity, that by Giddens in his *Consequences of Modernity*. Giddens gives especial attention to the phenomenon of 'disembedding', that is, 'the "lifting-out" of social relations from local contexts of interaction and their restructuring across indefinite spans of time–space'. One dimension of disembedding that particularly interests Giddens is that it requires us to place our trust, not so much in persons or in social groups, but in what he calls 'expert systems', that is, 'systems of technical accomplishment or professional expertise that organize large areas of the material and social environments in which we live today'. An air passenger, for example, is involved in what Giddens calls a 'faceless commitment': she entrusts her life to air crew, traffic controllers and ground staff with whom she is unacquainted and of whose knowledge she is almost certainly largely ignorant.[12] Now whatever reservations one may have about Giddens's larger social theory (mine are considerable[13]), he has here identified a relationship which all modern societies share and which is connected to other features – for example, their distinctive relation to nature and their involvement in a set of global connections. By comparison with this kind of analysis, Bidet's account seems like a deduction from arbitrarily chosen premises.

It might in fact be better to treat Bidet's contractualism less as an analysis of modernity than as an exposition of a political philosophy. One is indeed given the impression that his positive theory of modernity is strongly constrained by normative considerations. Bidet does try to distinguish between 'is' and 'ought' at the same time as he grounds both in the 'metastructure'. Thus: 'the "norms of contractuality" ... enunciate the conditions of legitimate universalization of the relations which these categories designate, the powerful and legitimate form of the relations inherent in the matrix of modernity and of their articulation' (123). Or again: 'they must designate an ought-to-be [*devoir-être*], but in making it appear as a possibility of being itself' (123). Note that once again the category of possibility is being put to work, this time as the link between the metastructure and the normative order appropriate to it. Once again, the invocation of the possible doesn't seem to help much. If the metastructure is a set of possibilities, on what ethical grounds are we to select one from among them? If ought implies can, can does not imply ought.

The reason why no clear account is given of the relationship between the analytical and ethical dimensions of Bidet's theory of modernity is, I think, that they are hopelessly intermingled from the start. Consider, for example, this sentence, part of Bidet's defence of contractualism against Hegel's criticisms: 'The rational need to constitute a political state is not of another nature from the need to have with another (individual) a contractual relation, for it is the condition of it' (295). A couple of sentences on he elaborates on this claim: there is 'no conceivable contractual order among individuals if it is not assured by a central will, which is only central because it supposedly represents the ensemble of individual wills' (295). We have here a striking non-sequitur: granted that the security of contracts depends on the existence of a state to enforce them, why should this state derive its legitimacy from a social contract? A utilitarian might, for example, believe that stable contracts were necessary for welfare-maximization and treat this belief as one reason for supporting the existence of a state, while strongly rejecting the idea of a social contract as the basis of political obligation. Bidet here confuses the actual dependence of private contracts on the state with one particular theory of political legitimacy.

It seems to me that Bidet's socialist contractualism shapes his theory of modernity rather than being an ethical specification of it. The actual fit between modernity and political theory is, I think, much looser than he is prepared to concede. There is indeed a sense in which even capitalist modernity implies a far more egalitarian treatment of persons than any previous form of class society. The organization of exploitation through the market requires either the constitution of capitalist and worker as legal equals or, where this is not the case, the development of a specific ideology (usually some variant of racism) to justify this deviation from the norm. But this egalitarianism does not entail any specific political philosophy. Contractualism has long been locked in conflict with a powerful antagonist, utilitarianism, which is also committed to treating individuals as equals but does not attach the same priority to persons and their rights. This old struggle shows no sign of ending. There are, in addition, other contemporary theories of equality – for example those advanced by Ronald Dworkin and Amartya Sen – which cannot be categorized neatly as either contractualist or utilitarian.[14] Bidet's Balibarian reformulation of Rawls is best seen as one contender in the struggle both to capture and to radicalize modernity's egalitarian potential.

My third major disagreement with Bidet concerns his attempt to dissociate the market from capitalism. His argument involves a close reading of *Capital*. He traces the incomplete process of revision through which, in successive drafts, Marx moves from the dialectical form of exposition characteristic of the *Grundrisse*. That text treats the relationship between the market and capitalism as a conceptual one so that 'the market realizes its essence in capitalism' (67). The move, however, from commodity to capitalist relations in *Capital* Volume 1, involves not an 'analytical continuity, but ... a constructive intervention' (71): it is not the abstract logic of commodity circulation but the particular character of commodity labour-power which makes possible the self-expansion of capital. Consequently,

> it becomes impossible to consider capitalism as the unique and necessary development (at the logical level) of the market. The operator of the connection is 'labour-power' and the strategic question is that of its status as a 'commodity'. It is to the extent that this status is realized that one can truly talk of capitalism. (73)

This transition to a 'constructivist' mode of exposition (71) is, however, never fully achieved even in *Capital*, Bidet argues. The influence on Marx of Hegelian essentialism is reflected in particular in his treatment of the sphere of circulation as a secondary and phenomenal form, even though some of his most important arguments – for example, the formulation of the labour theory of value itself and the concept of relative surplus-value – depend on an account of competition which he either banishes to its official treatment in *Capital* Volume 3, or tacitly invokes at points in the exposition where he is supposed to be dealing with 'essential' class relationships in abstraction from the market (151–66).[15] From this reading Bidet draws two conclusions: first, that 'logically it would have been advisable to consider competition *at each level* of the exposition' of *Capital* (160); second, that the relationship between the market and capitalism which would emerge from this kind of rereading of Marx is one 'of two dissociable structures in the sense that the market could operate in a non-capitalist society' (161).

There is much to be said for this interpretation of *Capital*. Bidet, both in *Théorie de la modernité* and more fully in *Que faire du 'Capital'*, provides a clear and detailed examination of Marx's progressive retreat from Hegelian forms of reasoning which nevertheless even in *Capital* continue to shape his discourse. As an overall reading of Marx's economic manuscripts it would be hard to fault, and it could indeed be substantiated in cases which Bidet does not discuss – for example, the Hegelian structure of even the revised version of the opening chapter of *Capital* Volume 1, on the commodity.[16] Nevertheless, this interpretation does not support the second of the two conclusions Bidet draws from it, namely that 'the market could operate in a non-capitalist society'. In the first place, to reject the dialectical treatment of the relationship between the market and capitalism is merely to say that imagining one without the other does not entail a contradiction. This is a statement about a relationship between concepts; it says nothing about whether the market and capitalism actually *can* be dissociated in social reality. Very often precisely what scientific discourse does is to demonstrate that the referents of logically independent terms are in fact indissociable. Bidet's critique of the dialectical mode of exposition does not rule out that this might be the case with respect to the market and capitalism.

Adequately to address the question of their actual relationship would require some consideration of what is meant by the market here. Surprisingly, however, Bidet has little to say on this subject. His attempts to reconstruct Marxian economic theory develop one of the main themes of *Que faire du 'Capital'?*, namely the necessity, never fully grasped by Marx himself, of analysing the wage-relation as a political relationship (167–232).[17] Through a subtle and illuminating examination of the concept of the expenditure of labour-power, the use-value of this peculiar commodity, he is able to show how capitalist production, 'because it is expenditure of labour-power, is always also the social constraint of this expenditure, and the institutional and discursive regulation of this constraint' (217). This is an analysis which, as Bidet notes, has a close kinship to the approach of the Regulation School (Michel Aglietta, Alain Lipietz et al.) and indeed, he believes, can provide it with a 'foundation' (214). Precisely for that reason it suffers from a characteristic fault of the Regulation School, namely the failure properly to integrate an account of competition between capitals with that of the wage relation.[18]

The point can best be brought out by considering what is meant by the 'market'. Renato di Ruzza has rightly criticized the vagueness of much recent discussion of this concept.[19] When Marx treats the market and capitalism as indissociable, he plainly does not mean by the market the kind of long-distance and local trade which, as Polanyi pointed out, are to be found in many pre-capitalist societies.[20] He means, rather, generalized commodity production, where 'the product wholly assumes the form of a commodity only'.[21] Under these conditions, the market acts as the principal means of allocation of social labour to different branches of production and thereby determines which and in what measure human needs will be met. The market thus understood functions as a form of social compulsion. Thus, in his discussion of technological rents, that is, the super-profits made by capitals which by introducing some new technique are able to reduce their costs of production below the average, Marx writes:

> The law of the determination of value by labour-time makes itself felt to the individual capitalist who applies the new method of production by compelling him to sell his goods under their social value; this same law, acting as a coercive law of competition, forces his competitors to adopt the same method.[22]

The odd thing is that Bidet attaches great importance to the case of technological rents (what he calls 'differential surplus-value') in his attempt to show how such 'essential' concepts as surplus-value are intricated in the 'phenomenal' sphere of the market; here 'Marx explains a *tendential* macro-economic phenomenon, namely the growth of relative surplus-value, by a *structural* micro-economic configuration, competition within each branch' (153). Yet Bidet barely considers this analysis, with its stress on the 'coercive law of competition', when seeking to set out what he calls '[t]he foundations of the Marxian theory of the market' (195–232). It is true that he talks of a 'double' constraint involved in 'the articulation of commodity and capitalist relations', of which the first is the 'constraint to produce determinate goods in a determinate time', but his attention is focused overwhelmingly on the second constraint, imposed by capital on labour in the process of production (211).

Bidet seems here to fall victim to a very common contemporary error, found, for example, in both the capital-logic and Regulation schools. As a corrective to the economism of the Second and Third Internationals, and even of Marx – 'who', Bidet tells us, 'is impregnated with the mechanistic and teleological epistemology of his century' (222) – capitalist relations of production are politicized by being reduced to the relation of domination of capital over labour in the process of production. I do not see how such a view can avoid a voluntarism in which capitalism is reduced to the clash of hostile class wills. The alternative would be Marx's own understanding of the interdependence of the two constraints, of the process of competition between capitals and of the extraction of surplus-value within the process of production itself. This understanding is expressed by specific observations – for example, Marx's statement that '[t]he influence of individual capitals upon one another has the effect precisely that they must conduct themselves as *capital*'[23] – as well as in the explanatory priority he implicitly gives to what Bidet calls the 'structure' of competition between capitals over tendencies such as that of the rate of profit to fall.[24] From this perspective, the complex balance of coercion and consent through which capitalist domination is secured within the process of production can only be understood in the context of the competitive process through which capitals are compelled to exploit and to accumulate.

Seeing things this way has political implications of the most profound importance. I can merely allude to two here. In the first place, a distinctive light is thrown on the rise and fall of Stalinism once we consider the global process of competitive accumulation. The era of the first two Five Year Plans, when the Stalinist system was forged, appears from this perspective, not as a bizarre aberration, but as the purest form taken by a general tendency towards militarized state capitalism against the background of a world market disintegrating into protectionist trade blocs: the Nazi war economy and the New Deal are best seen as variants of the same tendency, not the products of a different social system. Similarly, the collapse of Stalinism today appears once again as a limit-case of a general process – this time the cracking open of nationally organized economies under the pressure of the internationalization of capital: the convulsive and concentrated form taken by this process in the former Eastern bloc is to be understood as a consequence of the fact that, at the last point of transition in the 1930s, the USSR went furthest in the direction of national organization. The East European revolutions therefore represent, not a turn in Bidet's cycle, but a step sideways, from one variant of capitalism to another.[25]

This brings me to my second point. How are we to greet this development, the global triumph of 'the coercive law of competition'? As Samir Amin has recently reminded us, its consequences for most of the Third World are dire: the cases of the Far Eastern 'Four Tigers' (South Korea, Taiwan, Singapore and Hong Kong) stand out as exceptions to the general picture of misery and impoverishment.[26] The incorporation of Eastern Europe into the world market takes more and more the aspect of a free fall to the status of Third World debtor countries rather than an ascension to the doubtful delights of Western prosperity. It seems evident to me that the socialist project can only define itself in opposition to *this* market, the market of 'actually existing capitalism'. This leaves open the question of whether there is another kind of market compatible with, perhaps even required by, the achievement of the goals which socialists traditionally have set themselves. Bidet plainly thinks that there is. He conceives of the market as a rule, rather than the structure of compulsions theorized by Marx, and envisages the application of his version of Rawls's principles of justice involving the 'articulation' of market and plan.

Bidet is, in other words, committed to some version of market socialism. It must be counted as one of the weaknesses of his book that it offers no detailed specification of how the just version of the market economy it recommends would work. Bidet must in any case confront the most general challenge facing all market socialists, namely to show how transactions between units of production can be regulated by the purchase and sale of commodities without this giving rise to what Marx argues are the principal characteristics of capitalism, above all the exploitation of labour and chronic economic crises. Defenders of market socialism tend to draw pictures of an idealized market economy free of the ills of capitalism without explaining how such an arrangement is to be achieved in practice.[27] This is not to say, of course, that socialist opponents of the market *tout court* do not face challenges of their own. Chief among these is to provide an account of the mechanisms though which producers would cooperate to run a complex industrial economy while avoiding the traps of both market capitalism and the Stalinist bureaucratic command system. Some efforts have been made in this direction, but it is clear that considerably more research and discussion are required.[28] What is, I think, beyond doubt is that Bidet fails to show that the market can be dissociated. In that sense the great debate about modernity – are we doomed to oscillate between degress of *laissez faire* and bureaucratic control, or is there still a 'feasible communist' alternative to both? – remains open.

Notes

Earlier versions of this chapter were delivered at the colloquium 'L'idée de socialism a-t-elle un avenir?', organized by *Actuel Marx* and the Istituto Italiano per gli Studi Filosofici at the Sorbonne, 6–8 June 1991, and at the Political Theory Workshop at the University of York. I am especially grateful to Jacques Bidet for responding so generously to my criticisms, and to Chris Bertram and Andrew Chitty for their very helpful editorial comments.

1. Alex Callinicos, *Against Postmodernism*, Cambridge: Polity, 1989.
2. Marx and Engels, *The Revolutions of 1848*, Harmondsworth: Penguin, 1973, pp. 70–71.
3. For example, Karl Marx, *Grundrisse*, Harmondsworth: Penguin, 1973, p. 162.
4. Perry Anderson, 'Modernity and Revolution', *New Left Review* 144, March–April 1984, p. 113.
5. All references in the text are to Jacques Bidet, *Théorie de la modernité suivi de Marx et le marché*, Paris: Presses Universitaires de France, 1990.
6. Rossana Rossanda, 'Pour une analyse marxiste de la crise des sociétés de l'est', in J. Bidet and J. Texier, eds., *Fin du communisme? Actualité du marxisme?*, Paris: Presses Universitaires de France, p. 35.
7. See my critical discussion of Habermas in *Against Postmodernism*, ch. 4.
8. A. Giddens, *A Contemporary Critique of Historical Materialism*, London: Macmillan, 1981; and *Consequences of Modernity*, Cambridge: Polity, 1990.
9. Gilles Lipovetsky, *L'Ère du vide*, Paris: Gallimard, 1983. But see also, for example, Luc Ferry and Alain Renaut, *Heidegger and Modernity*, Chicago: University of Chicago Press, 1990.
10. Jacques Bidet, 'Capitalisme, communisme, marxisme, socialisme', in Bidet and Texier, eds., *Fin du communisme?*, p. 17.
11. Étienne Balibar, '"Droits de l'homme" et "droits du citoyen"', *Actuel Marx* 8, 1990.
12. Giddens, *Consequences*, pp. 21, 27, 88.

13. Alex Callinicos, 'Anthony Giddens: A Contemporary Critique', reprinted in A. Callinicos, ed., *Marxist Theory*, Oxford: Oxford University Press, 1989.

14. For example, Ronald Dworkin, 'What is equality?', *Philosophy and Public Affairs* 10, 1981; and Amartya Sen, 'Rights and capabilities', in Ted Honderich, ed., *Morality and Objectivity*, London: Routledge & Kegan Paul, 1985.

15. See also Jacques Bidet, *Que faire du 'Capital'?*, Paris: Klincksiek, 1985, esp. ch. 6.

16. See Alex Callinicos, 'The Logic of *Capital*', D.Phil. thesis, University of Oxford, 1978, ch. 8.

17. See also Bidet, *Que faire*, esp. ch. 4.

18. See Robert Brenner and Mark Glick, 'The Regulation Approach: Theory and History', *New Left Review* 188, July–August 1991.

19. Renato di Rusa, 'Le marché, quelques observations théoriques', *Actuel Marx* 9, 1991.

20. Karl Polanyi, *The Great Transformation*, Boston: Beacon Press, ch. 5.

21. Marx, *Theories of Surplus Value* Volume 3, Moscow: Progress, 1972, p. 74.

22. Marx., *Capital* Volume 1, Harmondsworth: Penguin, 1976, p. 436.

23. Marx, *Grundrisse*, p. 657.

24. Bidet, *Que faire*, p. 145.

25. The argument of this paragraph is developed at much greater length in Alex Callinicos, *The Revenge of History* (Cambridge: Cambridge University Press, 1991), which in turn draws heavily on Tony Cliff, *State Capitalism in Russia*, London: Bookmarks, 1988, and Chris Harman, 'The Storm Breaks', *International Socialism* 46, 1990.

26. Samir Amin, 'Le système mondial peut-il être réduit à un marché mondial?', *Actuel Marx* 9, 1991.

27. See, for example, David Miller, *Market, State and Community*, Oxford: Oxford University Press, 1989.

28. See, for example, Pat Devine, *Democracy and Economic Planning*, Cambridge: Polity, 1988. I explore these questions in more detail in *Revenge*, ch. 4.

9
The End of History: One More Push!
Christopher Bertram

In his *The End of History and the Last Man*, Francis Fukuyama has history taking place on two dimensions.[1] On the one hand, there is something resembling an orthodox Marxian story where forms of society flourish and perish according to whether or not they are conducive to scientific and technological progress; on the other, there is a Hegelian tale about history as the recognition of more and more people as possessed of moral standing – first one is free, then some, then all. The connection between these two dimensions is never fully worked out by Fukuyama, and it is not my intention to resolve that difficulty here. Rather, I want to concentrate on Fukuyama's dimension of recognition and argue that, by the internal criteria it offers us, history is not yet at an end. Nevertheless, I shall propose that by those same criteria it is almost at an end. I want to suggest that the justificatory discourse of modern societies already presupposes the free and equal status of human beings as such and holds out the promise of their liberation, even if the concrete institutions of modern societies fall short of the standards they themselves proclaim and impede the realization of those very standards.

My central strategy here will be look at the way that the writings of egalitarian liberals (such as John Rawls[2]), point to the need for a far more radical transformation of existing social institutions than they have perhaps bargained for. Rawls, in his most recent writings, seems to abandon the search for standards of justice that hold universally. Rather, he seeks to formulate explicitly the implications of convictions about justice that he thinks citizens of liberal democratic polities already hold.[3] Many have regretted the narrowing of focus and the limiting of ambition that have marked Rawls's recent work and have suggested that the elucidation of the 'common sense' of liberal-democratic societies is bound to have conservative implications, thinking perhaps that the elaboration of capitalist 'common sense' can only result in a theory that justifies capitalist institutions. Whilst I too regret the abandonment of the search for a less contextually bound theory of justice, I doubt that these allegations of *conservatism* are well founded. Rather, whilst it is true that an ideology that presents an underlying social reality as other than it is may serve to mask and legitimize, the standards proclaimed by the same ideology can also be used as a powerful weapon for the critique of that reality. It isn't, then, that capitalism fails to meet standards of some political theorist; rather, it fails to meet the standards of normative justification that it has itself generated. Capitalism fails by capitalist standards.

Since I have already given several hostages to fortune, I shall try at this stage to get one of them out of the way. Hegel and Kant were both able to see history as purposive, as goal-directed. We are unable to endorse such a view today although it seems that the very idea of the 'end of history' depends on it. Nothing I say here should be taken to imply commitment to a teleological view of history in the sense that some final goal is taken to play an explanatory role. I do believe, though, that states of completion or potential completion of processes have an important role to play in isolating what we are to discuss, explain and evaluate. Thus the processes leading to the extinction of the dinosaurs, the death of Lorca and the demise of the Soviet Union are all picked out for us as objects of inquiry by their outcome even though the outcome itself explains nothing. Our interest is also focused by potential outcomes, as for the German revolution of 1919 or the Chinese revolution of 1927. The 'end of history' here is just that state of affairs where all human beings come to be recognized in theory and in practice as free and equal. If that recognition corresponds to fundamental human interests, then the process whereby it came to be realized or frustrated is a plausible candidate for the greatest story ever told, even if that does not exclude the possibility of other stories, histories and, still less, the continued empirical unfolding of events.

Some Thoughts about Ideology

Let us return to the tension between capitalist standards of justification and capitalist social reality. Accounts of ideology – especially, though not exclusively, Marxist accounts – have tended to focus on the ways in which the beliefs generated by a particular social structure serve to reproduce that structure. If we look at a text such as his 'Preface' to *A Contribution to the Critique of Political Economy* (1859), we may appear to find Marx endorsing such a view. Now there is more than one account of ideology to be found in Marx's work and I don't want to get into a discussion of which view he ought to have endorsed, or which coheres best with his other commitments. We might, though, notice three rather obvious points about the functionalist theory of ideology, ironically points which it shares with the views of the 1950s theorists of 'totalitarianism': first, ideology consists of false beliefs; second, those beliefs stabilize the social structure by misrepresenting its true nature to the agents who participate in it; third, it becomes mysterious how those ideologically befuddled agents are going to effect transformative social change. We have what looks like a stable system, where the (ideological) outputs generated by the system reappear as inputs ensuring its unchanging survival, rather like the interaction between plants and their environment in a sealed glass jar.

This kind of relationship between a system and its effects is only one out of a range of possibilities. One relevant alternative model is provided by Sartre in his account of 'counterfinality'. In *A Critique of Dialectical Reason* Volume 1, he tells us how peasants in China, seeking to enhance agricultural production, act in such a way as to undermine its viability. Here, the outputs reappear as inputs undermining the stability of the system itself.[4] One can imagine a similar relationship between the sets of beliefs generated by a social structure and that structure. Perhaps we can think of this as a quasi-Hegelian model of ideology as opposed to a vulgar Marxist one. Here, when agents examine their form of life in the light of the ideas it has generated, they come to perceive its inadequacy and it gives way to a new form that better embodies the normative standards that the earlier one has generated. The new form in turn generates new variations on those standards which serve eventually to undermine its viability. Presumably, this process can only come to an end when the normative self-image generated by a society corresponds to its reality.[5]

Perhaps the most commonly found Marxian image of ideology in a capitalist society is one where false beliefs serve to mask the underlying reality of that society from people and especially from workers. Thus the wage contract is represented as a fair agreement between free and equal sovereign individuals, whereas in reality the unequal access that each has to the means of production gives the capitalist the possibility of exploiting the worker. We may appear to have a functionalist theory here, but this ideology can cut both ways. On the one hand, if the representation of capitalism as conforming to a contractarian standard of agreement between free and equal individuals is successful, this ideology can have a powerful legitimating effect: we appear to have a case where a system generates ideological outputs that reinforce its own stability. But if, on the other hand, people become convinced of the validity of norms that conform to the criterion of agreement between free and equal persons, but also come to believe that capitalist societies could not receive such agreement, the ideological self-representation of capitalism can serve to undermine support for it. Capitalism was portrayed by Marx and by the classical Marxists as bringing its own gravedigger into being; my suggestion here is that in normative terms it may end up digging its own grave.

The representation and reality of the wage contract offer one illustration of the double-edged character of capitalist ideology, but there are further ways in which capitalism comes to generate norms that begin to raise questions about its justice. E.P. Thompson's discussion of law at the end of his study of the Black Acts in *Whigs and Hunters* gives us an example. There Thompson faces the paradox that law is often, perhaps usually, an instrument of class rule, yet in order to carry out its function effectively it must be more than merely instrumental. Rather, it must in reality, and not just apparently, embody certain standards of fairness.

If the law is evidently partial and unjust, then it will mask nothing, legitimize nothing, contribute nothing to any class's hegemony. The essential precondition for the effectiveness of law in its role as ideology, is that it shall display an independence from gross manipulation and so shall seem to be just. It cannot seem to be so without upholding its own logic and criteria of equity; indeed, on occasion, by actually being just.[6]

Thompson goes on to claim that 'the rules and categories of law penetrate every level of society, effect vertical as well as horizontal definitions of men's [sic] rights and status, and contribute to men's self-definition or sense of identity.'[7]

Through the operation of contractual relations in the marketplace and though the way in which legal and political institutions operate in an increasingly rationalized way, capitalist (and perhaps 'modern') institutions do much to foster in individuals a sense of self and others as free and equal. We might also point to ways in which the capitalist labour process transforms the individual tied to a particular mode of life in precapitalist society into a someone who is more 'abstract' and 'universal'.[8] The conception of the person and her relations with others that issues from all this may be very far from the empirical reality, but it nonetheless offers a normative standard to which agents are at least tacitly committed in some of the roles they play.

Justification and the Conception of the Person

I now want to say a little more about this – admittedly ideological – conception of the person and the role it might play in political philosophy. I take the central concern of political philosophy to be the justification of political institutions and the normative standards that govern them (or ought to). Justification of norms and institutions is going to have a curious double character. If we are going to implement the idea that the appropriate test for those norms and institutions is whether they could be agreed to, then we will naturally be drawn to some sort of contractarian apparatus. But if that contractarian apparatus is going to be successful in the practical task of justification – in persuading its recipients – it will have to represent the parties to any hypothetical agreement in terms that the recipients of its justifications can identify with. Otherwise they will simply shrug their shoulders and regard the outcome of hypothetical deliberations and agreements among imaginary persons as having no binding force for them.

This justificatory task presupposes, then, an audience of a certain type. It would seem sensible to conceive of this audience in a way that allowed for the participation of more than just professional philosophers and political theorists. Nor does it seem satisfactory to construe the ideal recipient of justification as an individual possessed of full rationality and perfect information: in other words, an ideal individual possessed of superhuman cognitive capacities. Institutions have to be justifiable to those who might live in them; standards have to be justifiable to those who might live by them. On the other hand, it is clearly unsatisfactory to reject idealization completely and to require the actual assent of actual persons to proposed institutions or norms. Leaving aside the practical problems this would involve, we would be open to obvious counterexamples demonstrating the unsatisfactory nature of such agreement: people would, because of defective rationality or incomplete information, assent in circumstances where on any reasonable assessment of their best interests they should not do so, and their particular judgements of personal advantage would unduly influence them.

To whom then should the norms and institutions be justified? The proposal here is that they should be justified to persons considered to be responsible for their ends and actions who assert their right to be treated on the same terms as others and who recognize that right in others. These are the ideal recipients of justification and hence the persons to be represented by the parties to any imaginary contract. The grounds for asserting this are that such is the conception of self, others and agency that is in fact presupposed in many of their actions and relations by the citizens of liberal-democratic capitalist states and that is also affirmed by liberal-democratic capitalist societies in their normative self-image (even if that normative self-image does not correspond to the underlying reality).

I anticipate at least two sorts of initial objection: the first, which I shall call the realist objection, asserts that the beliefs about the self that people have are false and that we should base our normative political philosophy on a true conception of self and agency; the second, which I shall call the counter-normative objection, agrees that we should operate with an idealized conception of the person but denies that we have picked the right one.

Now the realist objection can come, and indeed comes, from many quarters. The postmodernist may insist that the conception of the person alluded to is, say, Cartesian and that the self is in fact some fragmented mishmash of identities. The rational-choice theorist may insist that a more appropriate model would be that of *homo oeconomicus*. The eliminative materialist may wish to replace our everyday conception of self and agency with one grounded at some more basic level. To all these suggestions the same set of replies will be given (although we shall shortly see the rational-choice theorist reappear in counter-normative guise). The conception of the person that I allege is presupposed in the justificatory discourse of liberal-democratic societies does not correspond to any empirical fact. Hence an objection that says that the facts about people are different is beside the point. We are engaged in justificatory dialogue with people who (at least when not engaged in academic discussions) presuppose that they and those around them are beings of a certain type. When Hume looked within himself and perceived not self but the stream of sensations, this did not lead him radically to reorient his political philosophy to take account of this worry about selfhood.[9] He recognized that, in their common enterprise of building institutions and justifying them to one another, people could not operate without a tacit view of self and agency that itself lacked empirical warrant. When Strawson tells us that certain attitudes towards persons (such as resentment) presuppose that certain facts are true of them (for instance, that they are autonomous), he does not at the same time believe that those facts are susceptible of independent empirical investigation.[10] Some people may believe that we will one day revise our conception of self and agency in the light of, say, neurophysiological discoveries. Whilst I am not committed to the view (indeed I am committed to denying the view) that the conception of the person presupposed by agents in their dealings with one another is unchanging, I find its widespread abandonment in the light of such discoveries implausible.

There is, however, an alternative conception of the person that has widespread acceptance and can also provide the basis for the justification of norms and institutions. I am thinking, of course, of the conception found in rational-choice theory, utilitarianism, and microeconomic theory. Here persons are depicted as utility maximizers and are considered as rational in so far as they seek to find and to employ the most effective means of securing their ends, and in so far as they are willing to modify their beliefs in the light of evidence.[11] The ends that they have are not themselves subject to criticism. I want to say a little here to motivate my employment of one conception rather than the other, although we will again meet the rational-choice conception at the end of this chapter.

At first sight the instrumental-maximizing conception seems to have at least two decisive advantages over its competitor: first, although admittedly an idealization, it can be deployed in both explanatory and normative contexts; second, it seems more general, capable of swallowing up the other as a special case where people have preferences for treating others as being of equal moral standing with themselves. (It is interesting to note in passing the way in which this conception has transmuted from being in its Hobbesian and Benthamite versions a 'realistic' revisionist reconception of human nature analogous to eliminative materialism in our own day, into today's surface-level folk-psychological idealization.) But the greater generality of the rational-choice conception of the person is no advantage if it is bought at the cost of ignoring some highly relevant detail. How relevant a detail is depends on what our theoretical and practical interests happen to be. The French saying that in the night all cats are grey may state a general truth about cats, but not one that is useful to someone trying to classify them into different breeds. The fact that rational-choice theory captures as much of human action as it does is certainly disturbing. But whilst we do have an interest in understanding how we act, we have other ones besides, not least an interest in understanding how we ought to act.

The interest we have here is in determining what claims we are entitled to make on others and what claims others are entitled to make on us. In this context it is important to explore the implications of the conception of persons as free and equal that people happen to have (even if we wish to reject that conception at the end of the day). But even beyond this, the key problem with employing the bare belief–desire instrumental model of rational choice in the context of our hypothetical contract is that it fails to give due weight to a fundamental and constitutive feature of the modern person, namely the desire to count, to have significance for others.

Recognition

The most basic level at which the striving for recognition conflicts with the purely instrumental conception of reason concerns the weight the desires of others have for us in our deliberations. In the instrumental conception, the desires of others ought to enter into the deliberations of rational persons first, in so far as those rational persons have desires to promote the welfare of those others. If I care about you, your desires count for me; if I don't care, they don't. Second, the desires of others might play a part in a person's deliberations in so far as the others are expected to assist or to thwart her in attaining her objectives. What I shall call the relational conception, by contrast, asserts that among my most important interests is to have it come to pass that the fact that I desire P provides others with a prima facie reason for also favouring P. If I am rich and powerful, or in a position to threaten or cajole, I may provide others with instrumental reasons for favouring P, but the fact that they favour P for those reasons is much less satisfying to me that they favour P just because I do. In other words, among my most important interests is that others come to recognize me as having the right to advance claims about what ought to be the case.

Now I may seek to monopolize this right for myself. I may seek to reserve to myself the right to originate valid claims, and may succeed in getting others to recognize this whilst denying recognition to them. The psychological story told by Rousseau and Hegel suggests that I will, however, pay a heavy price for this. Rather than having my own personhood confirmed to me in my interaction with others, I will have reduced all others to a status where they (at least from my viewpoint) lack the capacity to confirm my sense of self.[12]

There may be more than one type of social order where (some) persons find satisfaction for their basic desire to be recognized as valid originators of claims on others. Elites may find this desire satisfied amongst themselves whilst they deny recognition to an excluded mass. Persons may find that they are recognized as having the right to advance certain claims in so far as they occupy certain roles and stand in certain relations to others, but not as persons *tout court*. Dostoyevsky's underground man, who goes each day to the Nevsky Prospect determined not to give way before the officer who is purported to be his social superior, is typical of the modern conception of the self. He doesn't just seek to pursue the satisfaction of antecedently given desires; rather, his whole sense of himself is intimately bound up in his relation to other selves.[13] I would suggest that the degree of recognition implied in seeing oneself and others *as citizens* is the minimum acceptable to modern persons. It certainly often takes precedence for them over the pursuit of material well-being, as is evidenced by the mobilizatory potential of the demand for civil rights and universal suffrage.[14]

Communication and justification

Connected to the demand that we each make for recognition by others is the recognition we tacitly grant to others in many communicative contexts. Now I don't want to go all the way with Habermas and argue that something about language itself commits us to recognizing the free and equal status of others.[15] That seems much too strong a conclusion to draw. I would like to suggest, though, that since the business of political philosophy is justification, we seem to presuppose that the persons to whom our reasons are given are competent to receive our reasons and indeed to advance reasons and claims of their own. Our appropriate attitude to them as participants in a dialogue (or in a wider conversation) is not one of threateners, manipulators or whatever, concerned to produce a certain effect in our listeners in order to secure our instrumentally conceived best interests. Rather, if we are genuinely engaged in common deliberative activity in order to establish norms that we can share and live by, we must have a view of them as free and equal moral persons. We may be drawn into deliberation on norms by Humean considerations of mutual advantage, but once we engage in the task of justification we have to abstract from the contingencies of social circumstance to a large degree. To justify a norm to someone requires more than their grudging acceptance of it; justification implies that they would continue to regard it as binding were those circumstances to change to their advantage or disadvantage. We justify not just to empirical persons but to a model of the person possessed of certain attributes and stripped of others. (I am assuming, obviously, that justifications in terms of the word of God or the nature of an unobservable realm of Platonic ideas are not mutually acceptable to hypothetical justifiers.)

Some Implications of Rawlsian Philosophy

So my suggestion is that the appropriate conception of the person for normative political philosophy to employ is one that regards people as free and equal and, by (possibly controversial) extension, has a model of a just society as one that would be agreed to by persons so considered. In one sense this conception remains individualistic in that it regards individual persons as the appropriate moral authorities over the social system, but it is not atomistic: it does not see the good for individuals as being something attainable or even coherently describable outside of the possibility of their relations with others. As well as not being asocial, this conception is not ahistorical either. It is prepared to accept and live with the fact that this view of self and its relations with others is the product of some determinate historical culture. But this culture is our culture and we have an interest in exploring the implications of the normative presuppositions that it contains.

The most systematic recent attempt to work through the implications of the conception of persons as free and equal for political philosophy has been that of John Rawls. Rawls's theory is not addressed to Thrasymachus or Callicles, nor to the instrumentally rational maximizer of economic theory. Rather, it is addressed to persons who already possess a sense of justice. The original position, Rawls's ideal choice situation, is not some imaginary place outside time and space and inhabited by noumenal selves. Rather, it simply models restrictions on deliberation that we already accept in virtue of our subscription to a certain conception of the person that correspond to ideas 'implicit in the public culture of a democratic society'.[16] That conception of the person may not be a true one, but it is one that has a basis in the stories that liberal-democratic societies tell about themselves – in their legitimating myths – and perhaps (if Dostoyevsky's underground man is anything to go by) in the self-image of modern individuals more generally.

I won't spend much time going through the generally well-known details of Rawls's theory. He argues that instrumentally rational and mutually disinterested persons, placed behind a veil of ignorance that deprives them of knowledge of their own conception of the good and their own natural and social powers, and asked to determine principles to govern the basic structure of a hypothetical society that they are to inhabit, would hit on two principles. The first principle, which has lexical priority over the second, assigns to each person in society equally certain basic liberties. The second principle ensures that all positions are open to all under conditions of fair equality of opportunity and then, subject to the satisfaction of that, determines that the expectations of the least advantaged are to be maximized. Now there are many interpretive problems associated with Rawls's theory. What I want to focus on for a moment is one respect in which the theory doesn't work and how its necessary revision pulls us in a highly egalitarian direction.

Right at the centre of Rawls's construct, in the original position itself, there is a cuckoo in the nest. The cuckoo is, of course, the use of an instrumental conception of rationality. Now more can be made of this than is appropriate. Many critics have failed to notice that instrumental rationality is brought in as part of a construct that models the deliberation of persons who are themselves far from being pure instrumental maximizers. The primary negative effect on Rawls's theory is that, as John Harsanyi was quick to point out, persons in the original position would not choose the difference principle at all, but rather the principle of average utility.[17] The choices at this point are clear: either go with the principle and embark on some reconceptualization of the original position, or junk the principle and keep the apparatus unchanged. Numbers of sympathetic critics have gone with the principle. The most favoured method for doing this has been that of imaginary dialogue between the most and least favoured members of a just society who *ex hypothesi* share a commitment to justice (whatever it requires). Arguments based on natural aristocracy are already out of court, and desert-based arguments seem to fair no better because of the brute luck underlying the distribution of those capacities whose exercise gave rise to the desert claim in the first place. Nor do entitlement-based arguments do any better, because in the middle of a discussion whose ostensible purpose is to determine the nature of the rights people have, the conditions under which private property can be owned and transferred and so on, they simply assert the natural salience of one set of answers to those questions. If these arguments are unavailable then we are simply left with justifications of inequality in terms of the interests of everyone. Yet such justifications advanced in good faith among free and equal persons committed to treating one another justly are going to ground very little inequality. Such inequalities as they do justify are going to be limited to incentives without which the more talented are going to find it *impossible* to deploy their talents.[18]

Once we go a little beyond Rawls to some of the debates he has inspired, the dynamic of radicalization has become even clearer. For instance the 'What is Equality?' debate began with Rawls's proposed redistributions of social primary goods and the explicit leaving out of account of people's mental and physical differences. But a proper elaboration of the egalitarian ideal had to take these into account also. Once we have got inside the boundaries of the person, so to speak, it seems arbitrary to allow natural goods such as the capacity for effort to be the focus of egalitarian concern and the objects of redistributive measures, but to ignore the impact on individual well-being of such subjective factors as the unequally distributed capacity for enjoyment.[19]

I have skated very quickly over long and complex arguments. One thing that might entitle me to do this here is the fact that Francis Fukuyama shares my conclusion: namely, that Rawlsian liberalism is radically egalitarian. Fukuyama thinks this stance is a sort of irrational hyper-egalitarianism that people will continue to advance somewhat vainly even when history has ended. The end of history doesn't bring us freedom and equality in some absolute and unqualified sense, but rather freedom and equality to the maximum extent to which they are possible. But this is rather feeble and question-begging, seeking to appeal to the raw 'common sense' of his readers rather than to rationally supported distinctions.[20] It is entirely unclear whether Fukuyama thinks that a radical egalitarianism is unjustified or whether it is permanently infeasible because of the shortcoming of human nature. Certainly the mere fact of the existence of natural inequalities gives us no reason in itself for the social system to aim at or countenance some resulting unequal distribution of resources, enjoyment or opportunities. Fukuyama first presents the end of history as the realization or completion of an ideal: a state of affairs where free and equal persons accord one another recognition as such. When the implications of this appear more radical than he considers feasible or desirable history is allowed to terminate, uncompleted. Yet this terminated end is still presented as a completion.

Whilst Fukuyama appears to agree with Rawls that the implications of the modern conception of personhood are highly egalitarian, others would not agree. One difficulty is that the apparent consensus on this way of picking out the idea of personhood that underlies our idea of the appropriate moral relationship between individuals seems to break down on closer inspection. Those conceptions of freedom and inequality that command near universal assent are prescriptively imprecise; those that yield determinate prescriptions are the objects of apparently interminable disagreement. One author who seems to accept (in general terms) the characterization of persons as free and equal and indeed requires that morally competent agents accord to one another recognition as free and equal is Robert Nozick in *Anarchy, State and Utopia*.[21] Yet Nozick uses this to ground not an egalitarian political theory but a right-wing libertarian one. If an illustration were needed of the fact that garden-variety conceptions of freedom and equality will not do the work needed to get a radical egalitarian theory going, this would be it.

This might be to move too quickly, however. The difference between say Rawls and Nozick may not be that they understand freedom and equality differently, but rather that they differ as to the appropriate way to plug these conceptions into a political philosophy. Nozick, in good Lockean style, first determines the nature of the required moral relationships between persons and then requires that any permissible social and political structures fit around those core moral relationships. He implements this via his idea of rights as side constraints. So, for instance, if there are ways in which others may come to take legitimate possession of part of the external world that we are required to recognize as property, then the political realm must take that as a given and refrain from collectively implemented redistribution where individual theft would be impermissible. Rawls, by contrast, can be understood as following Rousseau rather than Locke. Here, rather then going directly from the conception of the person to a set of absolute rights, we take the totality of the social structure (including rights) to be the object of (hypothetical) agreement between appropriately described persons.

This is not the place to explore fully which of the two approaches is better. It does seem odd and perhaps irrational, though, to proceed as Nozick does with no regard for the foreseeable consequences of a set of rights rather than to attempt to implement the idea of justice between free and equal persons in terms of a set of rights and institutions that give all a chance of satisfying their most fundamental interests.[22]

In Conclusion: The Possibilities of Modernity

I promised earlier that I would return to the discussion of instrumental rationality. My claim has been that a society that delivered on the promise of a polity as agreed to by free and equal persons would be a very much more egalitarian society than capitalism makes possible. I said that the view of self as an autonomous agent amongst other autonomous agents was implicit in capitalist ideology and widely subscribed to by individuals in modern society. But some will think that I moved too quickly in excluding the view of self as individual utility-maximizer. This view is also widely subscribed to in modern societies, and not by different people but by the same people and even at the same time. In my preferred conception the individual's relation to the polity is as a citizen and hypothetical legislator, and the basic structure of society (including its economic institutions) is seen as the object of choice. In the instrumental conception the dimension of deliberation and interpersonal justification is absent and institutions are simply mechanisms for coordinating the interests of mutually disinterested agents.[23] This state might also happen to be a democracy, but the justification of democracy would be purely instrumental: the justification is not that it expresses the mode of life of the citizens, their conception of self and its relation to others (although the institutions remain expressive of the instrumental view of self). The paradigm for the 'universalizing model' – which I have been pursuing – is that of a deliberative democracy, that for the instrumental is a market economy. Although the instrumental model of society seems intuitively to correspond to the combination of night-watchman state and free market, it is nonetheless compatible with tyrannies in which irrational or arational desire or ideology subsumes societies which at the micro level are dominated by calculations of cost-benefit advantage.[24] Within a universalizing system, by contrast, other people appear as my interlocutors; they are ideally equals with whom I engage in dialogue oriented to the achievement of a consensus on our common interests. Within an instrumentalizing society others appear as obstacles or advantages to the achievement of my goals, and from the point of view of the state they are primarily the objects of policy rather than the subjects of discourse.

The schizophrenic nature of recent contractarian political philosophy, contrasting as it does instrumental and universalizing rationality (Gauthier), justice as mutual advantage and justice as impartiality (Barry), or system and lifeworld (Habermas), does not just correspond to some set of choices within political philosophy itself.[25] Rather, it corresponds to a very deeply divided conception of selfhood within modern capitalist societies. One possible end to history is with the triumph of the universalizing conception – not just in theory, but in reality; that is, the transformation of our social and political institutions so as to correspond to whatever free and equal persons would agree to. This might make use of all sorts of economic technologies (plan or market), but would make all norms and institutions the objects of choice by a deliberating citizenry. I need hardly say that if such is the end of history, it has hardly been achieved. Alternatively we might witness the victory of the instrumental conception, of calculation of advantage. In this case we would see a decline in interest in the institutions of mass democracy which would in any case increasingly cease to be the fora of public deliberation and would more and more become the objects of manipulation by interests using the tools of marketing, advertising and the media to create certain effects amongst a passive citizenry. Moreover, the passivity of the citizenry (so-called) would not represent agreement, but rather preoccupation with the private calculation of cost and benefit inside a framework set by the more powerful. Both of these seem to me to be possibilities latent in the present; both could come to pass. But we are not there yet. Dostoyevsky's underground man still confronts Nietzsche's last man.

Notes

1. Francis Fukuyama, *The End of History and the Last Man*, London: Hamish Hamilton/New York: The Free Press, 1992 (henceforth *EHLM*).

2. John Rawls, *A Theory of Justice*, Oxford: Oxford University Press, 1971.

3. See especially his 'Justice as Fairness: Political not Metaphysical', *Philosophy and Public Affairs*, vol. 14, no. 3, 1985, pp. 223–51; and, more recently, the material contained in his *Political Liberalism*, New York: Columbia University Press, 1993.

4. Jean-Paul Sartre, *A Critique of Dialectical Reason* Volume 1, London: New Left Books, 1976, pp. 161–5. See also the discussion by Philippe Van Parijs, 'Perverse Effects and Social Contradictions', *British Journal of Sociology*, vol. 33, no. 4, 1982, pp. 589–603.

5. Since ideologies typically fail to recognize any fact–value distinction, I think it appropriate to use a term like 'normative self-image'. I don't preclude the possibility of further analysing this. We might say that ideologies both proclaim standards and make factual claims about the world and offer a judgement about whether the world conforms to those standards.

6. E.P. Thompson, *Whigs and Hunters: The Origin of the Black Act*, London: Allen Lane, 1975, p. 263.

7. Ibid., p. 267.

8. See G.A. Cohen, 'The Dialectic of Labour in Marx', chapter 10 of his *History, Labour and Freedom*, Oxford: Oxford University Press, 1988.

9. David Hume, *A Treatise of Human Nature* Book I, part four, §6.

10. P.F. Strawson, 'Freedom and Resentment', in his *Freedom and Resentment*, London: Methuen, 1974.

11. The best-known recent attempt to deploy such a conception in social contract theory is David Gauthier, *Morals by Agreement*, Oxford: Oxford University Press, 1986.

12. For illuminating discussion, see N.J.H. Dent, *Rousseau*, Oxford: Blackwell, 1982, ch. 2; and Jon Elster, *Ulysses and the Sirens*, Cambridge: Cambridge University Press, 1979, ch. 4. The classic references are, of course, *Émile* and the discussion of the master–slave dialectic in the *Phenomenology*.

13. Fydor Dostoyevsky, *Notes from the Underground*. See also the discussion in Marshall Berman, *All That is Solid Melts into Air*, London: Verso, 1983, pp. 219–28.

14. Something that Fukuyama lays great stress on. See *EHLM*, pp. 143–4 for a representative passage.

15. See his 'Discourse Ethics: Notes on a Programme of Philosophical Justification', in *Moral Consciousness and Communicative Action*, Cambridge: Polity, 1980. See also Knut Midgaard, 'On the Significance of Language and a Richer Conception of Rationality', in L. Lewin and E. Vedung, eds., *Politics as Rational Action*, Dortrecht: Reidel, 1980, pp. 83–98.

16. Rawls, 'Justice as Fairness: Political not Metaphysical', p. 234.

17. John Harsanyi, 'Can the Maximin Principle Serve as a Basis for Morality', *American Political Science Review* 69, 1977, pp. 294–606.

18. G. A. Cohen, 'Incentives, Inequality and Community', in *Tanner Lectures on Human Values*, vol. 12, Salt Lake City: University of Utah Press, 1991; Thomas C. Grey, 'The First Virtue', *Stanford Law Review* 25, 1973.

19. Ronald Dworkin, 'What is Equality?' parts 1 and 2, *Philosophy and Public Affairs*, 10, 1981; Amartya Sen, 'Equality of What?', in S. Mcmurrin, ed., *The Tanner Lectures on Human Values*, Cambridge: Cambridge University Press, 1980; Richard Arneson, 'Equality and Equal Opportunity for Welfare', *Philosophical Studies* 56, 1989, pp. 77–93; G.A. Cohen, 'On the Currency of Egalitarian Justice', *Ethics* 99, 1989.

20. See *EHLM*, p. 294 n. 8.

21. Robert Nozick, *Anarchy, State and Utopia*, Oxford: Blackwell, 1974.

22. The commentary in Thomas Pogge, *Realizing Rawls* (Ithaca: Cornell University Press, 1989, ch. 1) is particularly pertinent here.

23. See Jon Elster, 'The Market and the Forum', in Jon Elster and Aanund Hylland, *The Foundations of Social Choice Theory*, Cambridge: Cambridge University Press, 1990.

24. Thus, according to Zygmunt Bauman much of the explanation for the participation in genocide of millions of ordinary and psychologically normal Germans lies in the way in which bureaucracies present individuals with choices as purely technical matters, susceptible to apparent cost-benefit calculation in terms of both individual and organizational goals, and distance individuals within such structures from an appreciation of the human reality of their decisions. (*Modernity and the Holocaust*, Cambridge: Polity, 1989.)

25. Gauthier, *Morals by Agreement*; Brian Barry, *A Treatise on Social Justice, Vol. 1: Theories of Justice*, London: Harvester Wheatsheaf, 1989; Jürgen Habermas, *The Theory of Communicative Action* (2 vols) Cambridge: Polity, 1984 and 1987.

Notes on the Contributors

Christopher Bertram is Lecturer in Philosophy at the University of Bristol. He is the author of a number of articles in political philosophy and is currently working on a study of contractarian theories of justice.

Andrew Chitty is Lecturer in Philosophy at the University of Sussex. He is at present working on a book on need and desire in the philosophy of history.

Joseph McCarney is Senior Lecturer in Philosophy at South Bank University. He is the author of *The Real World of Ideology* (1980) and *Social Theory and the Crisis of Marxism* (1990).

Frank Füredi is Chairman of Development Studies at the University of Kent. He is the author of *The Soviet Union Demystified: A Materialist Analysis* (1986), *The Mau Mau War in Perspective* (1989), and *Mythical Past, Elusive Future: History and Society in an Anxious Age* (1992). His book *The Silent Race War* will be published in late 1994.

Gregory Elliott is Senior Lecturer in Philosophy and Politics at the University of Brighton and a member of the *Radical Philosophy* collective. He is the author of *Althusser: The Detour of Theory* (1987) and *Labourism and the English Genius* (1993), and the editor of *Althusser: A Critical Reader* (1994).

Keith Graham was educated at University College London and University College Oxford. He is Reader in Philosophy at the University of Bristol. His publications include the edited collection *Contemporary Political Philosophy: Radical Studies* (1982), *The Battle of Democracy* (1986) and *Karl Marx: Our Contemporary* (1992). He is currently working on problems of identity and political allegiance.

Paula Casal has studied at the University Complutense of Madrid, where she recently completed a doctorate, and the University of Oxford. Her fields of interest are moral, political and social philosophy. She is currently studying ethical problems related to deceit, future generations and gender injustice. She is also an environmental campaigner and has published in this area.

Jacques Bidet is Maître de Conférences in Philosophy at the Université de Paris X. He edits the journal *Actuel Marx* and is the author of *Que Faire du Capital?* (1985), *Théorie de la Modernité suivi de Marx et le Marché* (1990), *John Rawls et la Politique* (1994). His *Théorie Générale*, which articulates a general theory of the modern social system and a political philosophy, will be published by PUF in 1995. He has also edited *Les Paradigmes de la Démocratie* (1994). His works have been translated into Japanese, Korean, Serbo-Croat, Italian and Spanish.

Alex Callinicos is Reader in Politics at the University of York. He is the author of a number of books on Marxism and social theory, including *Is There a Future for Marxism?* (1982), *Marxism and Philosophy* (1983), *Making History: Agency, Structure and Change in Social Theory* (1987), *Against Postmodernism: A Marxist Critique* (1989), and *The Revenge of History: Marxism and the East European Revolutions* (1991). He is currently working on a book on the philosophy of history.